FIVE LIVES

Frank Pakenham
Earl of Longford

FIVE LIVES

THE CATHOLIC BOOK CLUB
121 CHARING CROSS ROAD
LONDON W.C.2

HUTCHINSON & CO. *(Publishers)* LTD
178-202 Great Portland Street, London, W.1

First published 1964

© The Earl of Longford 1964

Printed in Great Britain by
The Anchor Press, Ltd.,
Tiptree, Essex

For
Elizabeth

Acknowledgements

I am grateful to Mrs. Martin Lambert and Miss Barbara Brierley who were my secretaries while I was writing this book; to the incomparable Miss Peggy Fitzgerald who looked after me for the previous eight years, including some months of preparation; to the following for advice of various kinds: Lord Birkenhead, Mr. Malcolm Muggeridge, Mr. Nicolas Henderson, Mr. Esmond Warner, Mr. Hugh Delargy, M.P., Mr. Robert Rhodes-James, Lady Charteris, Professor Agnes Headlam-Morley, Mrs. Joanna Spicer, and Mrs. John Betjeman; to my golfing companions and medical advisers for therapy of various kinds; above all to Elizabeth for continuing to persuade me that others would enjoy what I was showing her.

I would also like to thank the executors of the late Hugh Gaitskell for allowing me to quote from a letter written to my wife in 1928 and to the *Observer* for allowing me to make extensive use of an article of mine called 'Fallen Minister'; to the Editor, Mr. David Astor, for his sensitive understanding of all my causes and occupations, whether or not he approved of them. The Count de la Bedoyère, Editor of *The Catholic Herald*, and his successor have given me wide opportunities.

I am indebted to Harold Harris who suggested the book and the title, and who gave me a great deal of help.

This book was finished by October 1st, 1963. Amid the throng of events since then President Kennedy has been tragically assassinated, Lord Home has become Prime Minister as Sir Alec Douglas-Home and Lord Hailsham has returned to being Mr. Quintin Hogg. Apart from a few drafting changes, I have left the text unaltered.

January 1st, 1964   *LONGFORD*

Contents

Introduction   9

PART ONE
A SOCIALIST IN THE CITY

1 Into the Parlour   21
2 On Being a Chairman   30
3 Double Agent   41

PART TWO
THE REALM OF PEERS

1 Old Wine and New   67
2 The Paladins   79

INTERLUDE
AN IRISH MIND
95

PART THREE
'THAT PRISON PERSON'

1 Not What We Did . . .   111
2 . . . But What We Tried to Do   120
3 'I Was in Prison'   133
4 Quantity and Quality   145
5 The Sinner and the Sin   153

INTERLUDE

A TRUER TALENT

165

PART FOUR

PRINCIPLES AND POWERS

1   'The Honourable Stile of Christian'   177
2   'The Hour of the Timid'   195

PART FIVE

THE ANTE-ROOMS OF STATE

1   The Last Year with Hugh   215
2   Mr. Valiant for Truth   228
3   From Each According to His Ability ... 245
4   ... To Each According to His Needs   256

EPILOGUE

THE AUTHOR AS A FATHER
by Judith Kazantzis
263

Index   273

Introduction
(1951-   )

No DOUBT a number of us needed a rest. Kind friends, some of them medical, assured us that we would be all the better for it and 'return refreshed'. I expect they were right. The long-term compensations were obvious. But that didn't make the immediate adjustment any less dramatic or disconcerting. Simultaneously one had been relieved of a heavy strain and deprived of a mighty stimulus. People talk of the strain or burden of office. Before I was a Minister I never much believed them. From the purely personal angle it seemed to be a case of 'You've got the best seats: we want them'. But the strain or burden was real enough, and is rightly connected in the public mind with the great responsibilities involved.

The work itself is very hard today for a Minister, but probably no harder than that which falls on a senior Civil Servant. The tension, I'm sure, is very much greater for all Ministers except the very slack, the very insensitive, or the exceptionally wise and mature. One Minister will trace it primarily to the duty of final decision, another to the obligation of speaking and answering questions in the House, another to the everlasting bargains and compromises without which collective government is impossible.

My own view is that the real strain does not arise from what Ministers *do* but from what they feel they ought to be doing. The vigilance of the public operates powerfully on the subconscious. Imagine a devoted general practitioner under constant attack for gross negligence in the local Press and you will get a partial analogy. The occupational disease of the good Minister is the neurosis, not that he is doing anything wrong but that he is not doing anything like enough. A formidable sense of insecurity results. Mercifully the Minister is not left to overcome it alone. Teetotallers argue that alcohol is a narcotic rather than a stimulus. Office is a supreme example of both.

A tremendous lot is asked of you. You are swept along in a whirl of activity. Your officials, whatever their inner thoughts, show such sublime confidence in you that anything you have to give is drawn on to the uttermost. And other cares are suppressed. Your finances are left over for a more favourable moment. Your philosophical perplexities are allowed to mark time. Only a grave family anxiety really registers and then heaven help your Ministry while it lasts.

And when the strain, the stimulus, and the narcotic go, what do you miss most? Obviously the financial change varies enormously from acute hardship in some cases to positive gain in others. For those who have no organized work to return to the feeling of having nowhere to go in the morning is somewhat crushing. Even when the wolf has not actually approached the door the self-respect of most of us (in the home and out of it) sags perceptibly when we cease to be effective breadwinners.

Again, one had to get used to being out of things, to not being run after. For years one had been leaving word with head porters of clubs, head waiters at restaurants, stewards at golf clubs, that 'There may be a call for me from the Ministry'. One was never exactly sorry if by some odd chance there was, although naturally one was profuse in apologies to one's friends, and modest protestations that 'I'm quite sure it's not of the slightest importance'. One's own telephone number was ex-directory, of course. Now the whole world could know one's number without taking advantage of the priceless secret; and porters, waiters, and stewards had to be very old friends or very new chums to join in the make-believe of an emergency call.

But these are trifles. Surely the grievous loss was the work itself? The chance of public service? Yes, assuredly. But the tasks of Opposition are urgent and honourable. The greatest loss of all, I would say, was the comradeship. That with political colleagues happily continued, but the relationship with the permanent secretaries, Service chiefs, private secretaries, messengers, chauffeurs, and all the countless grades of Government service, was seen to be most precious at the moment it existed no more.

'And what,' asked an earnest young student, after an address at the University of Sussex, 'have you been doing since the Labour Government fell?'—which was clearly to him an event of the Dark Ages. Feeling that, for once, a piece of straight egotism was justified, I answered: 'For eight of the eleven years I have been chairman of one of the clearing banks. I have published three books, each, admittedly, smaller than the last: an autobiography, a book on the causes of crime, and another on the idea of punishment. I was one of the founders, and have for some years been chairman, of the New Bridge for ex-prisoners. Till last June I was chairman of the National Society for the Mentally Handicapped. I was first chairman of the Anglo-German Association and continued as such for over ten years. We were addressed by the Duke of Edinburgh, Mr. Macmillan, and Dr. Adenauer among others. I was chairman of various committees of enquiry including two which drew up plans for an International Police Force. One was organized by Federal Union and the other by the Wyndham Place Trust. I became chairman in 1961 of the Committee for London Government in the struggle against the proposed revolution. I have become a Director of the Alliance Building Society.

'I have spoken from the Labour front bench throughout the period. In retrospect hardly a Government report seems to have come out without my offering my opinions. Those of Monckton, Devlin, Albermarle, Crowther, Younghusband, Wolfenden (2), Radcliffe (2), did not escape.

'I was honoured, along with Professor Bodkin and Lord Moyne, with a doctorate of the University of Ireland and by membership of the Council of the University of Sussex. I returned to Christ Church for a short while as a don when the Labour Government fell, and I suppose that I might end my blurb by saying that I have contributed numerous articles to newspapers and often appeared on television.'

My family life is dealt with firmly by Judith in the Epilogue.

The eight children have grown twelve years older. Antonia has married Hugh Fraser, Conservative Secretary of State for Air, and Judith Alec Kazantzis, Labour candidate and lawyer. Antonia has four children: Rebecca, Flora, Benjamin, and Natasha. Thomas is on the *Observer*, Paddy at the Bar. He won the Bar golf tournament in 1962. Rachel is working with ATV, Michael is a classical scholar at Trinity College, Cambridge (a sensational departure), Catherine is at St. Clare's Hall, Oxford, awaiting, like General Grant and Dick Diver in *Tender is the Night*, 'her intricate destiny', Kevin is still at Ampleforth, where Thomas, Paddy, and Michael were also at school, all scholars or exhibitioners.

In 1945 I had ceased to be Frank Pakenham and became Baron Pakenham of Cowley on Mr. Attlee's nomination to the Crown. Early in 1961 I succeeded my brother Edward as the seventh Earl of Longford, with a seat in the House of Lords as Baron Silchester. I will come later to the tributes when he died. Among my sisters, Pansy lost her husband, Henry Lamb. His wedding present of a portrait of Elizabeth keeps our memory of him alive for us, as do his drawings of all our children. Pansy's daughters Henrietta and Felicia, and Mary's daughter Alice, are all happily married. Violet's well-received book, *Five out of Six*, joins Mary's *Brought Up and Brought Out* and my own earlier narrative in the steady documentation of our collective childhood. The prestige of Anthony Powell, her husband, as a novelist seems to rise higher and higher. Julia died very young, and looking still younger. Her son Ferdy (captain of the school at Eton, a First in Modern Languages at Oxford) is working in the Conservative Research Department. 'The best introduction to political life', as Lord Burlesdon said to Rudolph Rassendyll at the beginning of *The Prisoner of Zenda*. I have found it so myself.

The many visits to Ireland seem to have left very little time for foreign travel, though there have been short visits to Germany, Austria, and the United States, with longer ones by

Elizabeth to Italy and the Greek islands. The home base has been Cheyne Gardens in London and Hurst Green in the country. The main recreations, apart from seeing friends, have been reading, the theatre (not as much as one would wish), golf, nearly once a week at Rye, swimming (recently) and tennis (less than of old).

The problem of how to mention friendships defeats every autobiographer. Some of our friends crop up incidentally in these pages, but many who search for their names in vain must forgive me and take the will for the deed. Health has been good on the whole, apart from fibrositis, which has been fairly well kept at bay. At forty I had recently run a mile in under five minutes, which would end my life abruptly now. But swimming, which was beyond me till I was fifty-six, has taken the place of my old runs round Christ Church Meadows, and is a much better family sport. Anyone of fifty-eight should be rapidly undeceived, or have his head examined, if he supposes he is as vigorous as twenty years earlier. If he likes he can pride himself on his superior wisdom. Fifteen years ago, as British Minister responsible for Germany, I visited that country twenty-six times in twelve months. I doubt if I could do that now. But today I would not think that it was the most effective form of help.

I have told elsewhere how I was born a Protestant and became a Catholic, how I grew up a Conservative and became a Socialist, how I started as a member of the Irish ascendency and became an Irish Republican. If asked what else there has been unusual in my life I would suggest that I have pursued more careers than most people. I have called the book that follows *Five Lives* because it concentrates on five aspects of a working life, the life that I led from the moment that I left the house each morning until I returned at night. Yet I hope that those who want an inner life will not be altogether disappointed. It is certainly not a 'history of our times' or even a balanced record of my own activities. It covers, as I say, five selected aspects of my working life and I must diffidently point out that in each case I have rather unusual credentials which will be laboured all too blatantly as I cover the various topics. In the two interludes I have covered themes which run through everything.

But books are written by writers: how stand my credentials there? It is hard to say, if only because so many different standards are applied. I hold the personal view that hardly anyone is equally good at writing and speaking. I admit that there are intermediate art forms; conversation comes nearer perhaps to speaking. The subject bristles with interesting ramifications and refinements. Three superb talkers, for example, Lord David Cecil (who is a Companion of Honour for literature), Sir Maurice Bowra, and Sir Isaiah Berlin, write well and speak well by any standards. But conversation is their supreme expression. So perhaps conversation should be regarded as a third form of art. And then again, what of a great television man like Gilbert Harding, with whom Elizabeth appeared more than once? He was neither a speaker, nor writer of the highest quality, nor wholly fulfilled in private conversation. His medium was what one can only call public conversation, but there it will be perhaps years before he is equalled. And what of lecturers like Hugh Trevor Roper and Alan Taylor and Agnes Headlam-Morley as compared with political speakers?

But if I am allowed to judge from my own experience, and to make a straight comparison between politicians and writers, it is perhaps not surprising to find that the former class do not write very well, and the latter class speak no better. 'Most artists write well,' Evelyn Waugh said to me, 'Augustus John, for example.' (No doubt he would have added Yeats and George Moore.) 'All politicians write badly.'

'What about Churchill?' I asked him, adding, to show my awareness, 'I suppose you think he churns out clichés?'

He checked himself. 'I always think he is going to,' he replied, 'but, to be fair, he seldom does. At the last moment he gives his phrases an original twist.' I think we agreed that this might be due to his painter's eye, though I cannot remember whether Evelyn took him seriously as a painter.

I like to give myself, wherever possible, simple answers to simple questions. If I am asked—which doesn't happen very often—'Whom do you consider the best prose stylist in Britain at the present time?' I answer, as I have answered for years, 'Evelyn Waugh.' The fact that he did more than any other layman to bring me into the Catholic Church, and that I am the godfather of his eldest son, does not, I am sure, affect my judgement. It was natural, therefore, that I should seek his opinion on the manuscript of my previous volume of autobiography *Born to Believe*. He is a purist in all things remotely aesthetic. It was a pity, therefore, that in my excitement at the prospect of obtaining his opinion I sent him a typescript, which, through no fault of my secretary, had been thoroughly messed about with insertions and suchlike. His reply was not discouraging. Many of the anecdotes had great life, but there was a lot to be done. He would be at Brighton the following Sunday, and would be happy to come over for lunch and go over it thoroughly.

That lunch, or, as he would say, 'luncheon', was a painful affair. 'You must come to stay with me for a month,' he said. 'We will work on the manuscript together and produce something reputable. Otherwise I fear it will do you discredit.'

Alas, at that time my various public activities made a month with Evelyn impossible. But looking back I realize what a chance I missed. And what a generous offer it was! Here was he, a professional writer with a large family to keep, offering to place his instruction and art at my disposal. How many thousand dollars could he not have earned by offering the same facilities to rich Americans! When I declined his tone became blunter and he said things about my style, which in retrospect were salutary, but were bad for morale at the time. (A little of my pride was salvaged by the strictures he passed on the style of others. A high literary critic said to me consolingly, 'Evelyn has a very good taste in writing, but a narrow taste, so don't be too upset.')

'But what,' I asked him, 'is wrong with my style?' He gave an answer which I shall always remember.

'I suppose,' he said, 'it's because you're a politician; you think in sentences; a real writer thinks in words.'

I have often thought of that dictum when listening to professional writers giving addresses or making after-dinner speeches. They sound curiously artificial as they pick their

[15]

way usually from one carefully chosen word to another, still sticky with midnight oil. But, equally, there is hardly a politician whose writings do not seem incredibly verbose and slackly worded compared with the work of professional authors. Who is there in the House of Commons today who would be recognized as a stylist by professional writers?

A number of books, some of them outstanding, have come from dons, or quasi-dons, and many sparkling articles from journalists, of whom Michael Foot among others has written impressive books. But if asked to point to any M.P. who is a writer of English prose, in the sense used by Evelyn Waugh, my brother-in-law Anthony Powell, Rebecca West, or Cyril Connolly, I cannot do so easily. Among professional writers whose speeches are a pleasure to listen to I can think of Malcolm Muggeridge; he and Dick Crossman are exceptions to the aforementioned rule that no one writes and speaks equally well.

Evelyn was afterwards distressed at having spoken so plainly. He wrote to tell me that he could not see a man painting a gate without wanting to tell him how to do it better. And later, when my book appeared and was widely reviewed (and praised by low-brow rather than high-brow critics), he wrote again. He'd seen in *The Times* and *The Tablet* ('I don't read the radical Press') less than justice done to the book's wit and humour.

The Times review, in fact, had finished, after pleasing references to my person: 'Only an occasional anecdote, for which his ear is delightfully acute', revealed the book which my talents should one day justify. Randolph Churchill, writing with proper anonymity but with the indulgence of an old friend, in the *Times Literary Supplement* had hailed me as a master of political *rapportage*. The anecdotes indeed were what was praised in the daily newspapers. So was the benevolence, though the tributes and compliments were felt by many to be overdone. 'Not enough roughage', said Ian Fleming.

If this book had a signature tune it was discovered by Randolph Churchill in a quotation from Father Leen in the last few lines: 'Take it from me—and this is based on years of experience—people are always better than they appear.'

Father Martindale, writing charitably but unecstatically about the book as a whole, said I might never write a better chapter than the last one, which was called 'Things deeper than Politics'. From letters received, I should hope that *Born to Believe* had encouraged a number of people. But Evelyn Waugh was right: it could have been very much better. It is time to try again.

1

A Socialist in the City

I

Into the Parlour

I WORKED for eight and a half years in the City; for the last
eight of those as chairman of one of the eleven London
clearing banks. Our bank, the National Bank, came ninth in
size. Its growth during my period was more rapid than that of
any of the others—three times as fast in England and Wales
as the national average.

There are very few Socialists in the City on the director,
or higher executive, level. (The political opinions of the
thousands of middle-grade or junior officials are not known.
Perhaps half the bank officials belong to the National Union
of Bank Employees, N.U.B.E.; perhaps half of those vote
Labour, but all this remains hid.) You could work for years
in the City as a director, and lunch out every day, without
meeting a recognizable Socialist. 'I suppose,' a leading man
once said to me, 'you and Oliver Franks are the only Socialists
in the City.' In fact Lord Franks is usually regarded as a
Liberal, and in the House of Lords has taken his seat on the
cross-benches, which suggests that the City angle of vision was
far away on the right.

One high-class City institution has been presided over with
much success for a good while by a Labour peer, Lord Piercy,
but he has never been an active politician, and has spoken
seldom in the House of Lords in recent years. No admitted
Labour sympathizer, apart from myself, has ever come near

being chairman of a bank. My role in that sense was unique, and seems likely to remain so.

The position of Conservative politicians is vastly different from that of Socialists in their relationship with the City, and for that matter with industry and commerce generally; though outside the City names like Lewis Cohen, Sidney Bernstein, and Alan Sainsbury come to mind more easily. Endless Conservative M.P.s and peers are directors of one kind or another. In comparison, the Socialist quota, while it does of course exist, is tiny, particularly among the leading men. Conservative ex-Ministers, whether it is they or their Party who disappear from office, and whether their departure is voluntary or involuntary, are soon bedded out with lucrative full-time or part-time appointments in the City. If a case arose where this didn't happen it would be thought that something was seriously wrong.

Some of the most respected of them—Lord Salisbury and Lord Avon, for example—have moved in and out of their directorships as they have moved out of and into office. Lord Woolton and Lord Chandos are eminent gentlemen who made their great names first in business, then in politics, then in business, then in politics, then in business. . . .

A Socialist ex-Minister is hardly ever offered a business directorship when he leaves office. Sometimes he wouldn't accept one; sometimes he certainly would. But somehow, in spite of a general feeling among the best people in the City that this sort of thing ought to happen more often, it just doesn't happen.

A further refinement should be noticed. In the City proper, in high-grade banking in particular, it is difficult to point to a politician of *any* Party who has been a chairman or other full-time personage until his days as a Minister or potential Minister were over. Lord Harlech and Lord Monckton, successive chairmen of the Midland Bank, had been high Cabinet Ministers earlier, but by the time they went into banking were not expected to hold office again. Lord Balfour of Burleigh, when chairman of Lloyds Bank, spoke frequently from the Conservative benches in the House of Lords, but he had never embraced a political career, and was something of an exception in my day, though a much honoured one. On the whole, the trend towards non-political or ex-political bank chairmen seems to have grown stronger.

I was therefore an oddity in a double sense: Socialist in the City, and moreover a bank chairman whose political ambitions had not been fully extinguished. It was bad, or peculiar, enough, anyway, that I should speak constantly from a front bench in the House of Lords. The fact that I was speaking from the wrong front bench aggravated the eccentricity.

Why did it fall to me, as compared with all other Socialists, to embark on and live out this unparalleled destiny? For one simple, accidental reason. It will, however, require a lengthy explanation. Our bank—my bank, as it still is, in the sense that I am still a loyal and ever more deferential customer—our bank, the National Bank, was founded by Daniel O'Connell, the Irish liberator, in 1835 (he had a good deal of assistance in the City). In those days, thirty-five years after the Union of England and Ireland, and eighty-six years before the Treaty that brought it to an end, the two economies were in theory one. There was nothing, therefore, paradoxical in a bank whose funds were provided largely from Ireland but which had its head office in London. Long before the Treaty of 1921 it was quite natural that we should have come to run a branch system in both parts of Ireland and in England and Wales.

The distribution of our branches was and is very uneven between those areas. Today we have about 130 branches in the Irish Republic, more than any other bank; five in the North of Ireland; and thirty-one in England and Wales, where we have opened one new branch a year since 1957. We had not previously opened one since 1921.

Many of the Irish branches are small, with a staff of four, three, or even two, so that the figures given are no clue to the proportion of our business which can be described as 'Irish'. The London discount market is an important feature of our life and doings. No sharp distinction is possible between our Irish and English business, but one would not be far wrong if one said that two-thirds of it stemmed from Ireland and one-third in England. The great majority of our investments however are in British Government securities.

I said just now that there was no reason before the Treaty why a bank should not operate a branch system in both parts of Ireland and in England. But in fact we were the only bank to build up a system of that kind, and we are still alone in operating such a system today. There are eight banks functioning in the Irish Republic; all except one with branches in the North as well. Five have their headquarters in Dublin; one—ourselves—as already mentioned, in London; two have headquarters in Belfast. Of these the Ulster is owned by the Westminster Bank. This is the only case of a purely English bank which possesses even an indirect interest in banking in the Irish Republic. As already explained, none of the eight banks operating in Southern Ireland have any branch system in Britain—with the exception of ourselves. From the above facts it will be readily agreed that the National Bank is not quite like any other bank.

Nevertheless, there we were when I arrived. There we are today. There I am convinced we always will be. The Bank of O'Connell, regarded in Ireland as a leading national institution, yet a British registered bank, with headquarters in London, and a member of the London Clearing Banks system. Nor were we newcomers to that system. We had been members since 1859. Before the great amalgamations of the present century, from which our Irish affiliations presumably spared us, we were larger than some of those who became later the nucleus of the present Big Five.

The first time I ever went to a meeting of clearing-bank chairmen, the chairman of the chairmen genially remarked to me, 'I always say you oughtn't to be here.' Our bank was Irish, and out of place in this British holy of holies. He did not seem to mean it very seriously. No more was heard from him, or any other chairman, to that effect. In fact I never encountered even the *soupçon* of a tendency towards extruding us.

Goodwill and generosity apart, our exclusion could hardly have been effected without damaging the treasured 'image' of free and fair competition within the banking system. This image, indeed, corresponded to a genuine reality much more closely than I had imagined. I had assumed that there was much more 'ganging-up' than there proved to be; great care was in fact taken to avoid it. The 'self-denying ordinance' under which Bank A would refuse a loan to a customer who had already been refused by Bank B operated during much of my time, and this indeed restricted true competition. But this was regarded honestly if unimaginatively as a necessary consequence of the unwelcome credit squeeze, and a nuisance to be got rid of as soon as possible. Like the credit squeeze it has now been ended.

An additional factor confirming our position was the good-will of the Bank of England, prudently nurtured by my predecessor, my influential colleagues, and, as far as it lay in my power, by myself. I gained the impression that the Bank of England had quite a soft spot for us. We represented a residual link with Ireland, and we slightly mitigated the appearance and reality of a complete Big Five domination.

In the light of all this it may be easier to understand why I, an ex-Socialist Minister, aged forty-eight, an active member of the Opposition front bench, without any known business experience, should in 1954 have been asked to become deputy chairman of a London clearing bank with a view to becoming chairman in the New Year. It will be obvious by now that a chairman was necessary whose credentials would pass muster alike in England and in Ireland. And such a person was very hard indeed to discover.

The chairman of the National Bank, Mr. Michael Cooke, already over seventy and anxious to retire, had been looking in vain for a successor for quite a while, and growing ever more worried. He was an astonishing man: starting as a junior bank official in Carrick-on-Sur, he had worked right through the bank, come to England when things were bad after the First World War, and pulled it round. It was said of him that he could do any job in the bank better than any official. For twenty-one years he had reigned as chairman; a brilliant autocrat, immensely religious, on the worldly plane dedicated to the bank. He had worked himself almost to a standstill and was sure he could not carry on much longer.

He allowed himself one pious consolation: 'A guardian angel,' he used to say, 'watches over the National Bank.' But for a long time it was not easy to hear the beating of its wings.

Name after name was considered and turned down. This one might be marvellous in England, but what could he mean to the Irish? And vice versa. Mr. Cooke would have liked to call on Antony Acton, the member of the board with the widest banking experience, and later a tower of strength as my deputy. But Tony Acton very unselfishly, and I think very wisely, insisted that the new chairman must be in some sense Irish, and if possible a Catholic.

The Irish connection was clearly essential; the Catholic one only less so, though religion was as far as possible kept out of business. Our proportion of Catholic business, more particularly of religious-order business, was no doubt higher even in England than that of any of the purely British banks. But in a country such as England, where Catholics are only one in ten of the population, there was no question of the majority of our British business being Catholic (or for that matter having a specifically Irish flavour). The chairman of the National Bank must then in some sense at least be accepted by the Irish as an Irishman, and it would need an exceptional Irish Protestant living in England to be looked upon in that light. Possibly the connection with Daniel O'Connell, the supreme Catholic emancipator, clinched the case for a Catholic chairman.

Wanted, in short, a chairman prepared all the year round for daily duty in London; able to take luncheon at the Bank of England on a pleasant parity with the chairmen of the Big Five by virtue of his British air and standing. But wanted, at the same time, one who could pass himself off in Dublin, Cork, or Ballinasloe as an Irishman first, of whom Daniel O'Connell need not be unduly ashamed. The double requirement took some satisfying. And so the lot fell on me.

Somehow my Socialist aura must have lost its terrors. Other defects, maybe, were overlooked more easily. The fact, for instance, that Sir Robert Peel was my great-great-grandfather, and O'Connell once said of Peel 'that his smile was like the silver plate on a coffin'.

Still, it was Peel, after all, in company with the Duke of Wellington (married to my great-grandfather Longford's sister), who carried Catholic emancipation. He fought it hard, no doubt, but he carried it in the end. If one must have a

Protestant Ascendency background, Peel and Wellington had their redeeming features. And, after all, there was Paul Mary Pakenham, my great uncle, who brought the Passionist Order to Ireland. And my brother's name was already glorious through his years of immense labour for the Irish theatre.

Hence, then, the approach to me. But was I prepared to accept? At that time (1954) I was working for the Nuffield Foundation. I was ending the first year of a two-year enquiry into, roughly speaking, the causes of crime. It was in all the circumstances more than handsome of Nuffield to agree to my taking up the bank chairmanship a long time before my two years were up and to give me their blessing. Leslie Farrer-Brown, the director, told me sympathetically that a bank chairman had an ideal opportunity for pursuing social interests.

But did the bank chairmanship mean the end of my political career? I could be forgiven for considering the question. When the Labour Government fell I was forty-five; I had been a Minister of some kind for several years. I had been recently promoted to be First Lord of the Admiralty. The Conservatives had only a very small majority. We were living in an era when the swing of the pendulum was still regarded as a major law. The Labour Party might or might not win the election of 1955. I thought that they were likely to do so in 1959. I did a good deal of wrestling with my conscience, not to mention my ambitions, in the days that followed.

The approach came to me through John Dulanty, retired Irish High Commissioner, and by then a part-time director of the National Bank. It may seem frivolous to say that he was the best after-dinner speaker I ever heard, with the possible—though not certain—exception of the late Lord Birkenhead. I do so because the combination of gravity and gaiety insisted on, and so often demonstrated by, Lord Birkenhead himself, ran all through John Dulanty's life and career, and gave him a lovability, and at the same time a diplomatic finesse, which were entirely his own.

John told me that Michael Cooke, a personality then unknown to me, was anxious to retire for reasons we have already noted. He wanted me to succeed him. I gained the impression, for want of other guidance, that he had liked what he had read of my Catholic utterances, and accepted as authentic my Irish background. My Socialism seemed to have been overlooked or soft-pedalled. But there was one all-important proviso attached to the offer, irrespective of Party allegiance. If I came to the bank I must come for good. There was no reason why I should not continue to speak from the front bench in the House of Lords; that seemed to be regarded as a harmless spare-time recreation. But the bank must come first, not just for a while, but as a lifetime's option.

I went to see Michael Cooke at the Reform Club. Stocky, immensely vigorous in voice and gesture; thick, well-brushed grey hair; an old-fashioned nattiness of dress, including a well-knotted bow tie. He was famous for his rather hermit-like existence in the City, though very popular, as I discovered later, with other chairmen and such stockbrokers as the great Kit Hoare. He told me that in twenty-one years as chairman he had only once been out to lunch in the City, and then as a kindness to someone in trouble. He regretted, I think, the loss of the unblemished record. When I got to know him (he was seventy-three) he was very voluble, rather highly strung, and tremendously engaging, his eyes sparkling as he made his points. But there is no denying that he was capable of spreading terror. A rising bank official seemed to be talking too much; a brusquely incongruous question, 'What do the Jesuit balances amount to?' was flashed at him by Mr. Cooke, and we did not hear again that day from the unfortunate official. He has prospered greatly since.

On one occasion Mr. Cooke questioned the fortitude of those around him in resisting what seemed to him extravagant claims. He fumbled under the table for a moment, produced an ancient pistol, and threw it on the table with the words: 'There, that will give you the spunk to stand up to Mr. Blank!'

This afternoon he was full of persuasive charm. I could see that he was determined to get me, but determined also to get me on his own terms. He wanted to feel that another long reign would follow his; that he hadn't chosen someone who would use the bank as a stop-gap, a lucrative stepping-stone in the course of political advancement.

After I had left him I found myself very uncertain as to how far I could honestly promise to renounce Ministerial hopes for ever. I consulted Earl Attlee, not yet in the House of Lords and still Leader of the Labour Party. He advised me to talk to Hugh Gaitskell, of which more later on. But he himself saw no reason at all not to take a business appointment. There was always on these occasions the unspoken proviso, well understood in practice on both sides, that one would yield to a higher call if it were ever made, though one would not go out of one's way to seek it. 'The Tories do it; why shouldn't you?' was how he clinched the matter. I still cannot remember exactly how I satisfied Mr. Cooke and my own conscience and aspirations at the same time, but I convinced myself that I could turn in a performance that at the end of it all would justify me in his eyes, whether in this world or the next. I honestly felt, too, after talking to Lord Attlee and one or two sage relatives, that I could not reasonably be expected to promise that I would never, never, never leave the National Bank while there was still life in my body.

So duty and self-interest and inclination seemed to point together to my becoming chairman of the National Bank. I recognized that I must give the work an absolute priority for the indefinite future; that no personal calculations of mine must weigh for a moment against its interests; and that I must renounce political ambitions for as far ahead as I could see. It is not until you have renounced political ambitions that you realize what a driving force they may have supplied; how much colour they may have added to life.

2

On Being a Chairman

I SHALL be asked—what is it *like* being the chairman of a bank? An answer of a sort is not difficult. It's like working in a bank. It's also like being a chairman. Anyone who has any idea what it is like to work in any kind of business and to be any kind of chairman, even of a village darts club, can put the two together. He would at least have a glimmering of the experience. There is the routine life of the office, the journeys to and fro, the sense of earning a living for oneself and one's children in the same way as so many others. There is the duty and effort to draw the best out of one's team.

Is this the same as saying that to be a good bank chairman one must be capable of being both a good chairman and a good bank official? Hardly so, though no doubt there have been cases of such and may be more in the future. My predecessor Mr. Cooke, for example, and a very different, though equally strong personality, Tony Tuke of Barclays, were both the chief executive officers of their banks before becoming chairmen. They knew it all from top to bottom. And here I must digress for a moment.

It can be argued, and indeed I myself hold, that the top-level structure of our commercial banks is fundamentally wrong. There is a fundamental anachronism in the whole division into board members on the one hand and general managers on the other, with the latter 'running' the bank. This division stems from, and to an extent perpetuates, a quasi-feudal era in which boards, drawn primarily from outside commercial banking, are the first-class citizens. The rest of the staff, even though some of them will be receiving very high pay, in one sense at least are hewers of wood and drawers of water. The biggest decisions, on paper at least, are taken above their heads. The point remains true even though sometimes the top helots (chief general managers) themselves become first-class citizens (members of the board) when they retire. I feel sure myself that the commercial banks, as distinct, e.g., from the merchant banks, will never attract their share of the ablest and most ambitious young men while the present demarcation continues. I am aware that the chief general managers if 'polled' today would probably disagree with me. They prefer the substance of power without the shadow, but for all their well-earned reputation for efficiency and prudence they are a very conservative race. When one looks to the future I am sure that the view which, fairly or unfairly, I have attributed to them is distinctly shortsighted.

Ideally I am sure the leading members of a bank board should be full-time members of the company with part-timers added. From close experience I know well the knowledge and connections, the stimulus here, the restraint there, the mixture of patience and impatience which the good part-timer can bring. When the set-up suggested becomes prevalent in British commercial banks, as already almost everywhere else, the chairman is more likely to resemble Mr. Cooke or Mr. Tuke than eminent outsiders like Lord Monckton, Lord Franks, or *magno intervallo* myself. But while the distinction between the board and the general managers persists a bank will look to its chairman for qualities of wide viewpoint and public contact which it does not expect to find in its general managers. It will look to the latter for a background of technical knowledge and business acuteness which they will have acquired in a lifetime of management.

Without undue modesty I can say that there was no full-time post in the bank which I could have begun to fill but that of chairman. But I would resist passionately the notion, which I don't think would be propounded by colleagues, that I was a sort of front man or figurehead. What then did I actually do? What difference did I conceivably make?

In the first place I attended every day. Even after eight years I was sometimes asked, to my intense annoyance, 'How often do you actually go there?' I stayed all the mornings and for as much of the afternoon as was necessary, except when I was on tour in Ireland and the provinces. I was full-time in the vital sense that the bank had absolute priority. I was there whenever, and for as long as, I was needed. The routine of the bank occupied the bulk of the morning, with board meetings on Friday. I was an executive chairman, if not to quite the same extent as Mr. Cooke, who was a benevolent dictator. Every morning the main routine decisions of the bank had to pass through the committee over which I presided. Every decision, therefore, of any size, not only of 'policy' but of day-to-day administration, was approved by me and the director or directors present, after necessary discussion.

Delegation of lesser items to the general manager's committee was gradually extended during my time. Even so, we might seem to be bringing too much to the committee of the board, but a bias of this kind served the invaluable purpose of educating the directors and keeping us closely in touch. In practice the decisions seemed to come under headings such as these—staff, general, and individual problems; advances; investments; other use of moneys (the discount market, etc.); premises; advertising; general problems of expansion and progress including decision to open new branches; business of the London Clearing Banks Committee and, at certain times of the year, problems of the balance sheet and the dividend.

It will be recalled that half or more of our business was being obtained or conducted in Ireland. It came to us for information and, when necessary, for approval. It was part of my function to co-ordinate the British and Irish points of view, a task for which Ivone Kirkpatrick, with his house in Ireland, is still better fitted now. Social relations were of the easiest and happiest. We all came together at special boards in England or Ireland, if not quite as often as most of us would have liked. British concentration on traditional banking criteria sometimes appeared to suggest a tighter approach towards lending than was habitual in Ireland. Reconciliation was seldom difficult, but when it was I could reflect that as an Anglo-Irish chairman of Ministerial background this was what I was supposed to be there for. We were all at great pains throughout to make sure that the British credit squeeze did not affect our scale of Irish lending. In this we were successful, though care and thought were necessary.

Our Irish board was one of acknowledged distinction. They were all seven appointed by me, as were, by the end of my time, four out of our six English directors. John Leydon, our Irish chairman, is one of the four founders of the modern Irish economy. The others are Mr. Lemass, the Prime Minister, Mr. McElligott, ex-head of the Ministry of Finance, ex-Governor of the Central Bank, and Mr. Whitaker, at thirty-nine head of the Ministry of Finance and author of the far-famed Whitaker Plan. John Leydon's punctuality is notable, his piety still more so. We were amazingly lucky to get him. Arthur Quirke, executive director, had been picked out from the Law Department by Mr. Cooke. He and I drew very close as we toured Ireland in his car. A prolonged ovation from the staff at conference at Limerick was one tribute among many to his unending concern for every individual in the bank. Basil Goulding, head of a splendid business, brings a touch of insouciant brilliance to his many interests. Valerie Goulding, daughter of Walter Monckton, is admired everywhere for her polio clinic. And there was, too, Ned McGuire, senator, leading employer, ex-Davis Cup tennis player, the bold and sensitive collector. There was James Davy, chairman of the Gresham Hotel, high-ranking stockbroker and one of the most versatile business men in the country. There was Paddy Duggan, equally at home in accountancy and Thomas Aquinas. There was Gabriel Clery, a lifelong servant of the bank, slow of speech, shrewd, occasionally dissolving into uncontrolled laughter.

But to return to a day in London. In the days of Mr. Cooke the day-to-day decisions might fairly be described as his, and the bank had prospered during his long reign. I had neither the equipment nor the desire to emulate that part of his method, but he had left us a well-conceived system which could easily be adapted. We, then, that is the director or the directors, took the decisions as an act of collective mind, with the indispensable help, in the first place, of the chief official. That would be in the earlier years Mr. Jenkins and later Mr. Woollard. In the board room would be Mr. Prendergast, secretary of the bank, blessed with an upbringing in County Wexford, Mr. Wolfe, sometimes, when called upon, Mr. Warrell, Michael Cooke (son of the great Michael), chief accountant, and Mr. Marston, manager of the London office with a host of friends in the City.

What I am trying to say is that I shared in all the decisions of the bank but never took any of them on my own. I seldom if ever obtained agreement from reluctant colleagues. Sir Winston Churchill is supposed to have said that Professor Lindemann, later Lord Cherwell, was the other half of his brain. Mr. Woollard, a strong, retiring, gentle person, allowed me to think that our relationship was not dissimilar. Mr. Woollard is treasurer of his local Anglican church. If anyone wonders what kind of man is the backbone of the Church of England today, and whether one can devote one's working life to the City and one's private life to one's family and religion, Mr. Woollard is the answer to him. His quiet, acceptable relationship with the chief executives of other banks could always be relied on at marginal points.

But, looking back, I suppose that I displayed more initiative in some directions than in others. I was incorrigibly expansion-minded. I was determined to start new branches; our last one in England had been opened in 1921. I thought that we had somewhat neglected the business between England and Ireland and the potential customers moving between the two. We had the English and Irish sides of the bank too far apart. I was vehement for closer relations with the trade unions in England and Ireland. I was determined that women should get a better chance than of old. I pledged myself to see that no one doing the same job in the National Bank should be worse paid than in the Big Five, which had not always hitherto been the case. I was convinced that we were hiding our light too nervously under a bushel, partly through fear that if our true character as an Anglo-Irish bank was appreciated we would suffer in both countries. I was sure that we were a first-class bank with nothing to hide and that the more the public knew of us the more they would like us. On the other hand, left by myself and unprompted by Tony Acton, for example, I would have seriously underspent on buildings.

I was well aware that I had come into a well-organized bank, with a staff of great loyalty and customers firmly attached to us in both England and Ireland. We set special store by our personal treatment. One can't prove these things, but one of the advantages of a smaller bank (the disadvantages exist also) should be not only a more personal touch but more rapid decisions. Certainly we had been well equipped by Mr. Cooke for the double purpose. I well remember that at a dinner inaugurating one of our new English branches I boasted of our speedy methods. The mayor at my elbow pricked up his ears. Next morning the manager rang us up at head office to say that the mayor was on the doorstep, asking for a loan for his building business. 'I must have it at once,' he said cheerily, 'I was much impressed by what your chairman said last night. I want to test his bona fides.' He got his loan forthwith; his example seemed infectious.

What, then, of the personal responsibility which falls on the chairman? They are less, I am sure, than those which are felt by a political Minister. Leave out the general manager for the moment; the members of the board of a bank, after all, *share* the responsibility for policy and for results. The Board of Admiralty presents a superficial analogy, but that is recognized fiction. The only ultimate responsibility within the department is that of the Minister, i.e. the First Lord. In this sense a bank chairman could never feel the strain of personal responsibility in any way so acutely.

In spite of this consideration the life of the bank chairman *vis-à-vis* his general manager resembles that of a minister *vis-à-vis* his personal secretary in many respects. Some were surprised that I took to the life of a bank chairman so readily. But in fact it didn't seem all that new. Not that I adapted the words of Ulysses, 'Endure my soul still worse thou hast endured'. I said rather to myself: 'This is familiar ground. I have been here before.' The fact that I specialized in banking and currency at Oxford gave me deep down a basic grasp of what we were talking about which I never possessed at the Ministry of Civil Aviation or the Admiralty. I was much more likely to produce ideas which were really my own and not a careful extraction from the wisdom of others.

I have just mentioned one difference between the responsibilities of a Minister and a bank chairman. The decisions in banking are collective and not individual decisions. A second is still more significant; in business, in banking anyway, there is an absence of public knowledge and public discussion of the performance of particular institutions. This, while relieving the strain of public scrutiny, restricts, though it does not destroy, the field of public trust. Like other chairman, I used my annual speech to make as wide an impression as possible. I was among the first to propose ideas which afterwards bore fruit in the Radcliffe Enquiry, the system of special deposits and the Neddy type of planning. But I used my speeches particularly to enter into communication with the staff. Basically a Minister tends to be judged all too often by his speeches and replies to criticism, a bank chairman by results rather than words, which is fairer, though not absolutely fair. If your strength happens to lie in public debating you may regret the lost opportunities in the move from politics, but there is no denying the more restful mental existence.

On the other hand, the fact that one has no Prime Minister on top of one or Cabinet Ministers to carry along gives the bank chairman more freedom of action and perhaps more room for initiative. The absence of day-to-day pressure should make possible more long views. Certainly I found it easier as a bank chairman than a Minister to discuss at leisure and with a calm mind the question, Where do we mean to get to five years hence? It helps to know also that either oneself or one's nominated successor is likely to be in the chair for as far ahead as one can see. The Minister can never be quite certain when he gets back from the weekend whether he will find someone sitting in his chair. There are recorded cases of the latter occurrence—on one occasion the newcomer had been up to that moment the Minister's permanent secretary.

This is not the place to argue for or against nationalization—

a solution which no one seems to be proposing for the commercial banks. I cannot, however, resist referring to a combination of experiences which must be hard to match. I have presided over a public service, the Admiralty; a nationalized industry, civil aviation, where the air corporations were supervised and the aerodromes run directly by myself and my Ministry; and a private-enterprise industry, the private banks. My own professional life, apart from differences already noted, was very much the same in all three positions mentioned. The chairman's role, as I have suggested, provides the greatest freedom. It may follow, but does not always follow, that the chairman's use of this freedom coincides with the public interest. When we in the National Bank decided to start the majority of our new branches in the south-east of England we were undoubtedly looking after ourselves and our shareholders. Were we necessarily benefiting the State? In banking today I am sure that from the community standpoint freedom is worth the price; whether and how far this holds true of other industries must be settled by particular investigations and not in general terms.

The question was always arising in civil aviation: Are the corporations supposed to be governed by commercial or public-service principles? In business, unlike public administration, you have the profit motive as an incentive of action, and, still more relevant, the profit test as a criterion of the usefulness of what is done. The latter sounds inferior to the test of public value, but at least it provides a scale of public measurement which public benefit can hardly be said to provide in spite of modern refinements. Years ago Randolph Churchill told me of a conversation just held with his father. Randolph had been reading Bernard Shaw and told his father that he was disillusioned with the profit motive. 'What are you going to put in its place?' his father growled back. 'The loss motive?' I suppose the same rather crude defence could be put up for the profit test.

There is also a psychological difference between the public service and the business approach. The public-service man instinctively asks whether a proposition will help the country, the business man whether he and the 'other fellow' can do business together to mutual advantage on 'Do ut des' principles. But it's like the division between introverts and extroverts. Everyone is both, more or less. I associate Hugh Gaitskell with public service before all else and Harold Wilson with an instinct for business. But Hugh would have made a magnificent chairman of a bank, and I believe Harold Wilson will prove himself a fine Socialist Prime Minister. The bank man, from the novice to the chairman, has not chosen his profession to make a great fortune. He wants to be reasonably well paid, better than he has been, and the staff expect security. But the idea of public service is as strong in the good bank manager as it is in the Civil Servant. At the end of his career he will probably measure his success by the service he has rendered to his countrymen. Yet he is engaged in ever more strenuous competition with rival managers. The commercial motive and the public service are intertwined and are indistinguishable.

I have mentioned—boastfully, I am afraid—that during my time as chairman our bank in England and Wales increased its business three times as fast as the banking average. It was this, I think, that led Donald Tyerman, editor of *The Economist*, a good friend of mine, but no hander out of bouquets, to write to congratulate me at the end of my time on my enormous success as an amateur banker. And I suppose that it was mainly our results which led the *Daily Telegraph*, when my departure was first announced, to refer to the respect felt in the City for my business flair and shrewdness. From the public's point of view the service required is threefold. A bank must be safe for keeping money, handy for moving money, liberal in lending money. From the bank's angle it can render this service only if it makes a reasonable profit. This must come from collecting as much money as possible and as cheaply as possible, and using it, whether by loan or otherwise, as prudently as possible. In my experience the bank that succeeds best even by a purely commercial standard is the one which is most ardent in rendering the public the service it is looking for. But that ardour will in its turn depend on deep psychological factors at work in the life of the bank.

Evan Jenkins, a colleague but no flatterer, has seen me come and go. He has had wide and painful experience of human success and failure in peace and war. In a final comment on my 'reign' he selected our managerial conferences and my own many visits to branches accompanied by colleagues as a principal source of our strong collective endeavour. Indeed, I not infrequently found myself restraining the young managers in our branches from making a twenty-four-hour day of it and bringing themselves and their wives to breakdown. But it was a senior manager who said to me when I warned him against overwork, 'Oh, you mustn't stop me working, it's my great joy,' and a number of others spoke likewise.

It was naturally easier to keep in close touch with the English than the Irish staffs, in spite of seventy or eighty visits to Ireland during my time as chairman, and managers' conferences in all parts of the country. But when I feel regret at not having come still closer to them I console myself by looking at the presentation scroll which the Irish staff gave me on my retirement, along with their share of a Mini car in which the whole staff joined. The scroll stands on my dressing-table now. I will quote only one sentence, with understandable pride: 'They take leave of an honoured chairman and a great friend.' They have been much kinder than I deserve, but there was one step for which in my heart I take credit. When I became chairman there was a serious dispute between the Irish banks, including ourselves and the staffs. A 'go slow' was actually in progress when I delivered in Dublin my annual speech. I mentioned the difficulty, but went on 'even against the background of the dispute, the directors must not fail to express their appreciation for all the hard work done by the staff over a number of years'. The words seem commonplace enough today, but I can still feel something turn over in the atmosphere when I delivered them. I treasure the belief that they heralded a new relationship.

I end with the submission that one obtains a dynamic impulse in a business more by mutual confidence than by a restless expenditure of energy, though many journeys were made. A certain young man took £300 on a crazy impulse from the bank in Ireland and was dismissed. I was always ready to see anyone who was to be dismissed or compelled to resign. Indeed, I was ready to see any official who wanted to see me, but I liked a delinquent official to be specially advised of this (not that there were many such cases). I duly saw the young man, a heart-broken figure, about to set out for Canada. I gave him a rosary and said that I hoped he would keep in touch with me. Within four months he had repaid the money, working forty degrees below freezing point on an aerodrome in the far north-west before returning to Ireland. Later he has suffered much nervous trouble—I am sure that he would never have taken the money if he'd been in his right mind. He and I keep in contact and I see him when I am in Ireland. There is much spiritual seeking in his letters and conversations, along with much unhappy confusion. Nothing was further from my mind when I befriended the young man than the calculation that this or other forms of sympathy would 'go down well with the staff', but in my eyes it is this sort of personal identification with the staff which the chairman alone can offer.

Each chairman will have his own method. Some who are shy will prefer to do good by stealth, neglecting the personal credit. Oliver Franks surprised an East Anglian manager by putting up his feet on his desk and saying, 'Please talk to me for an hour about banking in East Anglia.' The manager will never forget it. It doesn't matter how it's done. It is the spirit that counts and it is the possibility of showing or not showing that spirit, and of spreading it or not spreading it, which gives the chairman the chance to do his job well or badly.

3

Double Agent

THE City, if I can use that dangerous abstraction for the moment, is very sensitive about its reputation for selfishness or unselfishness. It is confident, and fully entitled to be, about its reputation for honesty. The best autobiography to emerge from the City is that of Mr. Lionel Fraser. He ends it as follows: 'If I have helped my readers to detect the humanity which is to be found in abundance in City circles, the warmth, the kindliness, as opposed to the accepted picture of hard, unrelenting people working solely for their own enrichment and aggrandizement, I shall be even more content.' The passage, with what goes before, contains an idealism beyond cavil, but what is to me most striking about it is Mr. Fraser's reference to a City of 'hard, unrelenting, exceptionally self-seeking people' as the accepted picture. He has led a varied life, but I do not gather that he spent much, if any, time among left-wing enthusiasts. And yet he has found, or seems to have found, so low a view outside the square mile of the humanity within it.

Two other City men of high attainment are Lord Balfour of Burleigh, formerly chairman of Lloyds Bank, and Lord Drogheda, chairman of the *Financial Times*. Between them they have contributed much to public service and culture. Neither is as apprehensive as Mr. Fraser appears to be about the City's reputation outside. When I ceased to be a bank chairman, and a City man myself, each asked the same question: 'Don't you feel on the whole that there's as high standard there as you would find anywhere?' And they were thinking more of the moral than the economic factor, though not ignoring the latter.

The same preoccupation came out while I was writing this chapter, at a luncheon with a most successful customer of the National Bank, who had done great things in property. He was giving me lunch in the Junior Carlton Club; I asked if I would be relieved of my clothing if discovered there. 'Not at all,' he replied, 'I voted Labour till 1945, I have been utterly opposed to the Labour Party ever since because their way leads to dictatorship, but I am still a Socialist.' He went on to say that the only true Socialist was Jesus Christ, because He was the only man who gave up everything. Now I happen to know that this particular property chairman was a man of extreme personal dedication. Our New Bridge Society for ex-prisoners had not, and has not, a more active or effective member. In the face of a good deal of discouragement by his personal exertions he had just obtained a flat for an all-too-well-known ex-prisoner and his mother and father. He had personally guaranteed the rent, as he had done on other occasions.

What he was trying to tell me was that this kind of Socialism, in other words a life of service to others, could be found as readily in the City as anywhere else, and a good deal more readily there than among politicians of any Party. This use of the word 'Socialism', of course, was highly individual. I have never encountered it elsewhere in the City. But the conversation brings out the point that many of the best men in the City are well aware that a life lived exclusively in the City would carry its own dangers, and that a charitable philosophy must be consciously embraced, not just for the purposes of the image but for deeper and more Christian reasons. For my part I have never supposed that those who work in the City, at such an infinite variety of jobs and on an equal variety of levels, were likely to be better or worse than the general run of the British population. I have always been ready to agree with Mr. Fraser's additional estimate that they are normal, decent citizens.

It happens, however, that from my earliest days I have been inspired by and have unworthily sought to emulate one layman above all others. This was my mother's brother, the Hon. Arthur Villiers, who until he recently retired was a partner in Barings for many years, and simultaneously has lived—and still lives—in Hackney Wick. For all his extreme modesty he has long been known in the East End as the presiding genius of the Eton Manor Boys and Old Boys Clubs. He has received the freedoms of Leyton and Hackney. His moral influence has stretched far and wide, in and beyond those regions. From early days after the death of my father when I was eight, I saw far more of him on his return from the First World War than anyone else except my mother. Not unnaturally I identified the City with Barings, and Barings with my uncle. Incidentally, my mother's family, the Jerseys, owned Child's Bank until it was taken over by Glyn Mills. It would have been inconceivable, therefore, that I should have started life with a bias against the City, and through all my subsequent transmigrations in thought and politics I have never been in danger of acquiring one. When I was at Eton I seem to remember asking my uncle whether I might be wise to look for a career in banking. He warned me that even at that age my handwriting ruled it out. Later at Oxford I chose banking and currency as my special subject in Modern Greats.

When I 'went down' I cherished the dream of making a lasting contribution to financial theory, and with that in mind worked as a pupil in Buckmaster and More, the intellectual stockbrokers. I could not have chosen a worse moment—it exactly coincided with the tremendous slump of 1929—but I was an earnest, genuine inmate of the City for those few months in my hard collar, short black jacket, and striped trousers. I left a grateful, though a poorer, man.

Who shall measure the relative idealism to be found in the various professions? Three classic temptations are those of turning stones into bread, throwing oneself from the roof of the temple, and acquiring all the kingdoms of the earth. Wealth, glory, and power as they may be roughly interpreted. Imagine three brothers who enter business, politics, and the Civil Service. One might assume that the business man would be most subject to the first, the craving for wealth; the politician to the second, the love of fame; and the Civil Servant to the third, the yearning for power.

Such a generalization seems to me just worth making, to encourage thought, but hardly more than that. Take, for example, the English directors of the National Bank at the end of my chairmanship. The first two, Tony Acton and (Sir) Evan Jenkins, were there before me; the other four were my nominations. To say that Tony Acton is a typical City man would be misleading; he is much abler than the average man, in the City or elsewhere. He has had many advantages beyond that of the average or typical man, and made full use of them. He has travelled widely and intensively in Europe, America, Asia, and Africa. He was for many years a managing partner in Lazards, and since then has been a director of the Ottoman Bank, Bank of West Africa, Bank of London and South America, the Bank of London and Montreal, and the Standard Bank. He was a leading figure and excellent athlete at Eton; is indubitably wealthy; is fond of beautiful objects, and can afford to acquire them. He is the husband of a charming and popular wife. In short, the beau idéal of the successful old Etonian in the City, an inside member of the club if ever there was one. He and I were and are completely different types, in spite of the fact that we are both old Etonians of about the same age and background. But who shall say whether his ambitions are less pure than those of myself or my political friends?

For the whole eight years we were together he worked unceasingly but unobtrusively, just as my uncle Arthur Villiers would have done, for the success of our bank. In particular he placed the whole of his many years of experience unreservedly at my disposal. It would never have occurred to him to do anything else. It wasn't until we had been together quite some time that I discovered that he could have been chairman himself. He had indeed, as I have told already, been repeatedly pressed by my predecessor, Mr. Cooke, to succeed him, but in his objective, seemingly cold-blooded, way, he had decided that the chairman of the National Bank should have Irish blood and be, if possible, a Roman Catholic. And that settled the matter for him.

Evan Jenkins has found himself in the City by accident.
Coming of a family with high traditions of Government
service, he was a brilliant scholar, both at Rugby and Balliol,
serving and being decorated in the First World War in between.
He was secretary to the Viceroy of India, and the last Governor
of the Punjab. The end of the old Indian Civil Service cut
short a career of the utmost distinction. Since then he has been
chairman of the Eastern Bank, a director of the Chartered
Bank of India and of our own National Bank, bringing to
these later occupations the famous standards of his old profession. Not long ago a book appeared which dealt with the
last days of the British in India. Much of it concentrated on
the period and the area where Evan Jenkins was a central
figure. I asked him if he had read it. 'No,' he said, 'I doubt if
that kind of book could be helpful just now'—or words to
that effect. Finally I showed him a passage in the book in
which he himself was highly lauded, and described as the
epitome of all that was best in the Indian Civil Service. He
read it reluctantly and without enthusiasm. 'I see he's made
a couple of mistakes,' he remarked, as he handed me back the
book.

It goes without saying that I think highly of my own four
nominations: Sir Ivone Kirkpatrick, Cecil Rait, Norman
Biggs, and David Montagu. Ivone Kirkpatrick had been
permanent under-secretary at the Foreign Office and later
chairman of the Independent Television Authority. His
whole background, like that of Sir Evan Jenkins, had been that
of public service. Yet when I handed over the chairmanship
to him on my disappearance I could happily realize that he had
adapted himself without difficulty to City ways. There was
also the outstanding fact that amidst all his official success in
British service he had never abandoned his Irish home or
allowed anyone to forget that his roots lay there.

Cecil Rait had been twice a soldier, but is otherwise best
known in the City as deputy chairman of the Charterhouse
Company, and for helping Sir Nutcombe Home build up
this, one of the few completely new institutions that have
reached the top line in the City since the end of the First
World War. Yet much of his heart has gone into the work of

the Catholic Industrialists movement, which with Jack Gormley he has done as much as anybody to establish.

Norman Biggs, born in Newry, Northern Ireland, had left school earlier than our other directors, but had worked up through the official reaches of the Bank of England; had then become important in Kleinworts before becoming managing director of Esso. He was recommended to us by Kit Hoare, the one stockbroker picked out for special mention by Mr. Lionel Fraser. I will follow Mr. Fraser's example. Our bank has never had a better friend than Kit Hoare, and when he told me at the end of my time that I had made a great difference I valued his opinion more than any other. I should describe personal sensitivity as Norman Biggs's strongest feature; along with a knowledge of finance at all levels, a tendency to over-work an intermittent danger.

David Montagu, at thirty-three, was not only our youngest director but was said without contradiction to be the youngest director ever appointed to the board of a clearing bank. His flair for what is about to happen is extraordinary. He rang me up one afternoon and asked me whether Sir Anthony Eden was about to resign. It had never occurred to me as an immediate possibility, but, sure enough, it was so. I met him another day at a Mansion House lunch; he told me with a worried expression that he didn't like the look of things in the Middle East. Next morning I read that war had broken out there. I suppose that no firm in the City is more quickly alive to movements of sentiment in America and Europe than Samuel Montagu, but David possesses antennae all his own. David Montagu maintains an intense interest in Jewish—and not only Jewish—youth activities.

There was an additional reason why David's appointment gave me special pleasure. In a careful section of his book, sympathetic, though I am not quite certain whether he always leaves the impression intended, Mr. Lionel Fraser states with boldness: 'There are large numbers of Jews in the banking world.' That is, of course, true of merchant banking. The names of Rothschild, M. Samuel, Samuel Montagu, and, more recently, Helbert Wagg and Warburgs, to name only a few, are justly renowned. But it is not in the least true of commercial banking in Britain, or of the joint-stock banks. The National Bank has always possessed a more than average proportion of Jews among our most valued customers. I had been keen for a long time to appoint a recognized Jew to our board. As far as I could make out, the deputy chairman of Lloyd's was the only Jew on the board of any joint-stock bank, and he, a much respected figure, had come from Government service rather than a Jewish house. The position in the Bank of England, on the court and high-executive level, was as bad or worse. During my time in the City I would not describe this as deliberate anti-Semitism. In charity one might call it an evil legacy, but the result was the same. The highest positions in the City were virtually closed to Jews. I am glad to think that since David joined our board two of the Big Five have appointed leading Jewish merchant bankers to their boards. I have no grounds for saying that the step we took had any influence whatever on such developments, but I shall go on hoping it did.

One cannot describe or analyse a City personality who was that and nothing more. All the City men in the higher reaches of the City, whom one esteems most (alas! there are no women, although there is no reason why there should not be), are seriously concerned with the profitability of their institution, and in various degrees with increasing their private fortunes. But they would not be the men they are if that were their whole life, and for me, at least, it is other aspects of their life that attract me towards them. Yet in one sense the above is a slightly idealized picture. The same is true of Mr. Lionel Fraser's account of his main friends and colleagues. And this is not because both he and I are writing for publication; and not only because one is very unlucky not to become fond of those one works with over a period.

The truth is that the abstraction, 'the City', teems with ambiguities. The vast majority of those who work in the City are what used to be called 'clerks', now—in banking at least— 'officials'. A good proportion of them are now women. Something like half of them in banking belong to the National Union of Bank Employees, affiliated to the T.U.C. It was people like these in our own bank who joined with their

Irish colleagues and gave me, out of their not-very-high pay, a Mini car when I ceased to be chairman. I am not likely to forget their claims as human beings. But when one talks about 'City opinion' and the standards of the City, one is usually referring to the director or higher-management level. In making a comparison between their moral standards and those of, say, politics or Government service, one must remember that there is not the same scrutiny over the individual firm in the City as there is in the public field. There is, if you like, more freedom; more scope for initiative; more chance to go right ahead of one's fellows, but less restriction on practices unethical or near the line.

While the City, like the Commons, is in one sense a replica of national life, though in the case of the City the Conservatives are always in power, there may be a moral distinction when one comes to the weaker brethren of the City. Things can go on among them, though I am without first-hand experience, which would be eliminated more rapidly in politics by public scrutiny. The leaders in the City are, of all men on earth, the most anxious to eliminate any such defects.

During my eight years in the City I waged a rather timid but persistent campaign for better relations between the Labour Party and the City. My best effort, looking back, was an article published by the *Daily Telegraph* on 31 January 1958. Many conversations tended in the same direction. I had the honour of lunching at Rothschilds on different occasions with fellow guests who included Hugh Gaitskell, Harold Wilson, Aneurin Bevan, Frank Cousins, and James Callaghan.

James Callaghan has for a long time been considered the most probable Chancellor of the Exchequer in the next Labour Government. From my experience in the City I can testify that he is regarded as a 'very charming fellow', anxious to listen and study rival views. There is some danger, I suppose, in a Labour Chancellor of the Exchequer being too charming, but I have no fear on that score in James's case. His friendly disarming manner somewhat disguises his formidable size. He is a firmly integrated Socialist by training and conviction, with much intelligence, an easy power of speech, no chips on his shoulder anywhere, and an absolutely sound family life behind him.

I went with Harold Wilson to dinner with David Robarts, chairman of the National Provincial Bank, and at that time of the clearing banks as a whole. It was an evening of quick and shrewd appreciations and mutual tolerance and understanding. And there were other similar activities. My exertions may have made some difference. I cannot be sure. Naturally it was an issue close to my heart, and indeed to my peace of mind. Throughout the period I was a prey in my role of 'double agent' to many two-way feelings of guilt. I knew, or thought I knew, that many of my best and staunchest friends in the Labour Party could not believe that a true Socialist could be a banker at all. If they tolerated my City role it was on the cheerful, if unjustified, assumption that I was a sort of Wooden Horse, doing a useful job for the party inside the City walls. While many of my City friends (and the people I actually met were consistently a friendly multitude) accepted me in many cases as an old Etonian creditably concerned for the under-dog, but not a Socialist in any 'nasty' sense. It could be said, there-fore, that my battle for a better understanding between the City and the Socialists was at bottom a battle with myself. If this was true it was not the whole truth.

In one of my speeches in the House of Lords I argued that in the totality of misunderstanding and suspicion there was at once a rational and an irrational factor. Let me say a prelimin-ary word about the latter first, taking one example from each side of the fence. Working in partnership with my wife, I spoke up and down the country throughout the 1955 and 1959 general elections. On neither occasion did any Labour Party chairman ever refer to the fact that I worked in the City, let alone remark that I was chairman of a bank. (Curiously enough, this has begun to happen at one or two by-elections since I have left the City.) Yet no attempt was made to conceal my aristocratic background; a certain pleasure was taken— very sensibly—in presenting me as one example of the fact that the Labour Party was now the party not of one class but of the nation. The only secret too guilty to reveal was that I was in truth a bank chairman. This would have destroyed, I do not doubt, the atmosphere at the time. Yet if Labour were anxious, as they were, particularly on the second occasion, to win a reputation for economic responsibility, one would have thought that my bank chairmanship would have been a valuable card.

On the other side, there is the sad story of my candidature for a famous City club. It has never before been revealed, but as Sherlock Holmes used to say, 'The time has now come when no harm could result.' When I told the House of Lords that no one in my experience could doubt the depth of the City anti-Socialist prejudice I had this story, but not only this, in mind. Two relatives of mine, each exceptionally popular and respected in the City, proposed and seconded me for the club in question. I had been black-balled before now for clubs, but not since reaching adult life, and, frankly, I regarded the election as a formality. Indeed, I had not even bothered to find out the day of the election. To my astonishment and chagrin, however, I was rung up one afternoon at the bank and told on the telephone by the much embarrassed chairman of the club that things had gone shockingly wrong, and, not to put too fine a point upon it, I had been 'pilled'. I think he felt, apart from all personal factors, that the world of banking had been collectively insulted through this rough treatment of a bank chairman. Certainly no one could have been more tender in his expressions of sympathy. I gathered that it was all very much regretted by the committee, but that the names of candidates were stuck up in public, and that the members in true democratic fashion could exercise their power of protest.

If I heard a friend of mine tell a similar story I should wonder whether it always is pure politics or whether they have personally antagonized someone. On this occasion I know only what I was told. One member at least was heard to say, 'I love Frank, but I'm not going to have him coming in here and getting all the advantages of the City when he and his lot want to smash it all up.' And it may be that quite a number of others felt like him. I repeat that I am certain that the committee and other top people in the City were extremely annoyed. It is just one more illustration of the difficulty of generalizing about City opinion.

I would not say that the relationship between the Labour Party and the City altered appreciably during my chairmanship. The kind of views I expressed in my *Daily Telegraph* article, which came after my first three years, were those I held to the end. The circumstances of that article make it a convenient focus. It will be remembered that in the autumn of 1957, following the imposition of crisis measures, a great howl went up that the news of the increased Bank Rate had been leaked in advance, for financial gain. A tribunal had been set up, and had reported that nothing improper had occurred. When my article appeared the House of Commons were about to debate the report. But to understand why I wrote the article at all, and wrote it under some emotion, one must go back to the previous autumn and the crisis measures of that time.

The crisis first impinged on me directly at the meetings of the Clearing Bank chairmen. 'Oh, those Curzonian dissertations!' says Harold Nicolson, writing of Marquis Curzon of Kedlestone. 'Something has gone out of my life, now that they are no more.' I suppose I could say the same of the meeting of the eleven bank chairmen held at monthly intervals throughout my eight years, with occasional emergency additions. What are bank chairmen like when they get together? I am sometimes asked. To answer 'Just like anybody else' is a little unambitious. A few impressions must therefore be attempted.

When I became chairman of the National Bank four out of the Big Five were Old Etonians. The fifth, Mr. Tuke of Barclays, was an old Wykehamist. The chairman of the Lancashire Banks provided metaphorically a northern accent, but what I used to call in my own mind 'the U Banks'—Coutts and Glyn Mills—were in firm Etonian hands. And, of course, I was an old Etonian myself, though in some eyes a lapsed one. This kind of atmosphere was more or less preserved throughout my period, though diluted by the chairmanships of Lord Monckton (Harrow) and for the time of Sir Oliver Franks—now Lord Franks—(Bristol Grammar School). In any high level City grouping it was at least an even chance that one was talking to an Old Etonian.

Whether one likes the old Etonian ethos or not, no one can

be so blind as to fail to notice its existence. To avoid mis-
understanding, I would not think that any of these old Etonian
chairmen were appointed because their colleagues knew them
at Eton, or were determined, out of school loyalty, to see the
old school represented. The explanation is partly that the top
banking families have tended for many years to send their sons
to Eton; partly in financial and material advantages, which old
Etonians tend to possess; and partly, it could be argued, that
certain qualities of pose and leadership are acquired at Eton
more readily than at any other school.

What else can we say about bank chairmen, beyond the fact
that they were, or can easily be supposed to have been, at Eton?
They are likely to be well, if unobtrusively, dressed, well fed,
and well washed. Their manners are good; they are invariably
cheerful and friendly, certainly to one another, and presumably
to everyone. They are, however, a reserved, not to say cagey,
race, at any rate in their mutual dealings. I have often sat at
gatherings of politicians and asked myself, granting these
people the ordinary range of virtues and abilities, what is it
that distinguishes them from normal humanity? I have never
had any doubt about the answer—their loquacity; the urge to
make their contribution to the world's welfare through their
own uplifted voices.

With bankers it is precisely the opposite. Sometimes you get
the feeling with politicians that even the most modest measures
his achievement as he leaves a meeting by the amount he has
talked, by the extent to which he has imposed his ideas on
others. With a group of bankers I always had the feeling that
success was measured by the extent one gave nothing away. It
would not be literally true that any banker declines to offer his
ideas except in return for money, but a gathering of chairmen,
as distinct from a gathering within a bank, is inevitably a meeting of trade competitors. At such meetings one comes, metaphorically (I do not want to pretend to have been holier than
the others), with one's pocket book buttoned up. The most
common conversational opening in my recollection was, 'Do
you hope to get abroad this year?' In fairness, to compensate
for a somewhat satirical picture, I should mention that I have
never met a group of individuals who were more generous in

subscribing out of their own pockets to good causes, including mine, and bank chairmen are salaried individuals and not, by City standards, particularly rich men.

I served under four chairmen of the chairmen. None of them had worked up through their own bank (as, before my time, had Mr. Tuke of Barclays, a veritable giant of banking). Two of them were in every instinct business men: Lord Aldenham, a merchant banker of the old and dignified and Mr. David Robarts of the new and very lively school. Both of them kept our meetings short, the less anyone interfered with their business the better. They assumed that we felt the same, which was probably true of most of us.

Sir Oliver Franks—now Lord Franks—and Lord Monckton brought a wider outlook, though left to themselves they would probably have made much less money than their predecessors. Each has proved himself a great public servant and made a world-wide reputation outside business. Oliver Franks is popularily supposed to have refused at various times the editorship of *The Times*, the Director Generalship of the B.B.C. and the Governorship of the Bank of England. I happen to have come across one or two managers of Lloyds who spoke of him with reverence; the City felt honoured by his presence, if a little bewildered. He conducted our meetings in the highest traditions of the seminar, anxious that none of us should fail to make a contribution before night fell. He formulated our presumed thoughts so much better than we could express them ourselves that the rest of us were sometimes left in the position of the speaker who followed Edmund Burke after one of his speeches and could only ejaculate, 'I say ditto to Mr. Burke.'

'Don't you think,' Sir Oliver would begin, 'that we might tell the Governor that we see it this way?' Then would follow a perfect little disquisition, which some of the chairmen followed a little glazed of eye. It sounded right, but could these propositions really be their own inchoate thoughts? The only disadvantage of the Franks method from my point of view was that the proceedings took longer and sometimes I was secretly panting to slip off to the House of Lords.

Lord Monckton's methods are quite indescribable. In terms of time his meetings would be shorter than those of Franks, slightly longer than those of Aldenham and Robarts. I had experienced his famous charm many times before I met him in banking. I had assumed, however, that a desire to please, an age-old weakness of my own, detracted somewhat from his effectiveness in action. His inflexible support of the Duke of Windsor in his evil times should have told me I was wrong, and his leadership of the Monckton Commission proved it.

My Labour Party colleagues had always a great opinion of him. One of the highest told me at the time of the 1959 election that at some future date he might make a very good Governor of the Bank of England. I pointed out that he had been a Tory Cabinet Minister and met the answer, 'Oh, Walter's never been a real Tory.' Be that as it may, I completely revised my opinion of his strength of will after seeing him in the chairman's chair. The personal charm, while completely genuine, and indeed all the more because it was so genuine and based on so much good-will towards everyone, was used legitimately but designedly to promote the public good. It will be a tragedy if he is not given time to place the labour relations in banking on a new and far more satisfactory footing.

Certainly the collective attitude of the banks towards trade unionism in this day and age is indefensible. My predecessor, Mr. Cooke, was a very conservative gentleman, but luckily we had recognized the National Union of Bank Employees, N.U.B.E., years before I arrived on the scene. And we recognized no one else. Barclays recognized N.U.B.E. and a staff association; the other banks nearly always recognized staff associations. They not only refused to recognize N.U.B.E. but, in some cases at least, treated them with a certain contempt. And under this provocation N.U.B.E. were not immaculate in the tone of some of their replies.

When I first became a chairman I was freely told that trade unionism, while excellent in industry, was unsuitable for banking. This sounded, as was later to be seen to be, fairly good nonsense. The modern defence of the reactionary position is that the staff associations are trade unions, so that there is no need for N.U.B.E. That can hardly be swallowed. I am very proud to have been the first bank chairman to address a large gathering of N.U.B.E., receiving, predictably perhaps, but most acceptedly, a hero's welcome. Much more important, Lord Monckton, with all the prestige of his great work as a Minister of Labour behind him, was devoting himself, when I left banking, to a new understanding and new lines of negotiating machinery.

But I have wandered from our chairmen's meetings with their marked absence of 'ganging up' against the public, their personal friendliness, their sharp spirit of competition, and underlying all, of course, a British assumption that nothing must be done to damage the State. Once every three months we repaired for our meeting to the Bank of England and afterwards lunched there. The Governor, Kim Cobbold, had been roughly my contemporary at Eton and had won a classical scholarship to King's. His abilities and toughness were unquestioned. We always thought that he and the others in the Bank of England kept a special little place in their hearts for the National Bank. They certainly did not want to see the 'small man' blotted out of joint-stock banking. He was in my eyes curiously reluctant, though far from intellectually unable, to tell the bank chairmen what he wanted done. It was part of his whole philosophy, which is still, I suppose, the official line in the Treasury and the City, that only in the last resort does the Governor impose his views by the various techniques open to him.

The Governor who succeeded Cobbold, Lord Cromer, is more obviously positive and on more than one occasion has taken up a position in public with which the banks have disagreed. These, however, are slight differences of emphasis. It is the Governor's enormously difficult job to avoid as far as possible forcible measures while seeing that Government policy is carried out by the City and City opinion fairly interpreted to the Government. All this, without becoming himself a mere post-box. To perform these tasks perfectly in a period of British financial difficulty would be quite impossible, but both Cobbold and Cromer possessed the strength of character to stand up to the strain.

In my abstract way I reached the conclusion that the Government and the banking system should be in much closer touch. After all, the clearing banks had no representation on the Bank of England, no direct contact with the Treasury, and, therefore, apart from stray social encounters, no direct line to the Government at all. During my eight years—and six Chancellors of the Exchequer—this issue went through one or two phases.

We saw nothing of Mr. Butler (of course, I cannot say what private contacts he may or may not have had). Mr. Macmillan seemed much more anxious to meet the bank chairmen. I am told that he got quite a shock when he looked round the room and found me sitting there, an ex-Labour Minister, and member of the front bench in the House of Lords. If so, he concealed it perfectly and listened to my suggestions about a policy to unite the nation with proper gravity.

Mr. Thorneycroft carried it much further. In the financial crisis of autumn 1957 the whole tribe of us were summoned to the Treasury, where we sat confronted by Mr. Thorneycroft and other Ministers and high Treasury officials. The representatives of the Bank of England were seated sideways so as to emphasize their role as mediators. Great stress was laid on secrecy, successfully so, I think, but for whatever reason, the experiment was not repeated. On one occasion when I happened to be absent Mr. Heathcote Amory held an informal discussion with the chairmen after a Bank of England lunch. But Messrs. Selwyn Lloyd and Maudling dropped the practice, possibly finding it more convenient to talk to individuals privately.

Well, there we all were, we bank chairmen, in the early autumn of 1957. My personal recollections of the crisis are not very exciting, but one point always remains with me, which can safely be mentioned now. We are told a great part of the truth, we are told a lot of things in advance which we could have used to the advantages of our banks if we had been so minded. But, of course, that was unthinkable. So for a short while we were in a difficult position, with knowledge that was much more a nuisance than a benefit.

The one thing we were *not* told was that any change, let alone a startling increase, in Bank Rate was intended. I confess freely that this very fact of our not being told led me to suppose that no important change was intended. An older hand might have reached a different conclusion. Certainly the large increase, when it did come, was a complete surprise to me. If such a situation ever arose again I cannot imagine that bank chairmen would be so incurious about the most striking step to be taken as we allowed ourselves to be.

None of this bears directly on the alleged leakage of the news about a coming change in Bank Rate. Except in this way. I was surprised, as I have just said, when the Bank Rate was raised, but not at all when afterwards it appeared that it had been anticipated and the anticipations acted on. The news of far-reaching Government financial measures had been spread so widely that it was open to anyone of intelligence to expect as their natural supplement a big increase in Bank Rate. Among informed persons the bank chairmen were perhaps the least likely to guess correctly, just because they had been told so much else, and yet that one all-important thing had been so carefully withheld.

Then came the alleged leakage, then the outcry, then the enquiry and the exonerating report. Accusations flew readily both ways; among Socialists against the City; in the City against the Socialists, for charges, which it was held, were completely refuted by the report. Throughout this particular period my position resembled that of Sir Winston Churchill, who when he was asked which side he had been on in the Spanish Civil War replied, 'I was on both sides.' I still think that the Labour Party leaders, and Harold Wilson in particular, would have been grossly failing in their duty if they had not pressed for a report. This is not to suppose that every word they used was inspired. Though 'even the ranks of Tuscany'— in other words the Conservative M.P.s—reluctantly admired the toughness with which Harold Wilson defended himself amidst furious, and at first derisive, antagonism throughout the final debate.

But I did also feel, and am glad I felt, irresistible sympathy for the City leaders whose activities came in for such painful publicity, and whose characters and chance words were so suddenly brought under the public microscope. Is it wrong to admit that one is more influenced in this way if one knows the individuals than if one doesn't? The famous sentence in one of the published letters, 'This is anti-British ... but it makes sense to me', was naturally fastened on by Labour speakers as illustrating a conflict that could arise between the outlook of a particular business and the national interest. Its author was godfather to one of my grandchildren; I knew from first-hand experience his lifelong dedication and that of his family to building a fine business. Meeting him, and one or two others who were under fire at that time, I felt overwhelmingly, and still do, that they were being subjected, through accident rather than ill-will, to a species of criticism not inflicted on ordinary citizens, and one which they had no reason to expect.

It was in this mood that I seized my pen, or rather seized Peggy Fitzgerald, my private secretary. For eight years I was not only completely dependent on her but known to be so. She was selected as 'Private Secretary Number One' by the *Evening Standard* in a series of 'Top Secretaries'. And richly did she deserve her pride of place. She carried one virtue to an extreme point, in a fashion I recommend to other private secretaries. If anyone accepted an invitation from me she always told me that 'Mr. or Lord X would be delighted to come'. If he refused she gave me the impression he was heart-broken. It was not her fault if I did not appear throughout Westminster and Whitehall as the friendliest person alive. Mr. Tyrrell and Mr. Starkey, messengers at the bank, emulated her care for me. Her reputation extended far beyond the National Bank.

With Peggy's help, and without hesitation, I produced my *Daily Telegraph* article, from which I quote this passage:

'What is hard to convey, or indeed apprehend in full, unless one has worked in the City, is the pride that human beings in the City feel in their chosen profession; in its standards of professional competence; industry and, above all, honour. They believe, and are surely right to believe, that whatever changes may or may not be desirable in financial organization, no great country in the world except Britain could survive a grilling like the Parker enquiry and come out of it with its head held high. I am not coming forward to say that those I have met in the City are morally better than politicians, but I will certainly swear they are no worse.'

There was a sentence in the article which afterwards caused me some slight embarrassment in the House of Commons debate. 'Some', I said, 'of the most eminent of the leaders in the City have recently vindicated their integrity, never doubted by anyone but a fool or a knave.' This was quoted approvingly by Conservative spokesmen amidst loud applause from their own side as a fine debating refutation of Labour critics, particularly Harold Wilson, who was supposed to have done just that. I wrote in some distress to Harold, apologizing for any embarrassment I had inadvertently caused him. He assured me he had not in any way been disturbed. The fact that I felt bound to write is a small example of the horrible wariness one develops in politics through fear that any well-balanced statement will be broken up and some parts used out of context.

A lot of people in the City were grateful for that article. It fitted in with efforts that my brother-in-law Donald McLachlan was making at the time in the columns of the paper with his usual open-minded initiative and gift for a phrase to mitigate what he called 'the feud without a future' between the City and the Labour Party. In my absence from the next chairmen's meeting, Mr. Heathcote Amory, Chancellor of the Exchequer, told Tony Acton in front of the other chairmen what good service I had rendered. On another occasion at a large City banquet he stepped out of the procession and shook me warmly by the hand. And while I would call him friendly, I would not call him an ultra-effusive man.

Following that article, and following various speeches before and after it in the House of Lords, I received various letters, communications, and luncheon invitations among City people interested in some slight *rapprochement* with the Labour Party. I cannot pretend that the Labour Party showed a similar interest, although individuals were always happy to meet my City friends on social terms. I remembered lunching for the purposes of this kind of discussion at one of the most elevated of merchant banks. We were getting on quite well when the senior partner came in and asked what we were talking about.

'A *rapprochement*,' he was told, 'between the Labour Party and the City.'

'Oh,' he said, 'isn't that like expecting the Vicar General of the Jesuits to become a chum of the President of the Ethical Church?'

It was explained to him as gently as possible that this was what I had been asked to lunch to talk about. And every now and then I found myself interesting some high City personage in detailed plans for bringing one or two Socialists, ex-Ministers or economists, on to banking or other boards, which were always well stocked with Conservatives. But somehow these plans never came to anything. They tended to arouse most interest just before the election of 1959 and, when Labour lost, they somehow got lost sight of.

It is convenient here, perhaps, to sum up my thought about the gulf which separates the Labour Party from the City. The beginning of wisdom must be to regard the movement to better understanding as essentially two-way traffic. Socialist politicians make a mistake if they regard the average board room as a conscious extension of the Conservative Party. Any City group, collectively speaking, tends to talk of politicians, whatever their Party, with contempt. And this although many City men have had some active connection with politics at some time or other and many others are connected with politicians through schools, or family, or friendship. The image of a politician as a clever wind-bag who would sell his soul for a vote dies hard. It is a nice point whether this abstract type is disliked any more than the equally abstract figure of the Civil Servant or bureaucrat.

The combination Whitehall-Westminster, though it is only five minutes in the Tube from Westminster to Mansion House, is felt to stand for ignorant interference. It is the latter, the City men at all levels, who are really doing a job and earning the country enough to pay for a luxurious talking shop. It would be absurd, of course, to say that a view as extreme as this is held by the true leaders of the City. But you do not have to dig deep into the subconscious of the City to find an anti-politician complex, or at best a scornful in-difference.

Many years ago I was contemplating a political career (not at that time in Socialist politics) and I was wondering whether my training in a stockbrokers' office could lead in that direction. I was taken by Alec Spearman to see a well-known stock-broker, not in Buckmaster and More's. His angle was somewhat different. 'I once knew a fellow on the Stock Exchange,' he said, 'who went into politics. I believe that he got into the Cabinet but I never heard it did his business any good.' Most of us, in short, think our own profession superior to any other, and City men are particularly conscious of this in face of politicians.

All this, as said above, becomes considerably aggravated when the politicians in question belong to the Labour Party. It is inconceivable that I should ever have been asked to be the chairman of the National Bank if the demand in our case for an Anglo-Irishman had not reduced the possible selection to one. But this is no more than a reflection of the personal attitude of City men towards the Labour cause. If you took a thousand representative men in the City how many would you expect to find had voted Labour at the last election, or would have done so if commoners? A dozen? That would be an outside estimate.

Are there any special reasons why the City, in the sense of the partners and directors of City firms, should be so over-whelmingly opposed to the outlook of the Labour Party? I return to the distinction between the rational and irrational elements in the opposition or misunderstanding. The use of words like 'bias' and 'prejudice', which I cannot always avoid, produces a bias or prejudice of its own. Writing five years ago I said that a partner in a great City firm is as likely to be opposed to the Labour Party as a South Wales miner to the Conservative. It just happens, I wrote then, that one background and one way of life produces the other one, though I mentioned that an older Liberal tradition was long established in the City.

Between a bad, obviously worn-out, Conservative Government and a Labour Government fresh and vigorous I could imagine myself as a typical City man believing that the interests of my firm and my family would be benefited by Labour. That would be the extreme case. Ordinarily it is difficult for a man of substantial property not to suppose that the Party which favours a greater measure of equality is going to damage him. If you believe as ardently as do most City men that freedom to conduct one's own business in one's own way is the *sine qua non* of successful business achievement, it is difficult not to regard the Socialists, however mild and democratic, as the more collectivist Party; and one, therefore, which is most likely to interfere with freedom.

It is likely that these predispositions will continue. But a Labour Government would make a vast mistake—I do not believe they will make it—if they assume that the City is concerned *only* with economic issues. They tend to identify, as most of us do (whether we be the cotton trade, the railway-men, or the universities), the interests of their own group with the interests of the nation. City men are as patriotic and as democratic as the rest, but no more so. Any attempt to treat them individually or collectively as bad citizens would have fatal results, alike for a Labour Government and the City itself. There need be no question whatever of trying to placate the City by departing from Labour's economic policies. But the policies should be carried out, as I am sure they will be carried out, without provocation. Obstruction can be ruled out. The extent of positive co-operation could be very important and may prove surprising.

One issue of much complexity remains quite unsuited for personal narrative of this sort. There is the question of whether the interests of the City coincide with or inevitably differ from the general interests of Britain.

Here I would say only that there is no single answer which holds good for all time and under all conditions. There is no inevitable clash between the interests of the City and those of the nation, but no inevitable harmony. What is essential is that all who are in any way concerned should realize the possibility of conflict and the unlikelihood of a natural harmony unless positive steps are taken to bring it about. It surely goes without saying that in the last resort the interests of one section must be subordinated to those of the community.

Mr. Fraser will forgive me if I say that it is their oblivious-ness of this issue which causes so many champions of the City to become so indignant at the tone of much Labour Party discussion. 'To my mind,' he says somewhere, 'the strength of the City lies in its absolute integrity and profound experience.' But the same might be said of British Railways, yet the case for Dr. Beeching would not be weakened. The City possesses traditions on the material plane which are not surpassed in British life, and on the human plane are full of warmth and colour.

But the City must expect the Government, Labour or otherwise, to look at policies from the point of view of the country, indeed of the world as a whole. I have before now proclaimed the longing of the Labour Party to transform the lot of hundreds of millions of malnourished human beings in the under-developed countries. I have been pressed, not unfairly, in the House of Lords to say where this wealth is coming from and how it is to be transferred from the rich to the poorer countries. Certainly in face of these tremendous problems it would be folly and worse to neglect the services and counsel of those who between them possess so deep a technical understanding of the mysterious but indispensable mechanisms. Any Government worth the name should always pay deep attention to the financial and commercial expertise of the City, but it should not suppose that the City possesses a monopoly of such wisdom.

2

The Realm of Peers

I

Old Wine and New

PEERS make a fetish of describing themselves as 'new boys in the House' even when they seem to have been around an unconscionably long time. In my case the affectation would be merely tiresome. When I was made a peer (1945) I was, with Billy Listowel, the youngest to play a leading part at the time. I was younger by many years than the principal figures, such as Lords Addison, Jowitt, Pethick-Lawrence, and Stansgate (Labour); Lords Salisbury, Swinton, and Woolton (Conservative); and Lord Samuel (Liberal). I was at least thirty years younger than Lord Addison, leader of the House. At thirty-nine I was the youngest peer to be himself awarded a title since Lord Beaverbrook, who received one at thirty-seven in 1916. In my first few months Max Beaverbrook entranced the House, flitting round the dispatch-box like a ballet dancer, and sticking pins into all and sundry. But then, alas! he disappeared, frozen out one knew not how.

Today it is no good my pretending to be a novice or junior. I can boast, rather, to be with one exception the only member of any Party to have sat continuously on one front bench or another since the end of the war. The exception is Will Henderson, who had previously served in the House of Commons, a distinction denied me. We arrived in the House of Lords together and have stuck together ever since. I would need to be a poor fish, inarticulate, morbidly discreet, shamefully evasive, or of failing memory, if I had nothing to report of my eighteen years in the House.

Everyone from home or abroad appears to enjoy visiting the House of Lords; having lunch or tea or a drink there, or looking in on the debates. 'How well dressed they are!' they say to me, until I point out that they are probably looking at the clerks. Once I had seen Lord Salisbury wearing a dark blue jumper I realized that informal dress was permitted. The jolly club life is readily appreciated and envied. Leaving out those with high ambition in the Commons, I have never found anyone, man or woman, who did not respond with naive alacrity to the idea of membership, sometimes dangled a little frivolously before them. Nevertheless, one is often asked, 'Apart from the fun and the friendship, what does it all amount to?' I cannot imagine a harder question. Even members of the House of Commons are sometimes described as 'rubber stamps' by inside or outside critics.

The most vivid published accounts of the Lords in action today are those of Anthony Sampson (*Anatomy of Britain*) and Patrick O'Donovan who came in for one of our genuinely exciting days—a divorce bill at stake, with the Party lines absent, and a division in doubt till the end. The whole afternoon seemed to him 'a dream of wise legislation'.

My private secretary, Angela Lambert, who succeeded Peggy Fitzgerald when I left the bank and later handed me on to Barbara Brierley after the birth of her first child, reported on the Lords dispassionately: 'A really verbose and tedious speaker can frequently induce in almost every peer—with the exception of those already asleep—the urgent need for a cup of tea. But on the whole the standard of debate is high. The peers are well informed, even sometimes "with it"—their speeches are thoroughly prepared, and their wit, though highly specialized, is keen and genuinely funny. The humour is often that of a school debating society with Castleton Minor getting in a quick one at the expense of a slower-witted opponent, to the boisterous delight of his fellows; but unlike that of another place it is never malicious, and the House can show surprising tolerance in hearing out the views of, say, its sole Communist member.' (Whom, incidentally, I alone applauded—once during his speech, and again at the conclusion.)

Sampson is rather kinder than O'Donovan about the debating chamber itself though he describes it as 'extravagantly ornate, and reminiscent of a small private chapel'. O'Donovan considers that the chamber 'has gone in for splendour and failed. It might be the masonic room in some overweening station hotel.' Angela Lambert mentions the 'indifferent murals depicting heroic episodes in the history of the country'. All three are rightly complimentary about the magnificent attendants and their morale-boosting effect. I have seen many a peer creep in like a timid placatory lamb, harassed by the problems of home or lodging, and change into a self-assured, indignant lion by the time, half a dozen 'My Lords' later, he enters the debating chamber.

But to Sampson the legislators are basically unimpressive. 'There is an aura of contented old age—older than the oldest men's club.' O'Donovan finds the company as distinguished as anywhere in the world. He mentions Salisbury, Longford, and Hailsham among the hereditaries. Among first creations (who number 200 out of a nominal total of 900, but who do far the greater part of the speaking) he picks out Boothby, Montgomery, Gladwyn, Wootton, Attlee, and Silkin.

One need not quarrel with this list (especially if included in it) as far as it goes. It would be easy, but perilous, to extend it widely. Sampson for his part mentions 'a small group of Ministers (Hailsham, Home, Mills) facing Socialists like Morrison, Longford, Silkin'. Today one would start by mentioning Dundee, the hardest-worked senior Minister, before recording the loss of Home and Hailsham. One must certainly add the leader of the Labour Opposition for the last eight years, Lord Alexander of Hillsborough.

He made rather an unhappy start in the Lords. There was some feeling there that he was being sent there to supplant Lord Addison, but he has made his way by sheer character, Parliamentary astuteness, and the right kind of Oppositional militancy. Today he is deeply esteemed, as much for his Protestant morality as his British patriotism. The Baptist Church, the Co-operative movement, and the Royal Navy are equally dear to him. No peer (at any rate outside the episcopal benches) is so well soaked in the Bible, with special reference to the Prophets and the Epistles. It has happened before now that a front-bench speaker opposite has noticed Lord Alexander and myself deep in converse, and assumed that his remarks had troubled us. What he may well have been saying to me was more like this: 'But have you *read* the ninth Hebrews? If you have you must know that the sacrifice was to be once for all, not to be repeated; *not* to be repeated. There's no answer to that, you know.'

When the Labour peers gave him and Lady Alexander a dinner to celebrate their golden wedding he wound up, moved and movingly: 'As regards my wife it is all said better in the last chapter of the Book of Proverbs.' None of us, I think, had the passage in our heads, though some may have remembered that it referred to the 'valiant woman'. But all who looked it up must have found it thoroughly appropriate, especially the end: 'Work such as hers claims its reward; let her life be spoken of with praise in the city gates.' Just as happy is an earlier sentence: 'None so honoured at the city gate as that husband of hers, when he sits in council with the elders of the land.'

But when one tries to go further, and starts to build up an imaginary Lords team, the attempt breaks down, even in fancy. What place is to be accorded the Liberals? The graceful Phillip Rea; the sensible, outspoken David Ogmore, whom I had looked forward to working with in our own party for many years?

And then there are the Bishops. They work as a team, and a very good one, and exercise an increasing influence on the social debates. The benevolence of the Archbishop of Canterbury is irresistible. The Bishop of Exeter is not alone in bringing theology alive. The judges, apart from Lord Denning, interpret their duties narrowly. They speak too seldom, outside the law. We have missed them sadly in penal discussions, though in the great debate on capital punishment they testified both ways. I much envied their style.

And then there are the ladies, who must not be disposed of too quickly. Forgetting the rather malignant failure to appoint

Violet Bonham-Carter—one of the few orators, male or female, left to us—they have been cleverly selected. They have brought great credit on their sex, and much absurdity on the all-too numerous anti-feminists who doubted whether they would come up to our lofty standards, or prove bearable companions. 'We don't want to sit next to them here! We don't want to sit next to them in the library!' one grand old fellow had intoned, and though it all seems so silly now, it was only yesterday that his point of view was defeated. I asked the same peer not long ago, 'Surely you agree that they have worked their passage, and that your fears were exaggerated?' A slow smile crept across his ancient face as he mentioned one particular peeress. 'When I see that long neck bending over in front of me,' he said to me happily, 'I think of my chopper, and I say "Chop, chop, chop".'

All the seven ladies have spoken up—I was going to say manfully—particularly on social questions. Irene Ravensdale has braved the horrors of darkest Soho, and—what required still more moral fibre—her own party's displeasure in more than one division lobby. Kay Eliot, as a former Conservative Party chairman, has had most obvious influence with Conservative Ministers; Stella Reading with the high officials of Whitehall. Elaine Burton, an old national sprint champion, has given the gentlemen a lead in sport. Florence Horsbrugh, widely qualified, but attractively modest, has spoken less than the others. Barbara Wootton and Edith Summerskill were picked out by Patrick O'Donovan, which must be my excuse for doing likewise.

I first met Barbara Wootton thirty years ago when I was trying to become a W.E.A. tutor under London University. I was interviewed by a good-looking but severe young woman, who toyed with my letter of application a trifle disdainfully. 'Do you think,' she said, 'that the Carlton Club is the most appropriate address from which to seek a position with the Workers' Educational Association?' I muttered something inadequate and withdrew.

At that time I was working in the Conservative Research Department, and by sheer chance was instructed just then to report on the W.E.A. I recorded my drastic treatment at the

hands of 'a Socialist female don'. This by a typist's error reached
our chairman, Neville Chamberlain, as 'a Socialist female dog'.
He sent for me in delight, and when I entered the room was still
laughing immoderately—the only time I saw him amused.
But then I only saw him twice in the two years I worked for
him. Barbara was the only man or woman who obtained a
first-class with star in the Cambridge economic tripos. She was
a sophisticated adviser to Lord Beveridge during his full-
employment enquiry, 1943-4, while I acted as his general
factotum. Her evidence to my Nuffield enquiry into the causes
of crime was the firmest and most articulate we received, with
the possible exception of that of John Bowlby, the child
psychiatrist (who differed from her totally).

When she took her seat as a life peeress I was one of
her two sponsors—a position of some spiritual peril. She
warned me that as a humanist she would not be taking the
oath. 'Poor Lord Pakenham,' said the rationalists, seriously or
otherwise, 'they say he'll never be a cardinal now!' But what
was more disturbing was the long wait at the table in the Lords,
while the alternative form of words was searched for. We
seemed to stand there for an age, while elderly peers with
ear-trumpets bellowed questions and answers to one another
about Barbara's supposed beliefs or lack of them.

Barbara is the most arresting lecturer known to me. (I
have not heard my Oxford friends lately). She has played a
notable part in intellectualizing our debates, amidst general
applause. 'I wish I had been taught by her' is a regular comment.
A development of this high-brow kind was steadily occurring
in any case. Today the backwoodsmen of my earlier years do
little speaking except on transport and agriculture. These
happen to be almost the only subjects on which I myself have
had the grace to keep quiet.

Barbara and Edith take plenty of trouble over their appearance, with excellent results. I can see them both as Mothers
Superior (Stella Reading could be the founder of a religious
Order devoted to corporal mercy), but I see them also as great
headmistresses, Barbara perhaps of Benenden, and Edith of
Cheltenham Ladies' College. Edith, one must admit, was soon
at loggerheads with the House of Lords. One day she moved

an amendment on blood tests for illegitimacy. I supported her out of personal loyalty. But in the division we did not receive a single other vote. We lost officially by 72 to 2— I assume a record catastophe.

Soon after this, in a debate on Katanga, Edith followed a Conservative peer who had a financial interest. Edith began sweetly: 'I would like to congratulate Lord —— on declaring a financial interest. Too often noble Lords opposite possess financial interests but don't declare them.' Uproar at once. Lord Hailsham, leader of the House, demanded that she name the peers in question. 'I was just trying to be conciliatory,' said Edith in an aside to me, at the same time indicating that she had no intention whatever of giving way to the leader of the House or anyone else. There were prophecies on many sides that she would never 'get away with it'.

But now she has become completely part of the House; an accepted character. She attends without fail and sits listening carefully throughout the longest debates. She speaks a good deal, but always about subjects such as women, children, marriage, health, where she has not only strong feelings but specialized knowledge. Much to my surprise, and perhaps to hers, she is more and more found siding with the bishops' bench. I had supposed—wrongly—that a super feminist would have little sympathy with clerical morality. I should not have needed the reminder that Christian marriage is supremely the safeguard of the woman and her children.

By House of Lords standards, particularly those expected from the newer members, she can be distinctly rude. But our Labour benches needed someone to put some pugnacity into us—and it came more easily from a woman. I myself have been rebuked by Edith for being too mealy-mouthed, too anxious to please or be kind. She has reminded me and others that in a legislative chamber a measure of indignation, at times aggressively expressed, is indispensable. We were a little cowed, some of us, by the long years of being grossly outnumbered, not only in the division lobby—as we still are—but until lately in the speechifying. We were taught in our earlier days to humour the House, which meant the Tories, and with some of us the habit has lingered a bit long. We were more conciliatory perhaps than an Opposition should be, certainly than the Tories were in our place, or would be again. Our veteran leaders, Clem Attlee, Herbert Morrison, and, of course, Albert Alexander, have spoken out bluntly enough for anyone. No one could accuse Clem Attlee, for example, on Suez or on the Common Market—though I disagreed with him there— or Herbert Morrison on London Government of sparing the rod. Clem's speech of eight minutes at the very beginning of the Suez crisis was a small masterpiece of foresight and deadly exposure.

I must point out here that the balance in the debates has been mightily altered in the last five years. Day in, day out, we on the Labour side can now lay on a team who can hold their own not only in quality but in numbers with the Conservatives. The coming of the life peers has made all the difference. And this, though it is only a minority of the life peers who are Labour.

The question whether a peerage is passed on or dies with the holder is not directly important. The number of life peers who would have refused hereditary peerages is, I should say, negligible. The real point is that life peerages are awarded (in the Labour cases at least) on the understanding of services *to be rendered* instead of in return for services *already* rendered. This has brought into the House a group of peers in their late forties or their fifties instead of their sixties, committed to constant attendance, and rejoicing in the active encouragement to make speeches.

The names of Eddy Shackleton, Victor Stonham, Stephen Taylor, Harry Walston come first to mind. They and others have helped to transform the House, to step up the pressure on Ministers; to multiply the debates and the speeches. No one in the House is unaware of the change, least of all the attendants, who are now keeping long hours with unfailing, if sometimes wry, good humour!

But the voting is still as hopeless as ever, except in unimportant cases. Even when the whole House is utterly contemptuous of Government policy, as in a universities debate I initiated in 1962, there is no chance of a valuable victory unless a block of Conservatives secedes and joins us. When

[74]

Barbara Wootton carried by one vote a major amendment to the Children's Bill, the age of criminal responsibility was reduced from twelve to eight. We had, however, the advantage that Lord Ingleby—a Conservative ex-Cabinet Minister—had suggested a similar change as chairman of a Government committee. In the end the Government compromised on ten. That was a clear case of partial victory by argument, but the circumstances were special. The Government were easily beaten in 1963 on an amendment to the Peerage (Renunciation) Bill which brought it into immediate operation. But that time the two leading Conservative ex-Ministers, Lords Salisbury and Swinton, who had sat on the select committee, had always assumed that immediate operation was intended and took a strong line against the Government.

In this respect things don't change very much. In the passage of the House of Lords there is a picture epitomizing the dark side of its traditions. The scene is the debate on the Home Rule Bill of 1893 already passed by the House of Commons. The Lords are shown on their way to throwing it out by 419 to 41. (A staggering vote, out of perhaps 600 peers.) The largest votes in my day were those on commercial television and capital punishment. In the first case the number voting was 244, in the second 333.

In the 1893 picture Lord Salisbury, grandfather of the present statesman, is depicted moving the rejection of the Home Rule Bill. In a debate not long ago on Africa I was calling in the Irish analogy. I pointed out that by a curious chance the only three Labour peers on the front bench at that moment were all Irish earls: Listowel, Lucan, and Longford. Billy Listowel, much longer in the House than I, was a great success as Governor General of Ghana, and a model Socialist since his Eton days; Pat Lucan, one-time battalion commander of the Coldstream Guards, a Socialist of the same selfless type as Billy, was our gently effective shepherd. All three of us, I said, were grandchildren of peers who can be seen in the picture supporting Lord Salisbury in denying Home Rule to Ireland. With a characteristic touch, the present Marquess, Bobbety Salisbury, said to me afterwards, 'I appear to be the only back-slider.'

A year or two after the picture was painted, Lord Rosebery, the Liberal Prime Minister, in a well-known letter, informed the Queen that 'he is shut up in a House which is unanimously opposed to his Ministry, and for all political purposes might as well be in the Tower of London'. In one sense (that is, in the balance of the discussions) this is no longer true. But, for that very reason, the voting situation is more blatant today.

The most glaring case was the prolonged battle over the London Government Bill (summer 1963). New records of endurance were set up. We went on arguing till 2.30 one night, and 4 a.m. another. Partly for this reason we found ourselves sitting regularly five days a week by the end of July. A far cry from Anthony Sampson's pleasantry! 'The hours,' he wrote in 1961, 'are not strenuous. The peers usually sit for only three hours at a time, and never on Fridays.'

It happened that on that particular subject, London Government, our debating superiority was complete. Lord Morrison taught many of us a lesson in deadly ridicule and sustained opposition tactics. Lord Latham and Lord Silkin, along with George Lindgren and Joe Champion, helped him to lead a team organized to the last iota by Malcolm Shepherd, who himself showed to great advantage. Our collective knowledge of London government and other forms of local government was phenomenally strong. The Tories could only put up junior Ministers without local government experience. The Lord Chancellor shrewdly and benevolently kept down his own interventions to a minimum. The Conservative whips, indeed, made a virtue of necessity, and the few Conservatives who could have spoken from first-hand experience of London government kept mum. Lord Conesford, an interesting case of someone far more effective in the Lords than he ever was in the Commons, spoke strongly and well, but not always on the side of the Government. We could hardly have scored more heavily if we had had with us Michael Stewart, who gave such a superlative lead elsewhere. Lord Rosebery, returning to the defence of the L.C.C., of which he was the most illustrious chairman, would have found the atmosphere transformed since 1895, but the voting results were no different. An occasional amendment was carried, but always because some

Conservative group had sectional reasons for supporting it. It was noticeable that the one amendment (excluding Epsom and Ewell) which was carried in the teeth of Government opinion was moved by a Conservative of exceptional prestige, Lord McCorquodale, who had sat for that part of the world.

Patrick O'Donovan summed up the position with the epigram (I had said the same myself more clumsily elsewhere): 'It's a mixed company of those who were born to it and those who have made it in various ways. Its debates are dominated by the latter; its voting is at the mercy of the former.' That is profoundly true. It is just as true and even more relevant to British political history that (1) the parties are level in the debating; (2) the audiences contain far more Conservatives; (3) voting success remains a Conservative monopoly if they combine to make it so. And the art of combination under pressure is the outstanding talent of the Conservative Party.

But I have wandered far from the problem of choosing a House of Lords eleven. I have said in the House, and meant it, that the average I.Q. of our top hundred is much higher than that of the House of Commons. But the remark is a shade artificial. There are two distinguishing features of the Lords, apart from the strange mixture of hereditary and created peers, and the Conservative domination. They are (a) the part-time nature of our work compared with the relatively full-time work in the Commons; (b) the absence of an upper age-limit, which means that peers continue serving almost literally to their dying day, as would occur in no other occupation.

No one who worked alongside Lord Pethick-Lawrence and Lord Samuel can doubt the reality of such aged service. In their later eighties they were listened to with as much attention and profit as at any time in their life. And Lord Stansgate, not much younger, continued to sparkle like no one else. No one could rag the House quite so delicately. In a debate on the Press, when they were taking themselves rather seriously, he pointed out that they were unknown to the mass of the country. 'I must break it to you, my Lords,' he told them, 'that the temple of your fame rests on the columns of *The Times*.' When it came to the serious and, above all, unpopular causes, he could use the lash against the Establishment.

But if one tries to compare the quality of an up-and-coming life peer, such as those I have named, with that of a great industrial leader of fine intellect, such as Lord Chandos, the attempt breaks down. Considering that we include in the House about half the best-known names in the biggest kind of business, we hear from them but seldom. As I have said—perhaps unkindly—they seem to regard the House of Lords as a big platform for small men but too small a platform for big men. Again we have heard much less than we would wish from our intellectual giants, though Lord Robbins and Lord James have spoken nobly.

On the question of age, how measure the political worth of rising full-time Ministers, winning golden opinions, such as Lord Jellicoe, with elder statesmen who are already part of British history, like Lord Attlee and Lord Morrison? Yet the influence of these great people, if subtle, cannot be ignored.

The tradition is maintained that a big debate in our House is seldom conducted without a contribution from at least one national expert, often several. It is this background influence, never fully present, never quite absent, which draws from most of us the best we can offer, conscious, as we usually are, that by the highest standards of the House it is not likely to be high enough.

Great public servants have their limitations like the rest of us. But anyone who could consistently satisfy such Lords as Robertson, Gladwyn, Strang and Killearn could rest content.

2

The Paladins

THERE have been four leaders of the House in my time: Lords Addison, Salisbury, Home, and Hailsham; and three leaders of the Opposition: Lords Salisbury, Jowitt, and Alexander. (I leave out Lord Carrington, a very popular member of the House, who was appointed when this book was in typescript.) These seven have been the most effective speakers in the House during the period; the most formidable to oppose; the most valuable on one's side. Lord Samuel, leader of the small group of Liberals, deployed the neatest of epigrams and dispensed much wisdom, but was hardly as dominant as the others. This supports the impression that while the office of leader clearly derives from merit, it adds much weight of its own.

The House of Lords is kind to leaders. A strong regimental spirit permeates most of the Conservatives, and moreover as the only Chamber known to me without a Speaker or some kind of chairman, the House of Lords depends on strong if unassertive leadership and tends subconsciously to promote its leaders' success. In a curious democratic way it levels down all the others, however lofty their reputation outside. The only speakers outside the leadership who in my time have been listened to with personal deference, irrespective of their subject, have been Lords Halifax and Attlee. One was a former leader, another a former Prime Minister. Archbishops of Canterbury are listened to with canny respectfulness.

All the leaders I have mentioned rose at once and consistently to their responsibilities as speakers, but in other ways too. They have all taught me personally much. From Christopher Addison I learnt the difference between Parliamentary and other speaking. Everything here depended on getting and holding the House. Once, when I was fairly launched on a Ministerial speech, I was kicked on the back of the calf. 'Sit down soon,' muttered Christopher Addison, 'you've got the House with you now; you'll lose it if you go on.' He made it an iron rule (how I wish that we observed it better) that none of his 'boys' should speak for more than fifteen minutes—except the opener and closer, who should also concentrate on brevity. He realized to the full what sounds so obvious (yet none of us seem able to remember it)—that the speech which would be masterly as the sole item is far too long for an audience enduring a day's debate and yearning for new faces at short intervals.

These Parliamentary values are not the only ones. Government departments like their case to be expounded at length, and the Press is apt to notice one more the more one talks. But for sheer understanding of the House of Lords and what succeeds there I have not known Addison's equal.

He was as indomitable as he was benign and shrewd. The task of winding up in the groundnuts' debate was the hardest I remember. 'Leave that to me,' he said with professional confidence. 'There's only one defence here: attack.' He began by referring to the criticisms that we had had to put up with and by asking Conservatives whether they agreed with them. Yes, yes, yes. They chanted their approval. But as he proceeded to pick out attacks that were clearly unfair they became less certain. He produced, from heaven knows where, a letter which appeared to have been sent by a popular paper to employees of the corporation concerned. It seemed to instigate them to write anonymous letters to the paper criticizing their own corporation. Christopher Addison challenged the Opposition to justify tactics of this kind. They drooped in embarrassed silence. He pressed home his advantage, and he finished with a fine burst of virtuous indignation that such stories should be published about so patriotic a Government. Loud cheers from our side, with no response from the other. I cannot remember a cleverer or braver piece of debating.

William Jowitt, with his lovely modulated voice and splendid looks and presence, was a master of a slightly different technique. 'The secret of advocacy,' he said to me, 'is to find the worst thing the other fellow can say about your case, and then say it yourself in your own way.' In the House of Lords he seemed to identify himself emotionally with the huge Conservative majority, while he carried a long string of nationalization bills.

'My Lords,' he would say, 'you don't like this Bill. My Lords, I don't like the Bill. To be quite frank, I hate it. If any one of you could suggest another solution to the problem no one would be happier than I would. But as it is we are faced, as reasonable men...' (My fond memory may have touched up the phraseology, as with the Christopher Addison anecdote, but the spirit, I am sure, is right.) Bill after Bill would go through.

But he had many other shots in his locker. On occasion, in an atmosphere of harmony inconceivable without Bill Jowitt, as in his great speech on heroin, he would pulverize the Opposition.

I can still see him overturning a great friend of mine, a man of much distinction, by suddenly pointing his forefinger at him and exclaiming, 'The noble Lord looks confused!'

My friend, unwisely, rose to his feet. 'I don't look confused,' he protested, looking, I am afraid, very confused indeed.

'I must leave it to the judgement of the House,' said Bill Jowitt.

He was sometimes criticized, though the venom disappeared in later years, for his change of political allegiance, and his alleged lack of strong political convictions. It was true, of course, that he was short of Party feeling, but he performed prodigies for the Labour Party. He was, I am assured, a Lord Chancellor particularly admired for his judicial appointments. He was a most modest, friendly, unpompous, civilized, humorous man to sit next to hour after hour on the front bench.

Albert Alexander I have already mentioned, and shall return to elsewhere. Lords Salisbury and Hailsham I shall come to in a minute. Alec Home (if he had not become Prime Minister) might not have left a mark on the public mind at home—he meant more to foreign statesmen. He is the quintessential old Etonian, and whether one takes to his public image depends on one's reaction to the old Etonian ethos. When I was myself at Eton he was President of Pop, and in my recollection—not I believe accurate here—he was captain of the cricket eleven and of anything else that mattered. Although hardly two years younger, and very high in the school for my age, I would not have dared to speak to him unless he had spoken to me first. And I cannot remember that happening. All his life the boys and men who have known him well, and had plenty to pick from, have chosen him their leader. But he remains to those outside such circles an aloof aristocrat; to some before he be-came Foreign Secretary an effete Bertie Wooster, a supposed weakling; whereas in fact, like Lord Salisbury—another 'effete aristocrat'—he has a character like steel.

'Watch Home,' said my great friend Henry Burrows, later clerk-assistant of the House, when Alec first began to speak as an Assistant Minister for Scotland. Vaguely aware that he had not made much mark in 'the other place' (there were reasons for that), I ignored the advice. But how right Henry was! At the time of Suez Alec Home put up a better debating defence of the indefensible policy than anyone in either House. He laid all his emphasis on the one point in his case that could at least be plausibly argued: 'We stopped a war.' By getting the argument on to ground where some parity of debate was possible he deflected attention from the more profound enormities and extricated his colleagues with some show of dignity.

When he was appointed Foreign Secretary in summer 1960 there was general ignorance even in the well-informed Press about his capacities. Yet he had already been leader of the House of Lords for three years and not infrequently in his speeches carried the whole House with him—a rare feat indeed outside the field of mere generality or pious tributes. It is a curious truth that the Press have never felt equal to assessing personal reputations in the Lords as they would normally do in the Commons. They seem to be baffled by the unemotional air of the Lords' audience, and the mutual courtesies, albeit sometimes ironical.

If we regard him purely in terms of leadership of the House of Lords, Alec Home need fear no obvious comparison. He was less flexible and unexpected than Christopher Addison, though sharper and neater in phrase. Less intuitive than William Jowitt, and less deadly in pressing an argument, but possessed—like Lord Grey of Falloden—of the peculiar power of adding the force of his own character to the strength of his case. Less prophetic a moralist than Albert Alexander, but well equipped to represent the sentiment of the House of Lords in the expression of his Christian beliefs.

Less majestic than Salisbury, less glorious in vocabulary than Hailsham, narrower in range of subject and less fiery than either, he replied to a debate on *his own topics* more effectively than any of them. He dealt with the arguments of his opponents tersely and yet faithfully in the terms in which they conceive them.

When a friend in the Foreign Office asked me what he would be like as Foreign Secretary I replied, 'He'll be anti-Communist, and he'll write his own speeches.' I have not been proved wrong. He is, like Salisbury, a Christian Conservative statesman—with the accent on all three attributes. I would not say that a sense of the future is his strong feature. But when he told me that my speech introducing the Wolfenden Report was a superb performance I glowed with pride—and not merely because he was once President of Pop. Of his showing as Prime Minister under much more severe conditions, it is too early to speak dispassionately.

Lord Salisbury . . . Lord Hailsham. . . . The names symbolize crudely but not unfairly the large mutation that has occurred in the House on its way from an aristocratic to a professional chamber. Various noble families have their champions, the Cavendishes, the Russells, the Stanleys, the Churchills among them. But ask for the name of a great political family and the natural response is Cecil. Bobbety Salisbury has for many years embodied the concept perfectly.

[83]

I have mentioned the picture of his grandfather defeating the Home Rule Bill of 1893. In the same passage rests the bust of his father, like the grandfather and Bobbety, leader of the House, but remembered as much for his spiritual as political qualities. A number of his 'noble kinsmen', as he correctly refers to them, have been and are active members. He has defended more boldly than anyone else in recent times the hereditary principle in legislation and elsewhere. His own family are perhaps the best argument that can be produced for a case which, as a youth, I supported, but which I have long since lost the capacity to understand.

Not long ago I asked some clever young people of no certain politics to lie back on an imaginary couch and practice free association with the title 'House of Lords'. The result was revealing. 'Black Rod—ceremonial—red velvet—privilege—backwoodsmen.' In spite of all the changes, this aroma, for good or ill, persists in the public mind, and one must confess, in a class-conscious country like Britain, adds at once to the antagonism and the prestige. Once again, as with Home, one must reject any remote suggestion of effeteness about Salisbury. Like Home, and indeed more so, he can flash fire, and even make men quail. Connected or unconnected with the last quality, he incarnates the old aristocratic concept of the House of Lords just as surely as his father and grandfather before him.

Contrariwise, Hailsham prides himself on being, above all, a professional man. A gentleman, of course; an old Etonian like his father; but he never at any time wishes to be mistaken for an aristocrat.

His particular sartorial eccentricities are irrelevant here. His famous button boots, the collar stud visible above the tie—though less often now—the white panama in Moscow; these might as easily be discovered on the person of a duke. But once, when Hailsham was in controversy with Salisbury, he told me that the latter's tactics were worthy of a nobleman or, indeed, myself. I retorted, not seriously, 'I wouldn't know about that; I'm nothing higher than an Irish peasant!' To which Quintin replied, 'Yes you are, you're a beastly aristocrat like he is!'

Quintin did not come to the House till 1950. For years before and after that Bobbety ruled the roost. Even when we were in office, by virtue of his vast majority the fate of everything tended to hang on his attitude. Clem Attlee, who should know, and is judicious rather than lavish with compliments, has paid tribute more than once to Salisbury's statemanship during our period of rule, and he will be gratefully remembered by Socialists for two things in particular:

1. The immense trouble he took inside and outside the chamber to make Socialists, trade unionists in particular, feel thoroughly at home and equal. His celebrated charm was never exhibited to better purpose than when he stopped in the tea room to welcome unassuming visitors.

2. He taught by example a whole code of political behaviour: hard-hitting without personal hostility in the heat of battle, perfect amity the moment the dispute was over.

In the Lords, unlike the Commons, the rival parties sit down at the same table for lunch and tea. Some of us, new at that time to Parliament, may find ourselves pausing today on the borderline between the justified and impermissible in debate. We still ask ourselves instinctively sometimes how Bobbety would view it. And when he felt that he had hit too hard he would quickly say so. Winding up a debate in 1947, my fourth utterance in the House that day, I gained the impression that the House wanted to get away for dinner. I spoke briefly and lightly. Bobbety descended in full wrath and denounced my speech as the most deplorable he had ever listened to. It was the first setback in my upward progress, and I confess I was shaken. Later a note followed apologizing for his 'atomic outburst', but pointing out quite truly that certain seniors such as Lord Simon had been hurt by my tone of levity.

He himself felt that he had been leader or dominant too long, and said as much when he replied to a letter of mine regretting his resignation over Archbishop Makarios in 1957. 'Alec Home,' he said with prescience, 'will do it beautifully.' In his own opinion it was high time he went. But, if true, that was not the result of waning powers and staleness. It was rather that, like Eton among the public schools, he had got too far ahead of his rivals, with the help of various advantages. Even in 1945 a sycophancy, which he was the last to seek, had grown up around him. In that year there was a highly charged debate on the American loan, in which Lord Keynes, on his return from Washington, made a never-to-be-forgotten speech. It has been described as the most influential since the war in the House. One might place it with a much shorter one by Lord Halifax defeating a die-hard movement to hold up the liberation of India and potentially one by Lord MacNair on the illegality of using force against Nasser. Regrettably the effect of the last of these was ruined by events.

In the 1945 debate Lord Beaverbrook, not long before a member of the War Cabinet, was seated beside Lord Salisbury, Leader of the Opposition. In his own speech Lord Beaverbrook had aroused a delirious amusement by his attack on the loan and his open difference alike from the Government and his colleagues. Bobbety in reply to him remarked with sarcastic sweetness, 'There are many people in this country who cannot command even the resources available to the noble Lord and their lot might well be lamentable.' Roars of laughter from the court. Put in Beaverbrook from his seat next to Salisbury on the Opposition front bench, in a Canadian voice, 'Is not the house of Salisbury very rich?' (he pronounced it Sarlsbury). A horrified gasp from the whole House. One didn't say that sort of thing to a Salisbury in the House of Lords. Bobbety, never a man to shrink from an interjection or a combat, recovered quickly. 'I hope,' he said, 'we should all be willing to pull in our belts, but the fact that the noble Lord and I have more than other people should make us more careful about the advice we give.' Happy laughter again: Bobbety was back in the saddle. But I thought Max had scored. By 1957 this had all gone too far and become rather an infliction, not least to Bobbety himself.

But his real nobility has come out most clearly since his resignation. With no automatic support any more, though, of course, with great goodwill attaching to him, he has usually spoken for causes unlikely to enhance his popularity with either Government or Opposition. If anyone wondered before whether he were a *progressive* Tory the answer in these last years has been emphatically in the negative, except in the sense that he keeps up diligently with affairs. But if anyone is puzzled why he has counted, and still counts, so much in British public life they should study his apparently unrewarded labours in the place where he was once supreme. No left-wing idealist can fail to be aware that his dedication to causes and to politics as a vocation is as undying as their own. As Gladstone said of his grandfather the Prime Minister, 'Such a man will always be respected in England.'

Quintin Hailsham has been endlessly written about. In an earlier volume I described my defeat at his hands in Oxford in 1938. I told there how our long, chequered relationship had passed by the time I wrote into 'friendship unalloyed'. What follows is written from a still more cordial standpoint. Still, he found my earlier book 'agreeable but curiously unintellectual'. I will try to make up for that by one or two criticisms this time.

Like most of us he possesses many qualities and facets. But in his case four are transcendent. His brain, his Christian principles, his sense of fun, his temperament. His brain is unequalled for some purposes, and unsurpassed for most by that of anyone in public life. 'A great verbalist' was how a scientific professor described him to me recently; 'he thinks he has solved a problem when he has eloquently expounded it.' But he conceded his mental distinction. As who could not? He was the cleverest boy of his age at Eton. Robin Dundas, Senior Tutor at Christ Church, used to say that he was the ablest undergraduate there between the wars.

His Christian principles are beyond dispute. I have said elsewhere that I did not in any way like his scandal broadcast, which seemed to carry the duty of righteous indignation to serious excess. I think, however (though this I do not know), that in his eyes it is the soft-hearted Puritans like myself who try to have it both ways, and take the easy and popular line; the duty of denouncing evil, and even the evil-doer, is the last duty likely to be performed by a Christian today. At least, I suspect that is how he sees it.

His humility is deep-rooted, if not a surface commodity.

The night he became Lord President of the Council, Gilbert Harding and I proposed his health. We were all dining at St. Mary's Strawberry Hill, the Catholic Teachers' Training College where Elizabeth and I have been made so happy so often. When Quintin was about to reply, for the first time in forty years I saw him bereft of words. He was indeed overcome. 'No, no!' he said, 'I am not worthy!' I saw then what is meant by saying that a certain person in politics has high standards; in a worldly sense impossible standards. Certainly no one sets himself higher standards than Quintin. Which does not mean that he always lives up to them, any more than the rest of us.

I pass over rapidly his sense of fun. The one thing it is not is a cold-blooded gimmick, though as a thorough professional he knows how to make political use of skittish fancies, from his bathing drawers to his bell. (But I remember now that I myself have in these latter days been photographed by the *Daily Express* in the water, along with my daughter Judith.)

His enjoyment extends to his opponents' speeches. He is the most generous of listeners in the House, the readiest to appreciate the mildest joke across the dispatch-box—an extraordinary encouragement to anyone experiencing the loneliness of the long-distance talker. His emotional temperament is again at once a plus and a minus; certainly one cannot treat it as a mere liability. Nelson wept regularly, and so did Winston Churchill—for example, after the destruction of the French ships at Oran, and when he saw the Coldstream Guards on parade.

Quintin at his best possesses a true eloquence; a mind that soars and expands as it proceeds, and sets itself and other minds on fire. Though it is of the studied Churchillian and, in a different way, Gaitskellian type, rather than the sudden upheaval of a Bevan or Bevin, such oratory could not spring from a cold breast or brain. All those just mentioned were at times overpowered by feeling. Nevertheless his future as a statesman depends on how far he completely becomes the master rather than the servant of his emotions. From that point of view his old friends and opponents can only report a manifest and continuous improvement.

He was in the House of Lords for six years before he received an office in 1956. In the meanwhile he may or may not have rejected minor appointments. He did not mince his words about his own side. He was soon referring to his acting leader for the day, one of the most eloquent, respected and senior members, as 'speaking as usual with all the earnestness of an extinct volcano'. Early on the morning of the Coronation, as I entered Westminster Abbey, I found him jammed in cheek by jowl for the coming hours against the said volcano, who at the moment looked far from extinct. Each of them gave me a wry smile.

In a bitterly fought debate on commercial television he led off powerfully, but was teased by Bobbety into loss of control. Bobbety mentioned him playfully as having made a 'great forensic speech'. For some reason this got right under Quintin's skin, and he interrupted angrily. Later, when the last word fell to him, he was disconcertingly violent.

But that was 1953. As the years passed, and as fulfilment took the place of frustration, the famous temperament has been harnessed, controlled, sublimated. He had handled some of our older Socialists with unbecoming harshness when chairman of the Party. When he became leader we anticipated trouble. But he has won the heart of the House collectively by a kind of compère's inspiration which I had hardly suspected in him. Along with it has gone a resounding bonhomie and an instantaneous wit. If anything, his handling of the House has commended him more than his major speeches. These, though they read impressively for their various purposes, have sometimes been too long, and some of the best of them—on education for instance—have been delivered to small houses at the end of the debate. Sometimes, however, he has touched great heights, as on television, the nuclear peril, and more than once when religion has been involved. His short panegyrics on departed peers have been well-nigh perfect; for example, one on Lord Stansgate.

Only once in recent times did his old bellicosity assert itself. Salisbury, in a debate on Africa, sharply criticized his colleague, the gifted Iain Macleod, the Colonial Secretary. He referred to him as 'too clever by half'. David Kilmuir answered fully, and with immense effect, at the end of the first day. But Quintin was determined not to leave it there. 'I hear,' said Bobbety the next afternoon, 'that I am to be re-castigated by Quintin.' And for an age, so it seemed, Quintin lectured and rebuked him—I should say, to the general embarrassment. 'I know I oughtn't to have done it,' said Quintin afterwards, 'but I enjoyed it.' A friend who saw him at a party later said, 'He looked like a man who's just had a good day's shooting.'

Why the extraordinary depth of feeling? Bobbety had referred to Macleod's earlier profession as that of a bridge journalist. Was it again, as perhaps with the earlier reference to Quintin's 'forensic' speech, the fury of the professional man, lawyer or bridge journalist, at being patronized and derided by a great aristocrat? Karl Marx would have said so, possibly with some help from Freud, and for the only time in his life he might have been right. Be that as it may, there seems to have been no hard feeling. 'Quintin's so nice,' said Bobbety to me somewhat later. Quintin no doubt would reciprocate, apart from a reservation about the aristocracy in general. If any foreigner wanted to know what the House of Lords has to offer he might be told this story, and then shown Bobbety and Quintin chatting happily in the tea-room. (Now that Quintin and Alec Home have left us, this sight will be available less often.)

So back to the old question, how much does it all amount to? Very little, thinks Sampson. 'One forgets,' he says, 'how unimportant they are.' To O'Donovan: 'It still counts.'

To me there are three questions:

1. Can the House of Lords as a distinct entity assert its collective will against the Commons? That question can be answered at once in the negative. There is no such collective will in the House of Lords, and no chance, therefore, of its being asserted.

2. How far can the Conservatives use their overwhelming majority in the House of Lords to defeat or retard a Labour majority in the Commons? Theoretically they could do so, for what might be a crucial period of time at least. We remember

what happened last time to proposals to abolish the death penalty and to nationalize steel. Whether they would ever think that such a course was constitutional or moral may be discovered in the next few years. They would not try it twice if Labour were strong and confident. In that situation they would rapidly be brought to book. But towards the end of a Labour Government, with Gallup Polls running against them, as they have run against the Conservatives, it could be a different story. One hopes it won't be.

3. Can one or more peers, whether on party or non-party lines, exert a substantial influence on the minds of the House, and through our House, on another House, and on the country? I shrink from trying to answer that question in detail. The moral influence of the House of Lords, as a place of religious and social affirmations, is quite incalculable, and concrete cases are not much easier. In recent years I have myself initiated the first debates which can be traced in either House on the universities and the youth service; the first series in either House on prisons; and a debate on the Wolfenden Report, before the other House would touch it.

Incidentally, the influence of our House is always likely to be larger on subjects which the House of Commons shrinks from, or ignores.

I initiated in spring and summer of 1963—always, of course, from the front Opposition bench, and staunchly supported—a general economic debate, and the most comprehensive debate we have ever held on education. I have wound up for the Opposition debates on racial discrimination, women in industry, sport, the Press, the Finance Bill, and the World Police Force, and participated in plenty of others. And so back over the years, though I have spoken more often since leaving the National Bank. And I am only one, whose autobiography this happens to be. Lord Silkin, for example, could point to a longer list, and has done vastly more than I have on the Committee Stages of Bills.

One learns as time goes on that one peer acting on his own, however brilliant and incisive, cuts little ice. Two have more than twice as much effect, and four more than twice as much again. No one will ever know how much difference all this zeal and study and rhetoric has made to the lives of millions, or indeed of a single human being. But those of us who take the most active part, in spite of wishing that the House were very differently constituted, are seldom afflicted by any sense of futility. We believe, though we cannot prove, that it is all abundantly worth while.

Nevertheless, the House of Lords remains a strange, unjustifiable anomaly in democratic eyes, including mine. This, though the 'hereditaries' supply an atmosphere of courtesy, personal tolerance, and selfless attention to the speeches of others, which is entirely on the credit side. Ideally the House of Lords should be constituted entirely of those who have been nominated for services past, and still more for services to come. There should be plenty of non-party experts, bishops, judges, ambassadors, and representative welfare workers, with no one party allowed a permanent majority. But I recognize that in England today almost as many citizens would object to an unprovoked removal of all the hereditaries as would welcome it. And major constitutional changes should, if possible, be largely agreed.

For this reason I have advocated for the last few years—though I did not devise—the so-called two-writ plan. Henry Burrows must receive that credit. Those who inherited titles would be able to come and sit and speak, as now, but only those who were given a voting writ would be allowed to vote. The voting writs would be distributed so as to preclude the dominance of any one party, and at the same time make it reasonably certain that the Government could count on getting through its main legislation. In principle the created peers would receive voting writs, but hereditary peers who were political leaders could also receive them. So could other hereditary peers (Lord Arran, Lord Gage, or Lord Jessel to give only three examples), who had won their place by the stimulus of knowledge or authority they supplied. In that way, and without any real breach in continuity, the present quality of the House as a debating chamber could be maintained and enhanced but the shocking unfairness of one-party domination in the division lobby would be ended.

Interlude

An Irish Mind

An Irish Mind

'THERE was never a time', I wrote in *Born to Believe*, 'when I have not been proud to call myself an Irishman.' It has been easy to take a special pride in Ireland's international achievements since those words appeared. We have seen the Irish Republic a member of the Security Council led strongly and creatively by Frank Aiken; we have seen Fred Boland making a most civilized President of the Assembly, and General McKeown imperturbably commanding the United Nations troops in the Congo. We have seen Conor Cruise O'Brien, whom I described in the House of Lords as the 'Irish Lord Hailsham', crusading indomitably first at Elizabethville and then in wider and wider circles.

There was a moment when *The Economist* could say in a playful compliment that Ireland bestrode the world like a colossus. Years of hard diplomatic toil had gone into the winning of that position which is not likely to be lost. At home the first Whitaker Plan was intended to raise the growth of national income from 1 to 2 per cent per year. A rate of growth of 4 per cent has in fact been achieved. A second plan is now being embarked upon. At last there seems a prospect of halting the excessive emigration and the decline in population. Tourists and foreign business men are showing an ever-growing interest.

The end of partition is not in sight, but compared with what had gone before the South has fared better than the wealthier North. There has been some improvement in the atmosphere both between the North and South, and between northerners and southerners. I remain an optimist about the coming of Irish unity. Meanwhile the life of what Sir Winston Churchill has called 'an independent Christian law respecting state' goes steadily forward, Ireland remains perhaps the most religious country in Europe. The relationship between the overwhelming Catholic majority in the Irish Republic and the Protestant minority, small but talented and prosperous, is one which the Protestant North of Ireland and Catholic Spain might imitate with advantage. They have each shown some recent improvements.

When Elizabeth and I had three-quarters of an hour with General Franco in 1959 I argued vehemently, almost too vehemently, the case for better treatment of the Spanish Protestants, one of the indices by which Catholics in the world at large are apt to be judged. General Franco, very polite, very correct, very much the military man humouring an over-ardent civilian, gave me the impression that his mind was not closed on the matter.

Naturally, as chairman of the National Bank, I was much concerned in Irish developments. John Leydon as Irish chairman had left the Civil Service just before he joined us, but he was constantly being called upon by the Irish Government for vital assignments. The National Bank, with more branches than any other bank in Ireland, is a national institution there. We carry the same kind of influence, as, shall we say, Barclays or the Midland in England. My chairman's speeches, drawn up, of course, in close conjunction with John Leydon, were widely circulated and studied, whether I dwelt upon the niceties of Irish agriculture or suggested a bolder role for the central bank. The first was a subject on which my unaided wisdom would have been best ignored, the second one to which I had given much independent thought and where my views may have had some influence.

Perhaps I did render one concrete service to Ireland and to Anglo-Irish understanding during this period. I played a not-insignificant part in the return of the Lane pictures. It will be recalled that Sir Hugh Lane, the dazzling mercurial picture dealer and picture lover, went down in the *Lusitania* in 1915. An Irishman who had made much of his reputation in England, and quarrelled impartially with the stupider elements in both countries at various times, he had originally bequeathed his thirty-nine pictures, mostly French impressionist, to the National Gallery. They behaved in as elephantine a way as had certain Irish authorities. Renoir's 'Les Parapluies', which in the recent settlement was valued, and I should think much under-valued, at a quarter of a million pounds, was stuffed into the cellar, invisible to the public. And so on and so forth. Before he died (I must be allowed my own summary of highly controversial history) he made it plain—for example, to Sir Hugh Martin at the beginning of his last journey—that he wished the pictures, after all, to go back to Ireland, with whom he was by this time reconciled. When he was drowned a codicil to his will was discovered, under which he gave effect to his deeper, that is to say his Irish, loyalty. But though signed in three places, it was not witnessed, and therefore held invalid at law.

From that day until 1959 the controversy intermittently raged as to who should have the pictures. England admittedly had the legal right; Ireland, one would have thought, the moral one. I will not recapitulate the stages of the battle, in which many great names, not least those of Lord Curzon, Ramsay MacDonald, Yeats, and Lady Gregory, were involved. But through all the forty years, and more, one voice alone was never silent for long: that of Professor Thomas Bodkin, a dear friend of Lane, and an even greater authority on pictures. He was gallantly supported throughout by Sir Alec Martin, head of Christie's, whose testimony as an Englishman was of peculiar value where national passions tended to determine historical and artistic judgement.

Shortly before the war the Irish cause was espoused by Lord Moyne, ideally suited for the task of reconciliation between British and Irish claims. Living in both countries, a leading member of the house of Guinness, which operates in both, and has been perhaps more successful than any family business in either; utterly disinterested, devoted to all forms of beauty, in his gentle way a fighter, the fact that Bryan Moyne was the father of eleven children would be no disservice to him—in Ireland at any rate. A man very natural and unaffected wherever he found himself. I always like the occasion when he sat in the front row of the stalls of the Pike Theatre, Dublin, and put both his feet on the stage. The play was *Waiting for Godot* where Vladimir has to pick up the boot left by Estragon. This time, in error, he picked up Bryan's feet instead. In all our discussions, whether with Mr. de Valera, or the Trustees of the National Gallery, Bryan always seemed more at ease than anyone else and Tommy Bodkin more scathingly humorous.

I was very much a labourer of the eleventh hour. I was much honoured, if a trifle surprised, when asked in 1956 by Mr. Costello, then the Irish Prime Minister, to take a hand. I have always tried, as an Irishman living outside Ireland, to present myself as neutral between the parties, but ever since my book *Peace by Ordeal* (1935) there has been a disposition—certainly among the Finn Gael Party—to treat me as a crypto-supporter of Mr. de Valera and Fianna Fail. Naturally, I responded with alacrity. Again, I pass over various arguments and manœuvres. Already the indefatigable Hector Hughes had collected over 150 signatures of M.P.s for a motion calling for the return of the pictures to Ireland, but the National Gallery were tough and adamant. Many Irishmen wanted, or were supposed to want, all or nothing. At first there were no signs of progress.

A representative group of British politicians and other eminent persons got to work, with Tommy Bodkin stirring our enthusiasm. It was agreed at a private dinner that if an honourable compromise were available it should not be rejected. The Duke of Wellington, through Bryan Moyne, suggested a plan under which half the pictures would go to Ireland for a period, and then the other half. In the end, two years later, this solution was adopted. Many times before then it seemed the thing was hopeless, but I suppose, looking back, the corner was turned when I waited on Mr. Macmillan at 10 Downing Street, on behalf of our group in August 1957.

On previous visits to Downing Street during our time and

later I had always been struck by the air, if not of tension, at least of great things afoot. That had been true even in August, but this time the atmosphere was one of deliberate and profound relaxation. A charming aide greeted me with the words, 'I am afraid the Prime Minister will be a few minutes late.' (I think my appointment was 10.30.) 'He is having a long lie—a long lie,' he repeated, with smiling emphasis. This in fact was friendly play-acting; the Prime Minister kept me waiting about a minute, if as much. When I entered the Cabinet Room, and saw him sitting where Clem Attlee had sat so often, I was surprised to find that he treated me as a total stranger.

I had never known him well, but we had stayed with the Duke of Devonshire at Compton Place before the war. The Duke of Devonshire did not keep early hours. One night we did not leave the dinner-table until four in the morning. But we played four rounds of golf in two days. He used to twit me for a long time afterwards on my method of putting between my legs. Harold Macmillan had also encouraged us enormously at the time of the Munich by-election (1938). He came to speak at a meeting (at which, incidentally, I was in the chair) for Sandy Lindsay, the Independent Progressive, against the official Conservative, Quintin Hogg. An act of extraordinary political courage, whatever one thinks or doesn't think of Munich.

Later I had had pleasant dealings with him when I was chairman of the Anglo-German Association. I had taken the chair for him and sat beside him at our annual dinner. I had drawn, as I thought, a happy comparison between Harold Macmillan the Balliol scholar, the old Guards officer, the large business man, and another principal guest, Herbert Morrison, the man of the people. Harold Macmillan, when he rose to reply, described me with a dramatic uplift of the hands as one who had risen to great heights 'as University don, Minister and great Socialist intellectual'. Now I had descended—dropping his hands with the words—'to the life of a banker'. Happy, though not unkind, laughter at my expense all round. (I have never since questioned his powers of histrionic ridicule.) His letter to me agreeing to the interview had been friendly, so it was a little surprising to be looked at so blankly.

[99]

His tone at first astounded me. Not that it was personally offensive, but it was so completely blimpish. 'I gather,' he said in effect, 'you want us to do something for the Irish. What have the Irish done for us? What did they do in the First World War? What, for that matter, did they do in the Second?' And he proceeded for a time like the most reactionary member of White's or the Turf Club. I was only too aware that my time was limited, presumably to half an hour, and that it was slipping away. I ventured to put it deferentially: 'You will hardly expect me, Prime Minister, to reply on the wider issue, but I have come about the Lane pictures. As you know, the Duke of Wellington has suggested that half the pictures might be sent to Ireland for, say five years, and then the other half.'

His tone changed magically. In a moment he was the enlightened publisher, the forward-looking business man. 'There might be something in that if it led to a settlement,' he said at once. And in a few minutes we had covered a great deal of practical ground to excellent purpose. He left me in no doubt, and wrote to tell me so afterwards, in a letter which was not marked 'Confidential', that he himself favoured a solution on the lines suggested. But the Trustees of the National Gallery must be free to make up their own minds; the Government could use their good offices but could not coerce them.

Before I left his mood or tone changed for the second time. He had been the West End clubman; then the shrewd Scottish business type. Now, for a few minutes, he became the visionary, almost the original crofter peering out through the Western mists. What we had been discussing, even if it came off, was small stuff. Could it be a prelude to a much wider settlement? I reminded him of Cardinal d'Alton's interview that year under which an Indian solution would be offered to Ireland. She would remain a republic, but would be a member of the Commonwealth like India. The idea of Ireland returning to the Commonwealth stirred him visibly. 'I suppose such a thing has never happened before,' I remember his saying.

He realized that such a step on the Irish side was unthinkable unless it were accompanied by the achievement of Irish unity, or was destined to lead directly towards it. And that brought us back to the old stumbling block—though that was not how I described it—of Northern Ireland who could clearly be no more coerced than the Trustees of the National Gallery. I don't think that I realized quite how seriously he was taking a discussion which seemed to blow up so unexpectedly until I received the long letter already mentioned in which he not only expressed his goodwill towards the Lane picture settlement but discussed (albeit guardedly) the widest issues at the same time.

Even with this high-level British encouragement, and the known goodwill of the Irish leaders (Mr. de Valera had become Prime Minister but he kept Mr. Costello in touch), the Lane picture negotiations trembled more than once on the rocks. Lionel Robbins, the chairman of the National Gallery Trustees, was an old friend, as was John Witt who succeeded him. They both worked hard for peace, but there were other Trustees, names unspecified but guessed at, who seemed determined to die in the last ditch. I feared that if negotiations dragged on much longer the Irish authorities, who in any case did not think the proposal over-generous, would call the whole thing off. There was a dreadful moment when Lionel Robbins sent us a letter which seemed to me painfully legalistic. I sent it on to Dublin with a heavy heart.

I visit the cinema all too seldom, though I invariably enjoy it, but I was waiting in a cinema queue that evening when I ran into John Witt. I told him what a painful impression their last document had made. He was utterly surprised and acted promptly the next morning. The result was that Lionel Robbins sent me for forwarding a letter of extreme magnanimity in which he asked me to explain to any Irish friends who didn't like their initial letter that it was 'only poor old Lionel Robbins's way'. Feeling cooled down again, Lord Chandos helped to bring a larger outlook on the British side, and at the end all was rejoicing, with the crown rightly placed on the brow of Tommy Bodkin after forty years' faithfulness to death. In the Irish Ministry of External Affairs and the Embassy in London Con Cremin and Hugh McCann made essential contributions.

The last scenes well became both countries, with the National Gallery sending the more valuable half of the pictures to Dublin for the first period, and Mr. Lemass, now the Irish Prime

Minister, entertaining the British Trustees and the Irish team of negotiators at a magnificent dinner in Dublin. The Director of the National Gallery told me that it went to his heart to part with those pictures, but that they looked even better in the Irish Gallery where they were not so crowded. To our not inconsiderable relief we heard that the gallery was thickly populated while the British visitors were looking round; there might have been some argument at an earlier stage as to whether there was an Irish public for the pictures.

Professor Bodkin, Lord Moyne, and I were given honorary degrees by the National University of Ireland—supreme gratification—from the hand of Mr. de Valera, the Chancellor. But in the meanwhile Mr. Macmillan's interest in a wider settlement had seemed too incidental, too hedged round with British safeguards, to arouse any corresponding interest in the leaders of the Irish Government, or to seem to them to be in any way worthy of an initiative.

Another effort I made—one of many during the last twenty-five years and none of which has not borne obvious fruit. Jimmy Windlesham, later so tragically drowned and a brave Irish champion in the House of Lords, initiated a debate there in December 1960. I duly spoke and soon afterwards found myself writing a major article for the *Observer* in which I propounded once again the Cardinal d'Alton solution. There would be established a republic for a united Ireland which would be, like the Indian republic, a member of the Commonwealth. The article was warmly applauded by British ex-Ministers and by Irish friends of good standing not associated with the Irish Government.

I insisted that if there were to be any prospect of Ireland returning to the Commonwealth she must on no account be expected to approach Britain cap in hand and apply for readmission. The public invitation, the welcoming offer, must come from the British side. But when nothing of the sort occurred I was under no illusions. I was well aware that I must be repudiated in Ireland. Which is what happened, gently enough. Some Irishmen thought that I had been put up to it in England, some Englishmen that I was an Irish Government stooge. In truth, though this seems hard to credit, the initiative was entirely my own. Mr. de Valera, who had passed to the Presidency by the time of my article, told me that he was utterly opposed to my suggestion. Whatever the rights and wrongs of Ireland's leaving the Commonwealth in 1948, though he was not in power at that time, it was impossible to go back on that decision now. Any unilateral move would be the one thing that would drive him back to active politics.

In retrospect my article was not well timed. It came too late. Already thought in Ireland was turning to what I readily admit was a more promising, less controversial road to unity—the Common Market. If that had come off (or still comes off in the future) the barrier between North and South would fall. The strongest economic argument in Northern Ireland would disappear. The political unity might follow not long after. That particular hope is quenched—perhaps for the moment only. Personally I shall not be surprised if the improving world-wide relationship between the Protestant and Catholic Churches begins to transform for the better the whole psychological outlook of Northen Ireland. And then who knows what might follow?

Mr. de Valera has been so kind to me for many years that I must tell one story of him in gratitude. In the spring of 1963 I gave a lecture for Radio Eireann on the Anglo-Irish Treaty of 1921 in the Thomas Davis series. My book on the treaty (1935) had recently been used as a standard text in the Cambridge subject—Ireland 1920-5. Professor Nicolas Mansergh, creator of much undergraduate interest in Irish studies at Cambridge, had taken the chair for me at a lecture in December 1961, 'The Treaty Forty Years After'.

Naturally I discussed my coming lecture with Mr. de Valera. He was somewhat torn between his determination not to interfere in the slightest degree and his passionate desire that the truth should be told precisely. And there were things well known to him which would not be known at first hand to anyone else. Finally I recorded the talk in a London studio on a certain Thursday afternoon when already gripped by influenza and dashed back to bed for a week. On Sunday the talk was broadcast.

On Monday, beginning to feel a little better but still in bed, I was startled to hear Mr. de Valera's voice on the trunk line (he couldn't possibly have heard I was ill): 'I thought you would like to know,' he said, 'that your talk came through *well*. I heard it down in Limerick, close to the place where I heard that they'd signed the Treaty. Of course,' he added, with a characteristic touch of caution, 'it may not have come through so well in other parts of the country. It doesn't always. But down in Limerick it came through well.' I was greatly touched by the generosity of the thought and struck by his acuteness when he went on: 'Did you by any chance have a cold? I thought I heard you coughing once or twice.' No one else that I am aware of noticed this.

When I next met Mr. de Valera I asked him if his almost total loss of sight had improved his hearing. 'No, I don't think so,' he said. 'At my age [he was eighty in 1962] Miss O'Kelly [his private secretary] hears the telephone quicker than I do. But it makes me very attentive, so perhaps I hear little things. The only trouble,' he added, smiling, 'about having everything read to you is that after a while you're inclined to drop off to sleep.' But noticing once again his prodigious grasp of everything afoot I doubted if he slept for long.

Later in 1963 at a time of much family distress the telephone at Bernhurst rang one evening. 'This is Miss O'Kelly here,' I heard a lady's voice say, 'will you please hold on for the President?' Mr. de Valera came to the point at once. 'I know exactly how you feel,' he said and in a few sentences he showed me that he did.

In February 1961 my brother Edward died quite unexpectedly. Christine telephoned to me in London late one night to say that he had had a stroke. I was in time to see him lying in noble unconsciousness before the end came. President de Valera had made Edward a Senator and with Mrs. de Valera he had taken a continuous interest in the Gate Theatre. Seeing them together at a lecture which I gave at the Paul Mary Pakenham Centenary I somehow felt that Dev had a specially warm place in his heart for Edward and for what he stood for in Irish life. He sent a message of profound sympathy and respect to Christine. At the funeral the Archbishop of Dublin paid touching tribute to Edward's many public services, particularly those rendered to the Church of Ireland of which he was a most faithful son.

A large and representative congregation filled the church, a still larger and more representative one stood outside with bared heads in the February cold. We all came together at the graveside. Besides high dignitaries you could observe there priests of the Passionist Order which Paul Mary Pakenham brought to Ireland. You could observe Joan Littlewood and Brendan Behan and many other men and women of the theatre. A minute's silence was observed in the theatres that evening. The obituaries in Ireland were heart-moving indeed.

What was just as striking were the full and worthy admiring notices in the leading English papers, starting with *The Times*. John Betjeman wrote from a deep intimate understanding. 'Lord Longford was a man of brilliance, integrity, many interests, a warm heart and great generosity.' Evelyn Waugh described the startling house parties at Pakenham in the 'old days', but his conclusion was the same. 'It is not difficult', he wrote, 'to become an able figure in Dublin. It is rare to be regarded with real esteem and affection. That with Christine's constant support was Edward's achievement.'

Perhaps the last word can be taken from the *Sunday Independent*. 'When the financial going was hard, as it often was, he sought the help of the public. He stood quietly in our city streets with a collecting-box. It was not for his personal gain. It was for art, for culture, for Ireland.' I will only add that for all his store of erudition I have never met anyone who was quite so straightforward and natural.

Looking back to what I wrote in *Born to Believe*, I am not ashamed of the words I used there about Edward and Christine. But I am sure now that I underestimated the influence on my own life of such a remarkable brother. Like many other Anglo-Irishmen, I have led a somewhat schizophrenic existence. Perhaps this is true in a lesser degree of my Welsh cousins, of the Rhys (Dynevor) family, and of my Scottish son-in-law Hugh Fraser of the House of Lovat. You could hardly say in either case that they're English and nothing more. There is surely an additional flavour and an additional loyalty, but Anglo-Irishmen of the last hundred years (to go no further back) have had to solve as best they are able a deeper conflict. Which side would they take in the struggle for Irish independence? Which nationality would they choose when the break came in 1921, or would they choose both like Bernard Shaw, or for that matter myself?

My great-uncle, Paul Mary the Passionist, solved the problem in holy fashion in the 1840s. If, as alleged by a devoted friend in his Order, some anti-English feeling was the one blot on his sanctity, who shall be surprised at that in the Famine period? We still await his beatification.

Erskine Childers had to solve the problem in his own way by the time he uttered the final cry before his execution: 'I die loving England and praying that she may change finally and completely towards Ireland.' My uncle Dunsany solved it in a different sense from any of these and W. B. Yeats differently again starting with the first page of his autobiography where he combines his memories of Fitzroy Road, London, and County Sligo. 'The English boys at my school thought of Agincourt and Crécy and the Union Jack and were all very patriotic and I without those memories of Limerick and the yellow ford that would have strengthened an Irish Catholic thought of mountain and lake, of my grandfather and of ships.'

My brother's solution was to commit himself totally and irrevocably to Ireland. In the last thirty years he paid only three visits to England, flying visits in connection with his Irish theatre. What was deeply gratifying was that, as the obituaries testified, he had won so fine a name not only in Ireland but among all who care for culture in England.

I think I see more clearly now than when I wrote *Born to Believe*. I was a young Conservative in 1932 when I first met Mr. de Valera, and I was an ex-member of the Bullingdon, a member of the Carlton Club. I could never have conceivably espoused the Irish cause unless I had been psychologically prepared for it for many years by Edward's ideas and most of all by his example. I responded to his courage in facing obloquy and assault at Eton and Oxford (at the time when it hurt most) far more deeply than I realized for long afterwards.

By the time I myself embraced Irish nationalism we had reached and passed, to adapt Kevin O'Higgins, the last emotional phase of the struggle. We were near the end of the grim uprise of a submerged race. But for me, as told elsewhere, the effect on my total outlook was cataclysmic, it altered my approach henceforward to anything political and not just where Irish interests were concerned. Frank Gallagher, Irish writer and patriot, reviewed my book *Born to Believe* with kindness and insight in the *Irish Press*. 'He could not see things with an English mind', he wrote and referred to me as 'this Irishman in British politics'. Some of my 'Irishness' can be called sentimental, springing from love of an Irish home. When Edward died I was much younger than I had expected to be at such a moment. Even so, I was too old to start a new career in Ireland. It is best for everyone that by a previous arrangement Thomas should have inherited all my brother's property, including Pakenham, which he has rechristened by its old Irish name, Tully Nally. He is deeply in love with the place and determined to keep it alive. A full-time job on the *Observer*, following his much praised *Mountains of Rasselas*, does not deter him. My feelings for Pakenham or Tullynally retain their power.

But sentiment and Irish interests apart, does Ireland colour my outlook in these latter days? Nicko Henderson, boon companion, penetrating diagnostician, an expert, if anyone can be so described, on foreign affairs, tells me that my whole approach to international questions is very Irish. If Nicko and his wife Mary do not understand me who does? I would agree with him if he means that the holding down of one people, great or small, by another people will always be to me an outrageous denial of nature. It is some advantage perhaps to put oneself imaginatively in someone else's shoes, to know in one's bones how British foreign policy looks to at least one other country. That will be so whether the country held down is Ireland, Germany after the war, Poland, or one of the African peoples. The emergence of Irishmen at the United Nations suggests that they sympathize intuitively with the aspirations of the newer countries and are valued accordingly.

On the other hand, the old schizophrenia will not quite be

disposed of. It will continue to present its own strains and conflicts. Even when the balance is achieved it leaves its mark. One cannot expect to have everything, or perhaps anything, both ways. It is a supreme merit of modern British society that an Irishman who has something of his own to contribute is judged on that contribution. Others have demonstrated that the offering can be made so as to give Ireland reason for pride and England for gratitude.

3

'That Prison Person'

I

Not What We Did...

A NGELA LAMBERT, my private secretary at that time, spent a few days last summer in the maternity ward of the Royal Free Hospital. Four young wives shared the ward with her, of whom two had heard of me.

'Oh, he's that prison person,' said one of them brightly.

If I must have a single label I am well content with that one. In Ireland, when not confused with my elder brother Edward, I am quite widely known as the author of *Peace by Ordeal*, the standard work on the Treaty of 1921, though far more people there, I suppose, would think of me as Frank Pakenham than Longford. In Germany it seems that quite a few still remember me as the British Minister of 1947–8. In that capacity I recently contributed to a symposium on the occasion of Dr. Adenauer's retirement. In England I am introduced all too often and rather depressingly by well-meaning chairmen as a Minister in the Labour Government of 1945–51—an honourable but now ancient label.

But if I am asked without a special excuse to take part in television programmes it is usually because I can be presented as an alleged expert on crime, punishment, and prisons. The number of other politicians of this kind could be counted on the fingers of a truncated hand.

The day I heard about the 'prison person' from Angela I was visiting Grendon, the new psychiatric prison, with Jack

Donaldson. He is chairman of the Board of Visitors. I will
have more to say about Grendon later. Here I need only
mention that I was introduced by the chief officer to one
particular prisoner, who said straight away and without
affectation, 'I have just been reading your book, *The Idea of
Punishment.*' (I gather that it had been studied in one of the
therapeutic groups.) 'I wasn't quite sure,' he went on, 'whether
you preferred retribution or restitution.' This, as anyone who
has read the little book will know, was an extremely shrewd
comment.

'And what might you be here for?' I asked him. 'I hope
you don't think it impertinent of me to put the question.'

'Oh, I'm here for sodomy,' he replied. 'Of course, I don't
think the question impertinent, coming from you. *You* at
least are entitled to ask.'

Suppose I were told now, at the age of fifty-eight, that I
would be granted ten years of active public life, and another
ten beyond of some small influence. Supposing I were further
promised one impact, and one only, by which I would be
remembered thereafter. Supposing that I were asked where
I should wish to make it, I should unhesitatingly reply, 'Penal
reform.' That title must include the treatment of all who
come into conflict with the law, whether old or juvenile,
grave or trivial offenders. Prostitutes and alcoholics must
not be forgotten.

People often ask me how and why I got so much involved
in prisons. I never can give much of an answer. It is a matter
of record that I became an official visitor at the Oxford prison
about two years after I became a city councillor and about a
year before the war. I broke off when I was mobilized, in
September 1939, and resumed in the last six months of the
war, when my wartime activities, such as they were, had
come to an end. I gave up again perhaps a year later, when
my life as a junior Minister meant spending the whole working week in London. I returned to crime in a big way in
1953-4, when I carried out an enquiry, with a great deal of
expert help, for the Nuffield Foundation into the causes of
crime. This investigation, mentioned already and to be men-

tioned again, occupied most of my time for more than a year and a half, and landed me with a commitment for life.

Among these steps and decisions it was the first one which counted most, my becoming a prison visitor in Oxford in 1938. It was an initiative in which I was prompted by no one. Without Elizabeth I doubt whether I should ever have found myself becoming a Socialist, though I might have abandoned the Conservatives in despair. My Catholicism owes more than I can ever reckon to Father D'Arcy; my social work and perhaps my interest in finance to Uncle Arthur; my general academic allegiance to Cyril Alington, my headmaster, C. M. Wells, my housemaster, and Harold Salvesen, my economics tutor at New College. But I knew no one remotely concerned with prisons. That departure was entirely my own.

Curiously enough, I did not realize for years what it might mean to me. My autobiography *Born to Believe* was completed in 1952, published in 1953. I can find no mention in it of my prison visiting. I describe my fanatical immersion in every kind of social work in Oxford: 'Working men's clubs, old-age pensioners' associations, youth movements, political and discussion groups in town and university, in addition to immense Labour Party activity.' But prisons are left out. Yet by the time the book appeared I was about to probe the possibilities of a large-scale crime enquiry, as I shall explain a little later. And I am sure that I would never have ventured on so mysterious and forbidding a sea if I had not made a start in the front line as a prison visitor in 1938-9 and 1944-5. It may well be, moreover, that the earlier undertakings were a symptom of the same deep-rooted tendencies that prompted and sustained the later one.

Well, then, why did I choose prison work in 1938, when I already had more on my plate than I could manage, when no one beckoned me towards it; when it didn't connect with my academic studies, and couldn't help my political career? (It was and is generally supposed that prisoners have no votes. Quite a few of them have votes in fact, but up to the present it has seemed inappropriate or too much trouble to collect them.)

Why does anyone choose a vocation, a hobby, or a sport?

Psychiatrists can sometimes help, but they seldom take us far. Certainly I did not consciously decide in favour of prisons for any reason clear to myself or proclaimed to others. If I mention possible factors it is only surmise.

Certain headings of mental reconstruction are plausible. In one bracket I place the search for adventure and experience. In another, the sense of guilt and the goad of sacrifice. And all these requirements, for good family and professional reasons, but also in concession to temperament, had to be satisfied within the bounds of pre-war Oxford.

Among my friends, Peter Fleming had walked across Brazil and a large part of Asia; Philip Toynbee had fought in Spain and made me yearn to follow him; others took to drink as a form of audacity. In an earlier generation my Uncle Arthur and his friends had descended on Hackney Wick, where he lived, apart from the First World War, ever afterwards. I sought it all on my doorstep.

And there was an influence at work which is harder to explain. It arose from my ambivalent attitude to a political career. My circumstances, my faculties, my over-strong spirit of emulation prompted that ambition. But in an odd way I never counted the rigours of a day spent on politics as an honest day's work. Whatever my prejudices against Sir Oswald Mosley, when he announced that his party would make Parliament a working shop instead of a talking shop he rang a recognizable bell. Politics, then and since, have had plenty of glitter for me, but the suspicion, much of it irrational, has persisted that the glitter was largely false.

I was uninterested in the fact that one Prime Minister, Sir Robert Peel, had been my great-grandfather (as already mentioned), and that another one, the Duke of Wellington, had married my great-great-aunt. Much stronger was a mental formation based on an ingrained idea that as a younger son, even one with solid expectations from my great-aunt, I must find it difficult to marry early in life. I had grown up expecting to follow a money-earning career.

That last was certainly not a description I applied to politics. The possibility that as a young man I would be able to embark on politics never occurred to me until I had taken a first-class degree in politics, philosophy, and economics; had aroused the interest of H. A. L. Fisher, warden of New College, and had received the friendship of the Birkenhead family. The sense of uneasiness, of unreality, about myself as a politician, remained long afterwards.

And I was not only a politician but a Socialist convert, a figure whose claims to virtue were inevitably a source of torturing doubt to myself, if only because they were so suspect in the eyes of others. My lot was cast in pleasant places. I wore, metaphorically, the softest of garments, and lived in my own eyes in the houses of kings. (In my time an Oxford don thought naturally of his college as the centre of the universe, and his job as universally envied.) The contrast between my stern Kantian aspirations and preaching and the titillating pleasantness of my actual existence obsessed me.

I have described elsewhere my pathetic preparations for the coming war, and religious crisis of this period. But neither was directly related, as far as I can judge, to the prison-visiting decision. More significant were my efforts to *be* a genuine Labour man, not merely to *talk* like one. This meant, so to speak, forcing my way right through the working class, from the top downwards, and making contact with them at the bottom. Only then could one be sure that one's new identity was real; only then could one be sure that one was seeking no reward, and doing some incontrovertible good.

We used to be visited in our house at Cowley, after it was known that I had come into a bit of money, by quite a few beggars, itinerant vagrants from Glasgow and other places, sometimes with real or alleged Irish connections. One night one fainted on my doorstep. We took him in, and I gave him an overcoat, the second best of my two. He appeared grateful, and disappeared. A few days later I ran into an unemployed labourer, slightly known to me, with a coat over his arm that looked remarkably like mine. I asked him about it, and he replied: 'Oh, that filthy old thing—a chap from Glasgow gave it me the other night. He said he wouldn't be seen dead in it, and nor would I. I'm just looking for somewhere to chuck it.'

I don't know how I would react to that incident now. But in those days it strengthened my conviction that there were whole lost tribes in the ranks of the working class, and that it was my special vocation to live among them. About that time, Father Martin D'Arcy, s.j., my dear friend, gave me a kind of personal motto for life. 'Keep close to the poor.' On paper I have widened that conception steadily to include all prisoners and ex-prisoners; all mentally handicapped; and indeed all the deprived and afflicted. My practice is, of course, much inferior. But the light flickers; it never quite goes out.

Long and earnest were my talks with tramps and down-and-outs generally. But still there was this failure to get below the surface, to be one of the 'we's', instead of remaining one of 'them', to use a later expression. I was also moved by the pursuit of knowledge; here, as always, an ambiguous word. It was not scientific knowledge that I sought at that time; that kind of curiosity did not arise till fifteen years later. For instance, I met Leo Page, the king of our little prison world; responded to his lay holiness, but never read his books or knew he had written them. When working for Nuffield (1953–4) I was to be told by the permanent head of the Home office that Page, in his view, had written the best of all books on crime. Any knowledge that I craved to acquire was first-hand knowledge of prisoners, as individual human beings. The same kind of knowledge that my uncle and his friends had acquired in the East End as a by-product of their missionary endeavours.

Was there any conscious desire to equip myself to make a national contribution? That kind of motive had been at work when a few years earlier I lived and taught and studied education, as did Elizabeth, in the Potteries. But here there was little or no calculation. The action sprang from the emotions and the heart. Prison, like politics, for the outsider was full of glitter; but here the moral censor detected no self-interest and withdrew his blockage. And, as I soon discovered, the sheer immediate happiness that one could give by one's very appearance, friendly and diffident, in a prison cell, provided an intuitive reassurance to oneself. Whatever one did or said or failed to do and say, one was adding indubitably to the amount of good in the world.

I have fewer clear recollections than I could wish of my Oxford prisoners. I suppose I was very innocent—the prisoners told me a lot of demonstrable falsehoods about their prison records. All too often the conversation began by one of them, perhaps a solicitor, saying to me, 'Here I am; a few days ago a respected professional man, and now dragged by the scruff into this incredible situation.' One discovered later that he had had several previous convictions, and was just keeping up a front in my eyes and perhaps his own. Today that seldom happens. I suppose that by the time I meet a prisoner now, he knows a little about me, and thinks the truth more prudent. Or perhaps the shades of the prison house have hardened me, and written scepticism on my face. Or perhaps prisoners have become a more candid race, or less ashamed. I still believe that kindness is all, but now I look further ahead when I visit a prisoner. I don't know whether the maturity helps less or more.

A letter from one of my earliest prisoners reached me while I was writing this. 'The fellows here say', he writes, 'that Old Paby Pakenham has just changed his Monica.' (He refers to the move from Pakenham to Longford.) And much more in the same jocular vein. I guess that he has been in prison many times since I visited him. He seems incorrigibly cheerful, but he asks now whether I can help him with a regular visitor or pen friend. This could be the turning point.

When I was visiting Grendon, as described above, I heard of a prisoner, a desperate character in the public mind, who had just applied to come to Grendon in the hopes of a new start. A striking piece of news for those of us who know and like that particular prisoner. Old prison-service hands tell you that a moment often comes, perhaps in early middle age, when a man feels that the criminal life is getting him nowhere; when his aggressive urges and his physical toughness are ebbing a little. If you can catch him then, or, better still, if he will come to you, a whole life may be redeemed. So may it be with my Oxford correspondent. He was a cheery type. He still is, to judge from his letter.

Very different was a lay preacher, doing his ninth sentence for a homosexual offence. His religious passion, centring on the Epistle to the Hebrews, I never questioned. His sexual outbursts always occurred in the same way—in a desperate effort to relieve periodic depressions. Oxford prison in those days had nothing remotely comparable to psychiatric treatment. The staff were good-humoured, tolerant custodians.

Our ways parted. Before he left prison I had become immersed in government, and although we had known one another well, I thought of him seldom. There came a day when I was Minister for the British zone of Germany, when there was a food crisis in the Ruhr, and Sholto Douglas and Brian Robertson (our numbers one and two in Germany) had been urgently summoned to the Foreign Office. When the consultations under Ernest Bevin were at their height I was told a Mr. X had called, and must see me instantly. Not recognizing the name, I was taken aback to discover my old lay-preaching friend awaiting me in my vast Ministerial office. I suppose he thought I would expect him to be needing money, for he began eagerly: 'It's not bad news this time—it's good. I'm engaged to be married. The wedding's next week; I wanted to be sure you approved.'

I tried to conceal my feelings, while raising a few points. It emerged that the lady was a children's nurse, aged fifty-four (he was forty-six). She had never been married. He had not told her about his 'record', or his special problems. This was where I came in particularly. Did I really think that he must tell her? If he didn't he believed that it would never come out, and if he did it was very unlikely that the wedding would take place at all.

I know what I would say now. But I said the opposite then. After some humming and hawing I told him: 'Don't tell her if you feel that it would wreck the happiness of both of you. But if ever the truth comes out tell her it was my fault and ask her to get into touch with me.' I then shook him warmly by the hand, and scooted back down the corridor to apologize to Bevin for being away so long from the German problem.

Again I thought I had heard the last of our friend, but again I was wrong. Perhaps six months later I received a letter from his wife saying that she had discovered her husband's past, and that she could hardly forgive him for misleading her, except that it appeared that he had withheld the essential information on my advice. The story must be cut short. I entertained them both at lunch at Simpson's in the Strand. They bickered away, and I grew testy myself. But somehow, as they went off, I felt grounds for hope. His wife was seemingly strict, but prepared for sacrifice and fond of him. I have never heard of them again.

If the story has any point it is surely this: prisoners are not an exceptional class to be humoured from moment to moment at all costs. Many of them live all too often in the present only; lack of forethought is their gravest defect. Spontaneity and warmth are indispensable for winning their regard and confidence, but without forethought and follow-through the effect too often evaporates. In all the difficult cases the after-care or lack of it matters even more than the treatment in prison. Many thousands of prisoners never 'go back', whatever the community does or fails to do for them. But the lives of many thousands of others depend on whether we realize that the worst crime is to take no interest in them, and the next worst is to lose our interest halfway.

2

...But What We Tried to Do

SIR OSBERT SITWELL tells a story in his *Laughter in the Next Room* of his beloved housekeeper Mrs. Powell. A journalist, or what he calls 'a contemporary chat-spinner', had written this paragraph: 'The Sitwell brothers have achieved the impossible and persuaded their cook to work in a kitchen hung with pictures of the modern school.' Sir Osbert found a note from Mrs. Powell: 'Sir, please tell the young gentleman that servants are individuals like other people, and not a separate race. I happen to like modern pictures.' To recognize that prisoners are individuals like other people, and not a separate race, is the beginning of penal wisdom.

But it is not the end of it. It is as difficult and as dangerous to generalize about prisoners as about domestic servants, or for that matter about dons, bankers, or politicians, among whom I have worked so much. Yet most of us tentatively associate some characteristics with groups such as these. In so far as criminologists have taught us lately to distrust and despise all general statements about prisoners or other delinquents, they have performed a doubtful service. They are convinced that if only adequate facilities were made available for criminological research (if only they had a tenth of those at the disposal of the economists) we should be able to make our way on to firmer ground. Then, but not till then, will dogmatic pronouncements be tolerable. True enough in its way, but in the meanwhile crime goes on increasing until three times the pre-war figure has been passed. More and more prisoners are convicted and in due course released into the community. The present generation, however devoid of verifiable knowledge, cannot transfer to the next one its responsibility for preventive and remedial action.

My own penal activities have taken a quadruple form.

1. Public appearances.
2. Social research.
3. The New Bridge for ex-prisoners.
4. Friendship with individual delinquents.

These threads have been much interwoven and are likely to remain so.

My public appearances have centred on the House of Lords. I initiated in 1955 a long-continuing series of debates, more or less annual, on prisons and after-care. Helped by many, especially by Joan Bourne, I have spoken more largely on penal topics over the whole period than anyone else, though Barbara Wootton and Victor Stonham, since they joined the House, have brought a distinction in one case and a vehemence in the other to which I yield the palm. I have addressed numerous gatherings outside, including the Annual Conferences of the Magistrates' Association and the National Association of Probation officers, and have performed quite often on television.

In social research my biggest personal effort remains my share in the Nuffield Enquiry into the causes of crime, 1953–4, from which emerged my book *Causes of Crime* (1958). I can date its origin exactly. On December 1st, 1952, I read a turn-over article in *The Times* which brought home to me as never before that indictable crime had been increasing for many years. The increase had gone hand in hand with the establishment of the Welfare State but had started well before then. In a flash I knew that here was to be my greatest social interest of the next few years.

As one who had worked as personal assistant to Sir William Beveridge for three years, I felt that there was no one better qualified than he to investigate the question, 'Why have delinquency and material improvement and the abolition of extreme poverty increased apparently together?' The idea of

bringing in William Beveridge fell through, but with invaluable help from William Clark, and from David Astor, I
found myself in touch with Leslie Farrer-Brown, Director of
the Nuffield Foundation, a man of action and vision.

I embarked on a two-year enquiry into what was generally
called, in the Press and otherwise, the causes of crime. More
precisely, I was officially invited to make 'a critical appraisal
of current opinion about the causes of crime, and the reasons for
the increase of crime in recent years'. It was hoped to discover
which were based on tested evidence and which on unproved
assumptions. There was a difference of emphasis between what
I and other people thought I was doing, and my strict terms of
reference. This fact was not unimportant.

I wanted to use the enquiry to reach practical conclusions,
the typical politicians' or social reformers' approach. The
Nuffield Foundation were, no doubt, just as concerned as I
was about practical results in the long run. But they reckoned
that in the existing state of knowledge, the essential prelimin-
ary step was to find out how much, if anything, we knew
already. And this meant remorseless scrutiny of the views of
so-called experts. While splendidly open-minded on every
issue arising, they seemed to cherish more hope than I did of
equating the methods of the so-called social sciences with
those of the natural sciences, of being able to study crime as they
would study the soil or climate. They were much less ready
than I was to grasp at limited evidence with a view to immediate action.

With one or two of my small but deeply committed staff
I ranged up and down the prisons and other relevant institutions of England and Scotland. With expert assessors, two
psychiatrists, a stipendiary magistrate, and frequently the
director of Nuffield himself, Leslie Farrer-Brown, of the
penetrating questioning mind, I cross-examined at least a
dozen psychiatrists and many other authorities. Roger Opie
then, and still more since, a high-grade economist, came in to
help. He picked up criminology in a long vacation. He wrote
a considerable part of the eventual book and married delightful
Norma Cantor, my private secretary.

Of our witnesses, John Bowlby and Barbara Wootton

were among the few who enlightened us as much as we had hoped. Some of the others crumpled rather sadly. If a strictly scientific test, a test of verification, were to be applied, the total evidence of fact and opinion looked flimsy enough. If scientific categories were going to be insisted on in dealing with the questions, 'What are the causes of crime?' and 'Why has crime increased so much in Britain?', the total answer after a year was in one sense a lemon. And it was not likely to look much different a year later. I was genuinely committed to an enquiry lasting two years, but for all practical purposes we had got as far as we were likely to get in one.

Nuffield saw it differently. They were just as sceptical as I was about the scientific value of any conclusions we were likely to reach, but—at great trouble and expense—they had promoted an elaborate publicized enquiry. A scholarly report based on all the evidence available could reasonably be looked for. They kindly allowed me to become chairman of the National Bank, but they could not agree themselves to publish anything which was based on unfinished research. In the end a book emerged with their consent but on my own personal responsibility.

I was also chairman of the—I would think influential and (certainly) representative—Pakenham-Thompson committee on the whole problem of after-care, which reported in 1960. Its existence was entirely due to the sublimely bold initiative of a young public-relations man, Peter Thompson. Driven by a religious sense of hectic purpose, he wheeled into line a number of reputable personalities, most of them in penal work, but some from business. Somehow or other we all came together under my chairmanship. The report was drafted and much of the work done by the honorary secretary, Jack Donaldson. While still at Cambridge (first-class in moral sciences) he had received the dedication of Professor Broad's *Five Types of Ethical Theory*. There followed social work (the Peckham Health Centre), war service, farming, a directorship of Covent Garden. But apart from being one of the managers of an approved school, he came fresh to the penal field, and no one in my time has made an impact on it so quickly. I cannot shake off the illusion, if it is one, that our Pakenham-Thompson committee had much to do with the establishment of the Government's own enquiry into the after-care of prisoners. Their report was published while this book was going through the press.

A little later (1961–2) I was chairman of a no less representative and may it prove no less influential committee. It drew up a detailed plan for compensating victims of violence, on which subject I soon after initiated a debate in the House of Lords. We penal reformers are often accused of neglecting the victim in our concern for the criminal. Sometimes the charge is brought forward by those who have shown no great concern for either. But I am sensitive to the criticism when it comes, as it did more than once in the House of Lords, from someone like Eddie Winterton, who boldly said what a number of sincere people were thinking.

In all my efforts to clear the name of Michael Davies from his conviction for murder (of which more anon) I have reflected ruefully that the parents of John Beckley, the murdered boy, could only be caused further pain by keeping the issue alive. I could not hold back on that account, in fairness to Davies. I conceived the idea, however, of starting a Friends of the Victims Society. It has not yet eventuated. I am not sure that victims wish to be singled out in this way. But the Victims of Violence enquiry gave me and other penal reformers the chance to correct an impression that those who most deserved our sympathy were least likely to receive it.

Along with the social research has gone a deeper theoretic interest in crime and punishment. Stirred up when I was working for Nuffield by Sir Walter Moberley's lectures on responsibility, it has expressed itself most definitely so far in my small book *The Idea of Punishment* (1961). Christian and profane moral philosophers jostled one another in a short book list. The Catholic priests Rickaby and Hawkins, the Anglican bishop Gore, were matched by Lord Russell, the archetype of the anti-Christian, though gentler in these latter days; by refined Oxford verbalists like Nowell-Smith and Herbert Hart, philosopher and jurist; by Mary Warnock, authentically interpreting Oxford philosophy, but searching in Sartre and elsewhere for a deeper message. On the legal side the debt to Dr. Grunhut, the learned criminologist, and to Arthur Goodhart, a friend of many years, was obvious. In the midst of the Christian-humanist tension, the influence, and still more the stimulus, of Barbara Wootton was not concealed. The whole was lighted up, I would like to think, on its humble plane, by Papal and Thomist teaching.

The New Bridge is a society to help ex-prisoners, which is entirely unsupported by State funds, and entirely free from State or official control. In this way it differs from the Discharged Prisoners' Aid Societies whose work it seeks to supplement, and with whom relations, after an unpleasant beginning, are now cordial. Much credit for this happy state is due to Commander Hague, the present secretary of the Central After-Care Association, and the National Association of Discharged Prisoners' Aid Societies.

I would hesitate to describe myself baldly and arrogantly as the founder of the New Bridge, except that the title has been applied to me in the *New Statesman* by our vice-chairman Bill Hewitt. He writes under the name of C. H. Rolph, and is, I suppose, taken for all in all, the most respected unofficial figure in the prison and after-care world. Frank Dawtry, secretary of the probation officers? Hugh Klare, secretary of the Howard League? Jack Filmer, director of our own New Bridge? Honoured names indeed, but in one sense at least they are officials. Xenia Field? Since the Field Lectures were named after her Xenia is an institution. Bill Hewitt is just himself.

Assuming, then, the title of founder, I report that the founding moment came during a tête-à-tête dinner at the White Tower Restaurant in 1955, when I was entertaining Edward, ——, on his release from Wakefield. I had hardly known him before (he was barely half my age), though I had seen him about and we had common friends and acquaintances. His case had aroused a frenzy of interest. He, Peter ——, and a friend, ——, were convicted of homosexual offences under the 'consenting adults' clause, which is so bitterly criticized by so many. Two or three years later the Wolfenden Committee were to demand, so far vainly, that it should be repealed, and I was to open the debate in that sense in the House of Lords.

[125]

I had been struck from the outset by Edward's dignity during his court ordeal, as it reached me through the newspapers. I had learnt through official channels of the gallant show he had put up during his year in Wakefield prison. He has since become a happy husband and father, and made good abundantly in various ways, while never forgetting the prisoners or their cause. A little later than this, in a prison debate in the Lords, I mentioned that I had made friends on both sides of the fence, and referred to 'holders of honoured names who had borne themselves very bravely in their adversity.' I was thinking of Edward, Peter, and one or two others. But for some time afterwards every prisoner I met seemed grateful for a personal reference to himself.

By the time of the White Tower dinner I had come to know Peter quite well. I had first met him in Wormwood Scrubs on one of my Nuffield Enquiry rounds. I had obtained permission to visit him regularly, in connection with my studies. He has since written a book which will probably last longer than any other prison book of our time, partly because of the tragic starkness with which the homosexual issue is discussed. He refers to me handsomely and touchingly. He says that I helped to make him feel a human being again. Certainly when I first met him he was a man on the rack.

Though his prison clothes and his evident loathing of them were the first thing that struck me, my next and strongest impression was of a man who had quite unexpectedly been stripped utterly naked. A man whose innermost secrets had been dragged pitilessly and with the maximum distortion into the light of mocking day. In those days the tone of the Scrubs was much less civilized than it became under Governor Gilbert Hair, though the then governor was incapable of inhumanity. I can still see Peter being allowed to have a cup of tea with me, and then being forced to carry away the tray, holding it in front of him while a prison officer marched him out from behind. It was not deliberately cruel. Someone had to take the tray away, but the little procession and the way it was organized seemed calculated to underline the end of his thirty minutes of life on a par with other human beings.

And another time, when I was seeing several prisoners, I

remember discovering that Peter had been kept standing in the corridor for something like three-quarters of an hour. The first time we met we talked about homosexuality. I told him that I thought it was a sin, but between consenting adults should not be treated as a crime. We discussed the extent (rather hazy in my mind) to which Plato condoned or encouraged it, and the amount of it at Oxford. I felt—we both felt—that we had got to get that off our chests. In later talks we discussed everything else. It was a duty to probe the causes of crime, and I can remember more easily bringing messages of goodwill from Anne Fleming, who had originally asked me to see him, and from my daughter Antonia, who eventually obtained his book for Weidenfeld's. Her letter to him, though she had never met him, seemed to bring him back to life more positively than any other experience.

Once I visited him with his mother, thoroughly orthodox and all the more bewildered on that account, but utterly loving and loyal. I should say that Peter suffered in prison as much as anyone could suffer without real physical hardship during a fairly short sentence. The sheer injustice, indeed—as it seemed to him and so many others—the iniquity of his conviction, combined with his sensitivity to deny him any possible spirit of resignation. To him it was sheer, savage humiliation throughout. But his courage never faltered and his artist's brain was at work.

Returning to Edward and the White Tower, I told him that in all my travels—I had visited a score of prisons and Borstals —I had not found one single soul (outside the after-care organizations) to say a good word for our existing after-care arrangements. The goodwill of individuals might be conceded (it was in fact conceded less than was fair or decent). The opinion was virtually unanimous that the after-care as a whole was so gravely deficient that it might as well not exist. Indeed, I myself had reached the conclusion that it would be better if it did *not* exist. There would then be a better chance of making a new start. As it was, the existing set-up cumbered the ground and choked off anyone else who invaded it, and prevented a fresh beginning. Nevertheless, in anything we started we must work hand in hand with what was there.

Speaking from his first-hand experience of prisoners, Edward whole-heartedly agreed with me. He had not been 'out' long, but already he was being besieged by former companions in prison. They were desperately in need of help, and saw no hope in the official or quasi-official agencies. He was thinking of starting something, possibly on the lines of Alcoholics Anonymous. In that moment the idea of the New Bridge was born. The name came later and we owed it to Edward himself.

A dinner followed at Kettners with each of us paying for ourselves. There were several ex-prisoners, including Edward and Peter. There were Stephen Spender, Ludovic Kennedy and Mary McCarthy. There were David Astor, an unobtrusive friend of the New Bridge from that day to this, and Victor Gollancz, and one or two others who can be relied upon like them to champion any cause, opposed to the false logic and the dead-weight of conventional oppression and inertia. There were some, like Bill Hewitt, Cliff Tucker and Jack Filmer, who unofficially had worked for many years among ex-prisoners.

In particular, there was a psychiatrist called John Thompson, with whom I have since lost touch. He impressed us almost coercively, for all his gentleness of manner, with his French experience. We already were sure that what was needed was personal friendship for each ex-prisoner. John Thompson insisted that this must be supplied in groups rather than on a one-to-one basis. The group method reintegrated a man into the community. The one-to-one set up tensions of its own, and was at least as liable to isolate as to break down barriers. Through José Baird, the New Bridge has made much use of the group method, but help supplied on the spot through our headquarters has also figured largely.

We have tried to avoid—not always quite successfully—the provision of direct financial help, i.e. the handing out of money ourselves. (We have never had much to hand out.) But Jack Filmer and his heroic aides, in particular Dorothy Roberts, Phyllis Higgins and Jane Buxton, have tirelessly coped with every problem brought them, whether what was wanted was a job, a lodging, clothes, medical help, or just consolation.

It might simply be the need to feel, as Peter said I made him feel in prison, a human being, and the courage to go forward as such. In the end what matters most in the ex-prisoner is the will to help oneself. But how is that to be fanned back to life in face of what I have called before now 'the four great handicaps': the handicap of the initial temperament; the handicap of the prison experience; the inevitable handicap of the prison record, even in the eyes of the well disposed; and the brutally irrational handicap of that same record in the eyes of the unenlightened majority?

Jack Filmer must have a paragraph to himself. A small, quiet man, bespectacled like myself, formerly obituary editor of *The Times*, he possesses a deep knowledge of music and old furniture. This you would not be surprised to learn though you would not hear it from him. But you might be less prepared for the news that during the war, when not very young, he rose from the rank of private to that of Lieutenant-colonel. But if you saw him (I didn't, but I have heard it described) gently removing a broken bottle from a prisoner who had gone berserk in a public bar you would readily accept his statement, which I once extracted from him: 'I have never been frightened of a prisoner. If I have any trouble I just tell them not to be silly boys.' The same spirit animates his colleagues. The New Bridge tends to get a good proportion of the worst prisoners, including mental and quasi-mental cases, and we have never had any physical trouble.

But all this would seem to Jack and the others a melodramatic approach to their problems. They would pride themselves, if on anything, on their knowledge of individual prisoners, and with much justification. The other day an ex-headmaster came to see me, who had gone to prison for an offence against one of his boys. Otherwise a blameless and excellent man who was not likely to offend again. I rang up Jack about him, and though he had only seen him once, some eighteen months before, he at once replied, 'His trouble is that he lives in the country with his mother and another old crippled lady, and doesn't feel he can leave them, which makes a job difficult.' And so it proved. But what a memory for human realities! What makes the New Bridge tick? I can only say that the lives of those I have mentioned, and many others I have not, are given to helping prisoners because the prisoners can't help themselves, and they—the New Bridge staff and active members—can't help themselves helping them. Three years ago we were looking after about two hundred new prisoners a year. Last year the number was six times as great, and there seems no limit, provided we can find the resources. Many functions have been organized for this latter purpose. Belinda Norman-Butler, Joan Reed and Michael Croft have led and inspired our efforts.

For a long time we were viewed with suspicion, and so it seemed, resentment by the authorities. Our very existence seemed, not unnaturally, to the Discharged Prisoners' Aid Societies, to be a reflection on them, a criticism of their efficiency. And so I must admit it was, though I have always tried to explain that in our view there was nothing personal about our savage discontent. A revolution was necessary in the whole system of after-care.

What was needed was the acceptance by the community for the first time of a specific responsibility for providing a minimum standard of welfare for the ex-prisoner. That was the social principle. What was needed in administrative practice was a national network of after-care officers, supplemented by voluntary effort. Some of the voluntary effort should be State-aided, some of it, like the New Bridge, quite independent. It was not sufficient to assume that the Welfare State could look after ex-prisoners through the same services: the Ministry of Labour, the Assistance Board, etc., as were adequate for other citizens. Prisoners needed special help because they are specially handicapped. Progress has been made since then, but neither the principle nor the practice has yet been achieved.

We had other problems. The Alcoholics Anonymous idea did not work out in practice—to my regret. Our members as a whole were chary of being governed by ex-delinquents, though some ex-delinquents have been among our most loyal members; a number have worked unselfishly in our office. The notion persisted, however, in some official circles that we were a society of homosexuals to help homosexuals.

I remember well one of our cocktail parties at the House of Lords when I found myself introducing an ex-prisoner (homosexual offence) to Sir Lionel Fox, then chairman of the Prison Commissioners. Nothing could ever ruffle or impair Sir Lionel Fox's grave good manners. He would have treated the devil himself with old-world courtesy. I can remember hearing him say politely, 'I am only sorry that we didn't have time to show you a wider range of our institutions.' But I heard afterwards that he had been upset, and I esteemed him too much to feel any pleasure in the incident.

How much have we in the New Bridge accomplished? I treasure the thought of the human service directly rendered to many in dire need of it. I put just as high the spur, the goad, the irritation we have supplied to everyone else, including the Government. That, of course, cannot be measured, and there is not much credit yet to be distributed. The time for bouquets and prize-giving is a long way off.

In the House of Lords during the Criminal Justice Bill (1961) I described, without much contradiction, our national system of after-care as 'a nonsense, a shambles, and a mess'. I told Lord Montgomery sitting opposite that I had borrowed those words from his known vocabulary; I begged him to rise and confirm them. (I had bet Stephen Taylor sixpence that I would draw Monty on to his feet.) Monty sat tight and said nothing, but came up afterwards and said that he would back Victor Stonham and myself on the same subject next week.

He was as good as his word. He obtained a copy of the Pakenham-Thompson report, and delivered his maiden speech on prison after-care, a subject hitherto strange to him. He informed the House that the system was even worse than I had said. 'It was a dog's breakfast which,' he added, 'was a very different thing from the cat's whiskers.' Loud laughter, and large headlines next morning such as no one had ever managed to secure for after-care.

Monty once said to Sir Winston Churchill about myself, 'Don't you think his hair wants cutting, Prime Minister?'

Sir Winston spelt out his reply slowly. 'Your head, my dear Field Marshal, requires to be compressed under a military cap. He needs his for speaking in the House of Lords.'

But today Monty uses his head to much purpose in the House of Lords, and whatever one makes of his speeches, he is probably the greatest draw among the peers.

Let the last word rest for the moment with a certain accountant, eminent and eminent-looking, who called to see me at the National Bank about three years ago. 'You won't know me,' he said, 'but I'm Peter Baker's father.'

I pricked up my ears.

'I saw the governor of his prison yesterday,' he went on. 'The State's had my boy in its charge for five years. I said, "What are you going to do about him now that he's coming out?" The governor replied: "If you're asking what the State is going to do, the answer is nothing. You'd better go and see the chairman of the New Bridge." So here,' he concluded, 'I am.'

And I am very glad he was, for it led to my friendship with his son and it led also to my writing a foreword for a book which was not only highly readable but had the rare merit of being liked by prison officers. I hope that Peter will find an outlet for the qualities which helped him to achieve a fine war record and to show much promise as an M.P.

One laughs a shade too easily about the past and the present of after-care. It is in fact a scandalous story, with no one to blame, or, rather, everybody, except a handful of dedicated souls, all grossly overworked. A revolution is long overdue in this last neglected corner of the social field, ignored almost uniquely in the expansion of the Welfare State. As I write a great argument is in progress.

3

'I Was in Prison'

I COME now to my friendships with individual prisoners. Here my range is small compared with that of those who give their lives to the prison service, or probation, or similar work. But it probably compares well not only with that of other public men but with that of many criminologists and academic reformers. As long ago as the Nuffield Enquiry (1953–4), our chief criminologist, Dr. Grunhut, generously told me that my first-hand acquaintanceship with prisoners was a special asset in our discussions. In the years that have passed I have always tested penal theories and the encouraging pronouncements of Ministers by the reactions, elicited or imagined, of individual prisoners. It is an indispensable though not the only criterion. I have known a great many prisoners, in the sense that I have talked to them several times inside or outside a prison, besides countless more I have spoken to once in passing. But I have had the privilege, further, of knowing *well* a relatively small number of prisoners, some for as much as ten years, some for a shorter period but intimately.

I am no stranger to the lasting injuries inflicted all too often by prison.

'Yes,' said Gilbert Hair, in beginning an address. 'Yes, I am a prison governor. You don't think much of prisons as a way of treating human beings. No more do I. Perhaps you prefer execution or mutilation, or public humiliation in the pillory or stocks; or flogging; or you may have your own ideas. If so, I'd like to hear them. But if you can't suggest anything better, and if you want any sort of law and order, then prison it's got to be.'

And he proceeded to win their sympathy for the improvements he was trying to implement. Personally I don't think that the problem of finding a civilized form of punishment is as hopeless as that argument suggests. I believe that for most prisoners, leaving out the very helpless and the very dangerous, the ultimate answer lies not in incarceration but in compulsory work for the community. There should be no more denial of freedom, or of intercourse with one's family, than exists in, say, the Army. And large numbers of prisoners could live at home while doing this compulsory work. But that solution is opposed to many prejudices. It lies still in the future, and let me emphasize this: suppose it were in operation, but suppose that at the same time nothing more was done to help ex-prisoners than is done today. Their lot in the community when their sentence ceased would be little better than it is now. That said, let me repeat that I am no stranger to the cruel after-effects of many a prison sentence today.

I saw a great deal of Norman Hignett, a clever solicitor who some years earlier had developed grandiose ideas and grandiose expenditure to cope with them. By the time I knew him he had served several years for some kind of embezzlement. He was introduced by another ex-prisoner, much liked then and now by me, who testified to the strength and thoughtfulness with which Norman, then working in the library, had sustained him and others during their sentences. Norman had serious ideas about prison reform. He embodied them in a book called *Portrait in Grey*, for which I wrote a rather guarded foreword. It is a somewhat bitter book, a rather heavy book, but its genuineness, its thoroughness, cannot be denied, nor the suffering from which it sprang. It fell rather flat, though I still find students who refer to it gratefully. Already the problem of Norman's future was becoming a nightmare.

He could not practise at the law, except in what sounded like some near-the-wind connection. He was too able and ambitious a man to accept a minor clerical job, and I was well aware from our occasional lunches that he enjoyed a glass of brandy more than most men, and two glasses more than one. I heard rumours of difficulties; I did not desert him, but I did not fall over myself to keep in close touch. Then one day a letter arrived in the middle of a debate in the House of Lords. Like this: 'By the time you receive this, I will be no more ... I have tried; I have gone on trying, but every door is closed against me.' I hardly read it through; I made instant contact with the police. But it was too late. His body was discovered in the Paddington canal.

There were three or four mourners at the cremation at Golders Green, including one lady who had loved him. I retain and value the walking stick he left me; I often think that he would have been one of the hardest ex-prisoners to help back to an acceptable life, because he was alone, and he had notions too large for the real situation. But he had much ability, and, as his book showed, idealism. He had the instinct and the capacity to be of help to others. When I hear of any new scheme for reforming prison or after-care, I am apt to ask myself, 'Would it have been of any use to Norman?' Society can never be complacent when the existence of prison and the absence of after-care drive such a man to suicide.

But there are many more cheerful pictures. In front of me lies a well-written letter signed 'Christopher Craig'. (I wish my handwriting were half as good as his.) He tells me that he has settled down in an interesting job, with pleasant people near his new home. He writes to thank me for my support during his ten years in prison. 'I hope', he ends, 'we shall soon be able to meet under more favourable conditions than in the past.'

Christopher Craig. The policeman shot and killed in that roof-top tragedy of 1952. Derek Bentley, Craig's companion, hanged: a nice boy, well liked, as I discovered, at his approved school, but of pathetically low intelligence, and an epileptic. Derek Bentley, already in custody, is said to have shouted to Craig, 'Let him have it, Chris!' but played no part in the murder. Craig never heard the words which Bentley is supposed to have uttered.

I had seen Christopher in Wakefield prison early in his sentence. He tried to be cheerful. He told me that one of the assistant governors played billiards with him. He seemed to be getting on better than, as I afterwards discovered, was the case. I had kept in touch with him mostly through his mother. Much later on I had seen him in Wormwood Scrubs, where they told me he had developed a quite remarkable skill as a fitter. And I had more than once gone into the question of his release, the last time receiving a favourable reply from the Home Secretary. If the abstract justice of his remission had been insufficient his mother's letter, which I forwarded, would have melted a stone, as much by its argument as by its feeling.

I was prepared, therefore, for his release when it came. But I compare Christopher Craig today, aged twenty-six, and esteemed by those who know him best, with the same Christopher at sixteen, universally execrated outside his family. I find myself rubbing my eyes and recalling what Rosebery said when he looked at the dead Newman, who had been through so many traumatic vicissitudes. 'It seemed as if a whole cycle of human life and thought were concentrated in that august repose.' But, here, what was so moving was not an end but a beginning, a new life springing from a shattered old one.

I have been asked whether there is the slightest chance of Christopher Craig shooting another policeman. I reply, 'Not the slightest chance in the world; I am as likely to shoot a policeman as he is, and that not just because those who take life illegally hardly ever take it twice.' Here there were so many other special factors. First of all, then, the family background. So often one finds a broken home behind a delinquent, or else a delinquent home, or in adult life—as in the case of Norman Hignett—a consuming loneliness, an absence of any support when things go wrong. Here it was all quite different. Mr. Craig was a bank official and very respectable. Both parents were very devoted to their sons, as they have proved during ten long years of harrowing affliction and endless visits to different prisons. Christopher is one of eight children; six of them have led very normal lives. There are nineteen grandchildren already. But two of them, Christopher and his elder brother Niven, have been involved in serious crimes.

It may help to remember that Lord Balfour, the Prime Minister, was also one of eight children. (For that matter, I have eight myself.) Five, including himself and two of the daughters, were exceptionally brilliant and successful. One of the daughters who kept house for him appears from his last biography to have been a strong but difficult character; two out of the eight died of drink.

I first met Niven Craig in Dartmoor. As I looked into his face I could see nothing vicious, and I am sure nothing irredeemable. Bad luck contributed to his going wrong—separation from his parents during the war. Later, just as he was doing well in the Army, his youth prevented his seeing active service, which disappointed and frustrated him much. Be that as it may, he became engaged in a kind of war against society, and Christopher hero-worshipped him. The day came when Niven was sentenced to twelve years' imprisonment for armed robbery. One remembers Churchill's account of Lenin's brother, and the effect of his sentence on Lenin. 'This dearly loved companion dabbled in assassination, and paid the penalty. Lenin was at the age to feel.' So it was with Christopher. From that moment he began to keep dangerous company.

On the fatal night he set out with a gun, obtained illegally, and though he had no deliberate intention of using it, it is hard not to suppose that he had by that time become too reckless to care much what he did. And there was the other curious factor, that although he was just on sixteen, and came of a white-collar bank family, he could neither read nor write.

He had learnt to do both by the time I saw him at Wakefield. It is a strange commentary on our society that a boy should have to shoot a policeman to become literate. One hardly needs to be told that though he was a good-looking, athletic boy, a deep-rooted inferiority must have helped him to glorify a brother who was also an outsider, to side with his brother against the society that condemned him, and most of all, to wage war against the police. All this he has confirmed to me in outline.

Craig's first five years were spent at Wakefield prison. It's a prison specially equipped and staffed to deal with young prisoners, the emphasis being on treating them in all possible ways that will lead to their reform. Craig didn't respond to this at all. His record at Wakefield was distinctly not good. When he came of age he was moved to Wormwood Scrubs.

His brother was also there. It seems that the presence of the elder brother in the prison gave him a peculiar sense of family and security which he hadn't had before. Soon after he arrived there his behaviour began to change. He became a model prisoner, and everybody—by that I mean the prison staff, and people who visited the prison, and people like myself—believes that he's going to make good. A major factor in this has been the influence of Niven, though he himself had been in prison for five years. I have a letter here from a prison commissioner insisting that whatever is said against him, nothing can take away the fact that he has been enormously good for young Christopher.

When Christopher was sentenced he showed no remorse. His heart was hard. After he left Wakefield and went to Wormwood Scrubs he said to his mother one day: 'Up there they said I never said I was sorry. But who was I to say sorry to?' That was the first sign that he was thinking about how to behave. He told his mother that back at the first prison he used to hear the warders saying to one another, 'Watch him, watch him.' He hadn't bothered to mention before that he had heard this. He only mentioned it later, at Wormwood Scrubs, when he was becoming conscious that they were trying to help him. The point of asking, 'Who was I to say sorry to?' was that he felt that everybody was against him—you don't say sorry to the enemy. And he said to his mother just after he'd got to Wormwood Scrubs, 'Do you know, Mother, somebody smiled at me here the other day.'

And of course the governor of Wormwood Scrubs was one of the best in the prison service—Gilbert Hair. He transmitted his influence right down through the prison staff. And this is worth emphasizing because if Wakefield is—on paper—a prison specially organized and equipped for dealing with young prisoners, you would have thought that if Craig did badly there he would have done even worse at Wormwood Scrubs. But you can never tell.

So there is Christopher Craig at sixteen, convicted of murder and stigmatized by the judge as one of the most dangerous young gunmen he had ever encountered. And now, ten years later, discharged with general goodwill and respect surrounding him. No one can foretell his or anyone's future, but his recent past is an inspiring tale. No general principle can be proved by a single story, or by many such stories, but those who still support capital punishment may be reminded that if he had been eighteen he would have been executed. Could they not agree that in this case at least that would have been a horrible error, if not a revolting crime? And why should we suppose that Christopher is altogether exceptional?

But does the story suggest that ten years in prison are positively good for a desperate young character, as Christopher was at sixteen? Hardly so. In this case special factors were at work. First, and strongest, a tirelessly loving mother and loyal father, as is not always so with the parents of prisoners. In the second place it had been a series of accidents which had helped to turn Christopher at sixteen into a young delinquent. In terms of character he might otherwise never have become one. Even at that age, therefore, he was a much better boy than his performance suggested.

It is also true that if he had served six years instead of ten the same reformation would probably have been affected. It seems to me to have been running a risk to leave him in prison so long. But when all is said, and not forgetting the lack of progress at Wakefield, here is a case when the prison service can fairly claim that they had a human character in their hands for ten years, and did much to bring about his redemption. To their credit they do not hesitate to pay tribute to the uncontrollable rebel, Niven, for playing his part.

Since writing the above I have twice had supper with Craig, once at London Airport and once in the King's Road, Chelsea. I will only add (in my own words) one thing. He told me that there comes a time when a prisoner, if he is at all sensible, begins to 'screw his loaf' (that is, screw his head on the right way). He realizes that it is madness to bang his head against the wall indefinitely. One begins to conform externally, to act as if one were conforming internally. Later comes the moment when one discovers that one is conforming internally as well, that one has become inwardly and outwardly a law-abiding person.

.   .   .   .

I could ramble on about individual prisoners. In a lightning review the names of the best-known are easiest for a reader to focus. George Blake is now serving forty-two years. His mother was a neighbour and great friend of Lady Pethick-Lawrence. Pethick, who had 'done time' himself as a champion of the suffragettes, was a regular supporter of the New Bridge, and would have taken Blake under his wing with his usual undramatic chivalry. But at the age of eighty-nine he told me, 'I may not be there by the time he comes out.' So I took a hand (aged fifty-five myself). His sentence shocks me.

My meeting with George Blake in the Scrubs told me at a glance that there was no meaning in saying this man was a traitor. I have seldom seen anyone less English-seeming in accent or style, or one less likely to be governed by automatic British loyalties. He had indeed spent no more than two out of his thirty-eight years in England, and though legally a British subject, he might fairly be described as half Dutch and half Egyptian. The great tragedy of this man of many talents and attractions was that he had missed a university education in youth, and that Marxism came to him in a prison camp in Korea as his first real adventure in ideas. For two years he read Marx, the only author available, to the British Minister, also a prisoner, who had broken his glasses. The effect on Blake was catastrophic. He became a committed Marxist.

When I met him he was buoyant, astonishingly so. He told me frankly that he realized that in Russia he would have been executed. His offence was something that no country in the world could fail to punish heavily. He told me just as frankly, without retracting or maintaining a doctrinal position, that he was indeed sorry that he had let down those who trusted him. I repeat that I cannot think of him as a traitor to his country because his life had up to that point denied him a country. I was able to introduce his wife to the *Sunday Telegraph*, which published three articles of hers, impressively candid. I trust that I may be of some slight service to George Blake himself later on.

Donal Murphy and John Doyle were serving sentences of life plus fourteen years for their share on the raid on the Arbor Field barracks. A party of I.R.A. youths seized a large number of rifles, without firing a shot, after binding the guards. They have both since been released; Murphy after seven years and Doyle after nearly eight.

I visited Murphy in Birmingham prison, and Doyle in Walton jail, Liverpool. 'Murphy,' one governor told me, 'is practically a saint.' 'He is out of this world,' said another one. As I looked at his prematurely grey hair and into his sunken eyes I felt that this was true, and that his great sufferings had brought some of the blessings of martyrdom. He had never been in England till the occasion of the raid. He was described by the judge as possessing a gun which he would not have hesitated to use. I discovered, usefully, that he had never had a gun 'because they were one short'. No one was in a position to tell the court this because of the unanimous refusal to plead.

Doyle, small and unobtrusive, was said to be a dangerous type. I could not see it. The moral problem for each, by the time I saw them, was to give the authorities an excuse for releasing them without repudiating their comrades or principles. Murphy, after prolonged study, political and spiritual, had concluded that the achievements of Ireland at the United Nations and the prospects of a common market opened up possibilities of Irish unification without bloodshed. For Doyle, more tenacious perhaps in his older loyalties, things were made easier when the military I.R.A. went into voluntary liquidation and he could reasonably regard his military oath as done with. In my talks with Murphy and Doyle I found my mind going back to Michael Davitt and Thom Clarke, and other Irish political prisoners of the past who languished for so many years in British prisons as forgotten men.

One name stands on its own in my prison memories and friendships, that of Michael Davies. He was convicted in 1953 of the so-called Clapham Common murder. About 9.45 one July evening an unhappy youth, John Beckley, was stabbed to death with nine knife wounds in his body. This followed a prolonged running affray between two groups of youths, one much larger than the other. The jury disagreed at the first trial, but at the second Michael Davies, by this time standing alone, was found guilty of murder and sentenced to death.

He spent three months in the condemned cell; he was finally reprieved by the Home Secretary, David Maxwell-Fyfe, Lord Kilmuir as he now is. He was sentenced to imprisonment for life, and released after seven years in October 1960 (by then aged twenty-seven). In the meanwhile his mother and sister had fought for him tirelessly. I, and a much more influential figure, Lord Monckton, had wrestled with the Home Secretary to secure an earlier release, and at one moment had seemed about to obtain one.

Elizabeth and I met Michael at the gate of Wormwood Scrubs, and were swept off to a secret breakfast at the Star and Garter, Richmond, with him and a decorative young lady. The master of the revels was Harry Ashbrook of the *Daily Mirror* Group, who with Tom Tullett, their chief crime reporter, and my vital friend Matt Oliver, a private detective, laboured strenuously to discover and publicize the truth. A short, able book by Rupert Furneaux has already been published about the case, but mainly from the legal standpoint. A much fuller treatment of everything connected with it, including the social background, is now being worked on. What I write here is only an introduction.

When I was interviewed on Davies's release, I announced: 'I have never stopped believing him to be innocent. I hope and believe that his name will finally be cleared.' I began to press, and shall never cease pressing, for a free pardon.

Since then a good deal of fresh evidence, or what most of us would call evidence, has come to light. But formidable difficulties remain in the path of *coercively* demonstrating the innocence of a convicted man when there is no great will to believe on the official side. For some years I have never met anybody in the Home Office who will argue seriously to my face that Davies 'did it'. It is clear beyond argument that if the evidence now available had been before the court at his trial the jury not only might have felt but must have felt reasonable doubt. (After all, a jury had disagreed once already.) In other words, they would certainly have acquitted him.

But the Home Office say, in effect, that once a man is convicted, the boot goes on to the other foot. Now it is not the prosecution who have to prove him guilty; it is his champions who have to prove him innocent. 'Maybe,' they say to me in effect, 'the fact that we have released him after seven years does indicate that we now agree that there is some doubt about his guilt. But that is a long way from admitting that you have proved beyond reasonable doubt his innocence. We mustn't conceal from you, my dear fellow,' they finish blandly, 'that unless you obtain a cast-iron confession you have a very difficult task ahead of you.'

There seems to me something very loose and imprecise in their doctrine, and the way they apply it. I can imagine Home Secretaries who would take a different view of the evidence already submitted. But I accept the fact that if we are to succeed, informed public opinion must be aroused in Parliament and elsewhere. If possible, still more evidence must be collected. For over a year now I have had down a House of Lords motion calling for Davies's pardon. But it seems best to hold it up till the forthcoming book is published and the public gets a chance to study the whole matter carefully and slowly.

Why have I been so certain for so long that Davies was totally innocent of murder? (He had always admitted to participating in the affray, though he never admitted to possessing a knife.) It began for me by accident. In the course of my Nuffield Enquiry I was lunching with Dr. Mathieson, about the most experienced doctor in the prison service. As a psychiatrist, he had examined the six youths arrested in connection with Beckley's murder. He told me that he had liked Davies best of the six (he was at this time under sentence of death). Dr. Mathieson felt sure that Davies was 'not guilty, or, if guilty, then not guilty alone'. Later on he made it plain to me that he did not in fact consider him guilty.

I discovered—I forget how—that Davies was a Catholic and instantly made contact with Cardinal Griffin. He interceded strenuously for a reprieve—maybe he was doing so in any case. I am sometimes said to have influenced the reprieve when it came. That I should think is very unlikely. It is surely inconceivable that Michael Davies would have been executed for an unpremeditated murder when the jury had disagreed the first time.

Be that as it may, his mother and his sister Joyce were very grateful to me. We saw much of one another. I stood godfather to his sister's baby Charon when she was christened in West-minster Cathedral. It transpired that Michael Davies had himself been baptized there.

And what of Michael himself? When I got to know him and came to visit him regularly for nearly seven years in prison he was not a usual boy. Certainly there was nothing remotely violent about him, as I confirmed in many ways, though he came from a broken home, had undergone wartime disturbance, and had been in minor trouble more than once. His record in the Merchant Navy was excellent. But he seemed a solitary type; somewhat absorbed by his family, though possibly wanting to break out for himself and muck in with the wild, uninhibited youths who formed the so-called 'gang'. He stuck to the same detailed story with me and with everyone, then and since. What has impressed me deeply has been his desire to be confronted with anyone who might corroborate or challenge his story. This includes emphatically the boy, now a man, who, as Davies and so many others are convinced, inflicted the mortal wounds.

I have interrogated several of his associates, some of them in prison. Ronald Coleman, the leader—if there was one—of the gang, and 'Splinter' Wood, who gave evidence damaging to Davies at the trial, have both assured me that they are certain Davies is innocent. I am told that anyone in that part of the world believes that Mr. X was responsible. But how to prove it? What does proof mean, unless Mr. X himself comes forward or some of the witnesses? Who will readily admit that their evidence was perjured or completely mistaken? I have obtained assurances from the Home Office which would rule out subsequent prosecutions. And so the battle for truth continues.

Michael Davies, with his candid, rather sorrowful, gaze, the shadow of his long ordeal still heavy on him, continues to plead for unremitting enquiries. The coming book should force the kind of people to listen who in Britain, thank heaven, are always anxious to rectify injustice. This time let the last word rest with Ronald Coleman: 'The case was planted on Davies. I myself am convinced that he is innocent.'

4

Quantity and Quality

THE only man I ever met who admitted to enjoying prison was one of six prisoners in Cork jail before it was closed down for want of custom. There were six prison officers, one per head of prisoner. The jail, though it must have lacked modern conveniences, had been built to hold 200 prisoners, so there was no danger of overcrowding. I mention this to illustrate the tiresome truth that in prison reform the quantitative and qualitative factors are inextricably confused.

None of my prisoner friends of long experience doubt that the approach to the prisoner on the spot is much more human than it was a few years ago—which is not to call it satisfactory as yet. I will draw on the experience of one prisoner who has testified to the great improvement in prison conditions. Now, this prisoner's wife had long since disappeared. His dreams centred on his son, who was in the care of an excellent children's officer, far from the prison where the father was serving his sentence. The last reports on his son had been favourable. Suddenly, without any warning, he was sent for by a high prison official. He was asked to sign a form which according to him would have certified his son as insane. The high official knew no more about it than he did. The form had been forwarded from some authority somewhere with the request that the father's signature be obtained. The father instead tore up the form, and wrote to me in a state of appalling indignation, bewilderment and grief.

I shall be told that certification has been abolished under the Mental Health Act 1959; that the step being taken, the transfer to a small institution for disturbed adolescents under the care (as I have since found out) of the kindest of psychiatrists, was entirely in the boy's interest. It may indeed be so; my point is that no one but a prisoner would have been treated with the callousness accorded that father. It just doesn't happen to ordinary citizens. And yet I know most of the characters in the story just related. None of them would be capable of an action deliberately cruel. Take the same man again, a little later. A man who has been ill-treated by fate from the beginning, and has many convictions on his sheet, but is now setting out, I verily believe, to lead a worthwhile life.

In February this year he was told that he would be placed on the hostel scheme. That is the enlightened arrangement, hitherto much too restricted in scope, under which some long-term prisoners in the last few months of their sentence are allowed to work outside the prison. They return in the evening to the prison hostel, are paid proper wages, and are able to save something, as no ordinary prisoner can, for their release. My friend David was overjoyed and truly grateful, but five months later in July he was writing almost in despair.

There was still no sign of his going to the hostel, because no work could be found for him there. (They only needed to find work for nine men altogether, in X-town, a busy city.) It had been suggested to him that he might know how to get a job there for himself. A man, after years of prison, finding a job right across England! For the first time, if I could judge from his letter, his resolution to go straight was being strained. So this was the result of all those years of effort to be a model prisoner! Well, then . . .

I intervened on the highest level, chucking my weight about as I seldom venture to, or feel inclined to. Hey presto! (nothing to do with me, of course) a job was found for him in X-town! Once again I don't blame anyone in particular; his own authorities were just as annoyed as he was at the delay, and it may be, just as pleased at my intervention. But again no one but a prisoner would be treated in that way by those who were, as in this case, making some efforts to help him.

I can think of so much kindness, often far beyond the line of duty, and also of so much silly stuffiness in the attitude towards prisoners. On one of my Nuffield tours I found myself cross-examining in Holloway a dark, intense young woman. It emerged that she was to be received into the Catholic Church the following week. I offered to be present, and found myself enrolled as godfather. Later she had one or two adventures, including a period as a cook in a convent. The holy sisters adored her—and her cakes too, for that matter, as I found at tea there! But she led them quite a dance. Now all seems to be well. While writing this, I received a charming letter from 'your godchild Pauline' (and photographs of her lovely children). The governor, Charity Taylor, and her staff made a happy occasion of her reception into the Catholic Church. As we all took tea after the ceremony, I felt like a proud parent visiting a fashionable boarding school, on which my daughter had brought fresh honour.

Yet almost at the same time another young female ex-prisoner I was trying to help was not being allowed to write to her fiancé in prison because an ex-prisoner must not write to a prisoner. 'Besides,' added the male governor sourly in reply to my protest, 'I don't see how she could have got engaged to him here. Men and women are not allowed to make contact. They must have relied on ocular demonstrations in chapel, which is quite contrary to the rules.'

Brutalities still occur in prison 'on both sides' from time to time. A Dartmoor friend, already mentioned, then a prisoner, wrote to me after the last big fracas in that prison. 'I never thought,' he said, 'to feel any sympathy for the prison staff. But when I saw a string of them brought in to the prison hospital where I work, with dreadful injuries, I realized for the first time that they were human beings like I am.' He told me afterwards that comrades of the injured prison officers were far from squeamish when one of the escaping prisoners fell into their hands. Even under extreme provocation nothing less than perfection must be aimed at. High standards of restraint are laid down, and are better observed today than ever previously.

The real threat to the reform of the prison population lies elsewhere. What is much more degrading for the vast mass of the inmates are the small symptoms of inhumanity, of treating prisoners as second-class human beings which still vitiate, not through deliberate choice but persistently, so much of the purposes of reform. And so much of this is a function of archaic buildings, overworked staffs, and long hours without occupation.

Which brings us back to the quantitative factor, though this is no book to deal with it in detail. Ever since 1955, in our debate in the House of Lords, we 'Penal Reformers' have laid chief stress on what I have called 'the three evil ones'—overcrowding, understaffing, and shortage of work. In the summer of 1956 Stormont Mancroft, Under-Secretary at the Home Office, best known till lately as a scintillating after-dinner speaker and master of wisecracks, but thoroughly serious on prisons, admitted that much was wrong.

The Times, in a strong and stern leading article, described the prison service among the social services as 'last in the queue'. I always think of that as a turning point in the public attitude.

Mr. Butler became Home Secretary soon afterwards. He proclaimed a new era of penal reform. In particular he announced a new outlook on research which has been sustained, though the help received in that direction from the Wolfson Trust has made the State contribution look rather petty. He singled out our own three evil ones—overcrowding, understaffing, and shortage of work—as his three special targets to be attacked at all costs. He specifically took the number sleeping three in a cell as an acid test of overcrowding. Fairly soon he had secured—and perhaps no other Conservative could have done this—an increase in the building programme estimates from £1,100,000 to £4,400,000. The biggest building programme for a century was launched. Not saying much, perhaps, for only one new prison had previously been built in this century, but all praise to Mr. Butler, none the less. Little did the poor man know that just about the time he was becoming Home Secretary the crime figures, and with them the prison population, which had been tending to fall, began to rise rapidly. Crime has continued rising ever since. Curiously, the number of children born in Britain, after falling from 1947 to 1955, also quite unexpectedly turned upwards in 1956, and has also continued rising. Possibly a sheer coincidence; possibly in each case there has been at work a deeper cause not yet understood.

And so, through no sin of commission by Mr. Butler or the Government, the number sleeping three in a cell, rather more than 2,000 when he became Home Secretary, was between 7,000 and 8,400 when he left (now under 7,000). The supply of prison officers is still short, though recruiting has lately been better. The work position was described in a splendidly frank White Paper of 1959 as 'bad, and deteriorating'. It is little, if any, better now. Two or three hours a day are all that is worked in the larger local prisons. Sisyphus has pushed quite hard, but again and again the stone of reform has come rolling back down the hill.

A political opponent and disgruntled penal reformer is not the fairest judge of Mr. Butler's record as Home Secretary. He started like a great Home Secretary, and finished like a merely good one. It was obvious long before the end that he did not regard it as a full-time job. There was room for new responsibilities in Central Africa, and much else besides. If he had been entirely engrossed in penal work he would hardly have acquiesced so tamely in the frustrating of his high and genuine ambitions. He would have tackled the staff situation, and the work situation in detail, and called the attention of the nation to both. He would never have failed to mention the staff altogether in his comprehensive speech on his responsibilities to the Conservative Conference in 1961. He would have faced up to the need for a total transformation in the system of prison work and prison payments, instead of leaving such topics to an advisory committee with a very limited mandate. Indeed, he carried to extreme lengths the delegation to advisory committees or councils, as those who have waited so long for a complete revolution in after-care know only too well. Such methods make sure of a wide measure of agreement; they make equally sure of an intolerable measure of delay.

But when all is said he will go down to history as the Home

Secretary who took more palpable interest in penal reform than any predecessor since Winston Churchill fifty years earlier. He risked, and maybe permanently impaired, his whole political reputation to defeat the flogging elements in his party; the majority supposedly female. He imposed from high an atmosphere favourable to reform which is never likely now to be dissipated.

Lloyd George was once asked by Lord Riddell what he regarded as the finest opening of a speech. He mentioned one of Bryant's: 'Some may say that I have run my course. Some may say that I have not fought the fight. But no one can say that I have not kept the faith.' That can fairly, and I hope not ungenerously, be said of R. A. Butler.

Meanwhile enlightened experiments have been pushed forward, if too slowly and timidly for some of us. The Norwich experiment, with prison officers responsible for the welfare of their section. Group counselling and group therapy, with utterly frank discussion, in the one case under the auspices of prison officers; in the other, of a psychiatrist. Let me take Grendon, the psychiatric prison, the latest exhibition piece, opened more than twenty years after it was recommended, but none the less a place of inspiration. Here I am in danger of premature enthusiasm. In a remarkable report on it by an inmate (prisoner) I read that the prisoners come 'Hoping for help'. In few cases are they disappointed.

There are things I myself didn't like the look of; locked gates between the various parts of the prison are unpleasantly in evidence. But the approach and demeanour of the higher staff, including the senior uniformed staff, was splendid. They were mostly, though not entirely, 'medical'. Either they were doctors, or they came from the hospital side of the prison service, which rightly or wrongly is more curtained off from the rest of the service than is usually realized. The gentleman in charge, who would elsewhere be the governor, is a medical superintendent. The one in office served under the great John Vidler of Maidstone. He told me that he was trying to follow the same philosophy at Grendon as that with which Vidler—a layman, of course—had accomplished so much at Maidstone.

This raises a vital point. How far is the medical ethos of Grendon essential to its success? The prisoner reporting said that the inmates come 'hoping for help', and for help from those who were medically qualified to give it. Part of the course was individual psychiatric treatment, and another part—in his eyes much more valuable—was the group therapy under a psychiatrist's guidance. It was through the group pre-eminently, in his view, that the inmate broke out of his personal isolation and became a normal member of society. Everything depended on absolute frankness between members of the group, and absolute confidence that nothing said there would be repeated outside.

It may well be that these particular prisoners, who after all volunteered for Grendon knowing roughly what was involved, require medical, i.e. psychiatric help. I leave aside the unanswerable question, all too familiar to me since my Nuffield days, When is crime 'medical', and whom can psychiatry benefit? I raise another wide issue instead: Does Grendon provide a clue to the whole future of prison treatment? Could all, or at any rate most prisoners, reasonably 'hope for help' when they come to prison?

At present, of course, that hope would be an illusion. One can only hope that prison does not do most of them harm. And here one is back once more at that old quantitative factor. Grendon, when I visited it, had a ratio of one officer to two inmates, or one officer to every one prisoner receiving treatment. (Half of the inmates were a working party.) It was the best staff-prisoner ratio I have heard of since the jail at Cork was closed down, and the prison buildings were thoroughly up to date, though not necessarily to everyone's taste. At any rate, one reporting prisoner considered that the cells were 'like rooms'.

On the other hand, the prisoners, while enlightened enough to seek help, must be supposed to have more than their share of psychological problems. The working party prisoners were too apt to refer to the other inmates, i.e. the patients, as 'nut-cases'. One ribald commentator used the word 'nutters' once too often. He suffered a heavy fall down a flight of stairs in suspicious circumstances. In contrast, a gang of mail-bag robbers on first reaching prison might appear to present fewer mental problems but would be far less likely to suppose themselves in need of help. So analogies and inductions from Grendon must be made with caution.

Nevertheless a moral is plain. If you wish to reform prisoners the will to reform must exist on both sides, and it will be exhibited on neither side, neither among the staff nor among the prisoners, until the material conditions, including the supply of staff, make it credible. Otherwise it will be as difficult to persuade oneself, or persuade prisoners, that 'you come here for your own good' as it was to persuade most of the Germans when I was their Minister that we were genuinely seeking to re-educate them. At that time we were proposing to dismantle their factories in conditions of near-starvation. In each case the spiritual effort and response will not be altogether absent, but it will require exceptional virtue or wisdom to make them flourish.

5

The Sinner and the Sin

NOTHING but autobiography and the professional egotism implied in that undertaking could justify the full
quotation that follows from a letter received last August. It
came from a lady of high repute in the Society of Friends and
the world of education. I did not know her at all well, though
we had worked on an international committee together. It
came completely from the blue:

'Quite by chance', she wrote, 'I heard you give that little
requiem on Dr. Stephen Ward, and as I find myself still
thinking about it a week later, I feel I must write and say just
how important it seemed to me that it should have been done,
and done so beautifully . . . here was the essential and eternal
Gospel. Facts weren't shirked, but the air was cleared by
humane understanding and the refusal to judge . . . the
necessity of forgiving unto seventy times seven was implied, and
the healing Christian power of generosity was testified to—it
was all there in a very few words. . . .'

I received other welcome messages of praise or thanks (the
critics left me alone). None was more valued than that from Pat
and Richard Llewellyn Davies, who disguise, unsuccessfully, the
warmest of hearts under the strictest of Cambridge cultures.

What gave me special pleasure, what I had not deliberately
worked for, were several references to my remarks as notably
Christian.

'How splendid of Frank', wrote Dorothy Woodman, Kingsley Martin I hope and believe concurring, 'to speak like a rational human being and a Christian.' Coming from one of Christian upbringing, but illustrious humanist associations for many years, this made me ponder long and gratefully. For years now I had been intermittently obsessed by the problem of the sin and the sinner in all its aspects. It runs like a thread through so many of the other everlasting puzzles, the place of retribution in punishment; the meaning of forgiveness by society; justice and mercy; the proper distinction between crime and sickness, and between crime and sin.

I had begun to scratch at it in the last chapter of my *Causes of Crime*, published 1958, but mostly written earlier. I had made other shots in various addresses, such as one on forgiveness to a regional conference of probation officers. I had dwelt on it at length in my *Idea of Punishment* (1961), but I had never quite found the words I wanted, or fully clarified the thought. It was gratifying, and much more than that it might point the way forward to better thought, if in this tragic personal case I had said something specifically Christian. Something recognizably such; and something which non-Christians of talent and earnestness were disposed to accept.

Before turning back to trace my own connection with the problem, I cannot refrain from quoting a passage from Blake which comes into Victor Gollancz's heart-piercing pamphlet on Eichmann. I do so to provoke thought on the matter I am trying to discuss, rather than because I agree altogether with either Blake or Victor. 'There is not one moral virtue', wrote Blake, 'that Jesus inculcated, but Plato and Cicero did inculcate before him: what then did Christ inculcate? Forgiveness of sins. This alone is the Gospel, and this is the life and immortality brought to life by Jesus.'

In my 1958 book I had shown much scepticism about our alleged advance in knowledge of the causes of crime. But I claimed that we *had* advanced substantially in our attitude to the delinquent, were beginning indeed to show a new approach altogether. What did this amount to in practice? It arose from a new or much clearer recognition, assisted by the psychiatrists, that we were almost certain to be wrong in assessing or imputing degrees of moral guilt. We were, or ought to be, much more aware than before (though the truth itself was as old as the ages) that human justice would seldom if ever approximate to the Divine.

While making every allowance for the mental factor, I rejected totally the idea that all crime, or that crime as a whole, was disease. I repudiated along with it any other doctrine that threatened the freedom of the will. I assumed that the vast majority of criminals were morally blameworthy. But the *degree* of their guilt—that, I insisted, we could never begin to measure.

I quoted with gusto the Sermon on the Mount: 'Judge not, that ye be not judged.' If I had studied by then the *Devout Life of St. Francis de Sales*, I should have found fresh grist to my mill. 'The judgements of men', he wrote, 'are rash because the malice of sin depends primarily on the intention, which is kept secret in men's hearts, and as far as we are concerned, is hidden in darkness. They are rash because we have enough to do to judge ourselves without trying to judge others.' It is true that St. Francis accepts the necessity of courts of justice; there it is God who is the Judge; the magistrates must pronounce only their judgement; they have learnt from Him. He leaves us without much confidence that magistrates are likely to have access to the divine wisdom required.

It was this side of my argument that drew a friendly reference from Baroness Wootton in her mighty classic *Social Science and Social Pathology* (1959). 'Lord Pakenham,' she said, 'writing as a devout Catholic, has found it necessary in the same context to wrestle with the same problems, and has apparently reached much the same conclusions as so thoroughgoing an agnostic as myself.' I resisted this generous assimilation a shade gratuitously when I reviewed her book in the *Observer*. A poor return for the warm welcome she had given to my own small book a year earlier in the same paper. Indeed her article at that time gave it an indispensable professional launching. By the time my *Idea of Punishment* appeared (1961) I understood her meaning better and drew somewhat closer accordingly.

I must shorten our argument now. The difference in practice can perhaps be narrowed down to this: as I see it, we can never be sure that someone who commits a wicked crime is in the sight of God any more wicked than we are. But we shall provide a better justice, and certainly a more widely respected justice, if we make some allowance in our sentencing policy for the degree of guilt or redeeming merit which we must suppose to have operated. It will be rough justice, imperfect justice, a long way from the Divine Justice, but nearer to it than if we made no such effort. Barbara Wootton, I take it, will agree with the first or negative proposition about our ignorance, but she would reject the second in any ideal sentencing system. This should concentrate solely on the future (deterrence and more particularly, reform) of the delinquent, and ignore the past, including the guilt, real or imaginary. She might, however, admit that at present some allowance for supposed degrees of guilt is unavoidable.

Penal reformers and those who work among prisoners (distinct, if overlapping, categories) are of all sorts and sizes. But the finest spirits, and indeed the general run, are governed pre-eminently by concern for the criminal, in which compassion figures largely. The source may be Christian, or strictly secular, or something between the two, but its genuineness, wherever it springs from, is the one guarantee that human good will follow. There is also the scientific or criminological interest; its benefits I am far from disparaging. It has been grossly starved of the necessary finance in England, as in most other countries, though the Wolfson Trust has set a splendid example, and I have much reason for gratitude to the Nuffield and other foundations. But where the criminologists have been of the truest service their compassion has been as strong as their scientific curiosity. I need only instance my own advisers at the time of the Nuffield Enquiry, Dr. Grunhut, for example; Mr. Frank Milton; Dr. Stafford Clark, and Dr. Gibbens.

Barbara Wootton and I have disagreed on many points of theory, as a humanist and a Catholic must. But very seldom in practice in anything which concerned the treatment of the convicted, or for that matter of other unfortunates and deviants.

I have sat in her court and admired not only her endless patience and kindness but her clear enunciation of what I will call impeccable Christian morality.

Christian compassion towards convicted criminals has taken various forms in history. For sixty years from the very beginning of his journal John Wesley's interest in prisoners, especially condemned felons, was unremitting. But what concerned him was their future in the next world. On December 26th, 1789, we find him preaching the condemned criminals' sermon at Newgate. A few days later he reports: 'Twenty died at once, five of whom died in peace.' That appears to have been his overwhelming, indeed his sole concern. A little later he is reading the life of the famous Mr. George F——. 'I never heard before of so cool, deliberate, relentless a murderer! And yet from the breaking of the rope at his execution, which gave him two hours of vehement prayer, there is room to hope he found mercy at last.' That again seems what mattered to Wesley. It would be wrong to blame the Christian Churches directly for the execution of small children as late as the early years of the nineteenth century in this country. But one must admit they have taken a long time to reach their present enlightenment.

As late as 1930 all the bishops in the House of Lords were, with the exception of William Temple, in favour of capital punishment. Archbishop Temple's 'Ethics of Penal Action' is still the best single lecture ever given on penal philosophy, and no one has done more for prisoners and ex-prisoners than Mrs. Temple. Today the position is completely reversed among Christian leaders in the House of Lords and elsewhere. The sympathy for the delinquent is unequivocal. But the cause makes slow progress in the nation. There are still opposed to it the older forms of collective vengeance and selfishness, and more respectably, if just as regrettably, the old-fashioned, unthinking, ordinary decent men and women who still find it a great deal easier to hate the sin than to love the sinner. We have had many debates on penal questions in the House of Lords. Everyone who speaks is a reformer. The Minister exhibits profound sympathy. But our success has been limited and when the abolition of capital punishment became a live issue the House was flooded with excellent fellows who trampled us underfoot.

If the above creates an impression of intellectual or moral smugness let me hasten to dispel it. If one had any doubts about the existence of a moral dilemma in the whole idea of social condemnation, the summer months of 1963 surely forced one to admit that such a dilemma exists. As long as one is concerned with prisoners already convicted, the issue is straightforward. They have been and are being punished and made to suffer, rightly we can assume. Pity and help are their bounden due. What was there in him, cried Leopold, the American author of *Life plus 99 years*, who served thirty-four years in prison for murder, what was there in him which led so many to make such tremendous efforts to help him and rescue him? 'Only,' he concludes 'my great need; that is apparently enough for real champions.'

But when and where should the condemnation begin and end? How far is it the business of the criminal law to impose morality, or defeat immorality? And, short of criminal prosecution, when and how should public opinion impose its no less formidable sanctions?

Now few of us in politics, if we tell the truth, can claim to have altogether divorced our feelings from the party situation during the early stages of the prolonged affair that culminated in the Denning Report. The Labour Party's line of conduct was made a little easier by the existence of a Security element, albeit a minor one. They were entitled to use Security as a platform from which the whole issue could be fought. In their place the Conservatives would no doubt have done the same. But leaving out the Party interest, the Security element, and the unhappy lie in the House of Commons, how far can we go with *The Times* in describing the whole affair as a moral issue? There is certainly a moral question: whether a Prime Minister should retain in his Government a Minister whom he supposes to be guilty of private impropriety in the present or recent past. If the answer to that is yes (i.e. he can retain him), while the matter remains hidden, does it become no (i.e. he must get rid of him) when the public get a shrewd idea of what is afoot? Is there one rule of public morality and another of private morality? And does private morality become public morality when it becomes public knowledge?

In all these arguments I am on the puritanical side, but what I am concerned with here, what has come much more home to me as an individual, is this: when a Minister is condemned by public opinion to the point of forced resignation should one join in proscribing the unfortunate man, or should one try to befriend him? In this case I could have few doubts. Many much esteemed persons, though not, to be fair, the leaders of the Labour Party—were for a time full of savage condemnation, though the pendulum has now swung back. I listened to Quintin Hailsham denouncing the Minister with passionate vehemence. Quintin's Christianity is to me not only strong, but strengthening; yet at one point we diverge, and this was the point, beyond question. When I read Harold Balfour's brave and telling letter in *The Times* about the Minister's good qualities and shattered career, I knew that I must be with those who wished to help him out, rather than those who wished to shove him down still further.

The ghoulish interest shifted. For weeks the nation lived with the Ward case. And in the end poor Stephen Ward was broken and slaughtered, though not one human being, I am sure, either intended or foresaw the final outcome. No one can seriously deny that many of his activities had been violently anti-social. But it will be long argued whether he was rightly convicted, whether the jury reached the right decision, whether the crucial evidence was rightly obtained. Again it will be disputed whether the law ought to be altered to make what he did more clearly legal or illegal. Once again I side with the puritans at every point. It is true that I moved the adoption of the Wolfenden Report in the House of Lords in 1957, a year before the House of Commons would touch it. And that would have liberalized the law and removed the criminal ban from consenting homosexual adults. But that was an attempt to remove the special discrimination against homosexual sinners as compared with heterosexual sinners.

Be all that as it may, as the various court hearings in the Ward case were reported and became for many of us obsessional reading, one became more and more conscious that here was a man whose particular challenge to society had booked him for a prolonged torture. One had to sort out one's emotions and formulate one's attitude towards him.

I met Stephen Ward three times: each time staying at Cliveden with Bill Astor, a very old friend from New College onwards, and with Bron, a delightful host. I was asked, when I spoke about him on television after his death, what sort of man was Stephen Ward, and I replied, 'A friendly man, an obliging man, a man anxious—perhaps over-anxious—to please and impress.' I said that he wanted to get a lot out of life, and in the end got too much, but he was a giver as well as a getter. I was aware, I said, of many kindnesses he had performed, and I mentioned one in particular. The Mother Superior of a convent suffered from bad arthritis, and Stephen had treated her for a year without fee. His brother tells me that while he lay dying, and after his death, the family received many messages from women, now respectably married, who were grateful to him for the services that he had rendered, though these must often have taken, one supposes, an irregular form.

The first time I met him he was holding forth about the kind of people who suffered from fibrositis.

'You look,' he said to me, 'like one of them.'

I was foolishly rather irritated by this sudden diagnosis, all the more because it happened to be correct. I have no doubt that if I had agreed with him he would have given me treatment gratis. And certainly not for snobbish reasons. I accept the word of those who knew him best that the charge of 'snob' was very unfairly levelled at him. He undoubtedly revelled in glamour, but no snob could possibly have led the life he did, or kept the kind of company with whom he spent so much of his time. Even his accusers seemed to realize before the end that he was totally uninterested in money, which makes the charges all the more ironic on which he was—rightly or wrongly—convicted.

On subsequent occasions we got on well, though amidst a good deal of coming and going there was no approach to intimacy. The third time he brought up Ivanov to the house, somewhere after six o'clock, on Cuba Sunday. I can place the time approximately because the rest of the house party had just heard on the news that Khrushchev had climbed down, and Ivanov was unaware of this on arrival. We had the unusual advantage over a Russian diplomat there, but, as Boofy Arran wrote afterwards to the Foreign Secretary, we felt quite sorry for the poor fellow, who was obviously much disconcerted. He kept saying that he couldn't understand why Khrushchev had given way without any corresponding concession, over Berlin for instance. It simply never crossed my mind, in that most respectable company, full of Eton masters, ambassadors, and friends in some slight need of help, that Stephen Ward suffered from the obsessions which ultimately wrecked his life. I gather that that kind of thing began for him in Hamburg, where he went as a youth on leaving school in the thirties, and acquired strange ideas from the Germany of the period.

When the storm broke, or, at least, when rumours of the coming storm reached me, I was completely taken aback. For a time I confess to a half-conscious hope that he would be convicted. He seemed to me, even in this extremity, to be challenging and defying the conventional morals of society, which in my eyes are fundamental to Christian conduct. But as his ghastly ordeal proceeded my emotional attitude to it changed. It was not just a feeling of compassion, though who with any heart could withhold that from a man with society's hand on his throat in the glare of world publicity? I also seemed to sense something rather noble and all the more dignified, because unexpressed, in his refusal to drag in anybody more than strictly necessary; or to exploit his influential connections. He was determined to take his punishment alone.

When he was found guilty, and was lying unconscious—but I assumed that he would soon recover—I telephoned his barrister's clerk to let him know that I would be happy to visit him in prison if he wished to see me. *Dis aliter visum;* all that week I was haunted by the newspaper picture of him being carried into the hospital unconscious. So young-looking, innocent, and, indeed, beautiful. Somehow I felt, and I have since discovered that this feeling was widely shared in the community, we had brought him to this by dissociating ourselves from him. At the end of my *Idea of Punishment* I preached so high a doctrine. The one solution to the problem of the sinner and the sin was to identify ourselves with the prisoner. We must, 'like Father Damien—fall down beside him and wash his feet, as those of the disciples were once washed by the hands of the Master'.

I asked the Independent Television News if I could say a few words in the event of his death. Some of his activities, I concluded, could not be tolerated in the interests of the community and particularly of our children. 'But with him lying dead at our feet how can one fail to ask, "Which of us is qualified to cast the first stone?" Surely we can all join in prayer that his gifted and tormented spirit may rest in peace.' But words, however deeply felt, signify less than deeds. His brother, who sat beside him for three days, has told me of his inexpressible gratitude to the hospital authorities for their super-human efforts, and, above all, to the governor of Brixton prison, who telephoned continuously with tender enquiries; and the prison officers who kept their appointed vigil in his room with infinite delicacy and kindness.

Interlude

A Truer Talent

A Truer Talent

THE last twelve years have seen a striking expansion of Elizabeth's repute as a writer. She has always had since I have known her, three priceless literary assets, all three denied to me. She has been steeped in good literature, particularly the English poets, since she was a girl. She has a natural gift of observing everything, people, houses, furniture, and perhaps most keenly, nature. And she has a firm, beautiful, utterly legible handwriting, a pleasure to read as it is to her to make use of. There is nothing she looks forward to more, which calms her so sweetly, as a long undistracted 'write', if and when she can get it.

Whereas I had read comparatively few first-class works of English literature before I had left Eton. Intelligent company at home, Uncle Eddy Dunsany, and C. A. Alington at Eton had sown a seed which was to flourish later. Philosophy, politics, and economics (including recent history) gave me a strong start. There was to be plenty of theology, psychology, and sociology. I am a faint but pursuing student of literature. Yet it is the early reading, as Elizabeth has shown me, which supplies so much imagery and helps so much with style. Again I am extremely unobservant, except of people. There what *The Times* so kindly called my acute ear comes in to help the eye. To be fair to myself, I take much more interest in women's looks, clothes, and general style than appears to be expected of me. I am more likely than the average politician to notice if a woman has come straight from the hairdresser's. I have often chosen and bought a dress for Elizabeth on my own with popular results, and I am, in an untutored way, alive to beauty in nature. Otherwise an inattention of the eyes, developed through a reluctance to wear glasses as a boy, has sadly persisted, except for my following ball games with unremitting zeal. And my handwriting is the worst of anyone known to me, except that of an old friend, now in a mental home. (There is nothing wrong with the formation of *his* letters. They just happen to be much too small to be read.)

Elizabeth was as literary as anyone could be at school, though at the same time captain of netball—a tribute she insists to her character rather than her athleticism. At home her brothers John and Michael and her sister Kitty provided stimulus in plenty. She won a national poetry prize presented by John Masefield. She won an open scholarship in English literature to Lady Margaret Hall, preferring that to a career at the Slade. (An additional qualification, this last talent, for a writer, if Evelyn Waugh is correct and if no one with a painter's eye writes badly.)

At Oxford she turned to Greats, learning Greek for the purpose. She concentrated on ancient history and classical inscriptions in particular, to which for a moment (mercifully brief) she thought of dedicating her life. Her reputation was so widespread and so extraordinary that *Isis* made her their chosen 'Idol' for the week. She was almost the first woman to be so honoured. *Isis* reported on Elizabeth Harman as follows: 'Artistic, beautiful, cultured, decorative, enigmatic, fashionable, even headstrong. If in full womanhood she fulfills the wide promise of her brilliant maidenhood then she will take her place in the honoured band of female worthies.' The last phrase finds a curious unintentional echo in Sir Winston Churchill's obituary tribute to Neville Chamberlain, Elizabeth's first cousin once removed. 'We salute the memory of one whom Disraeli would have called an English worthy.'

There were friends already deep in politics, for instance Quintin Hogg and Randolph Churchill, though it was to me that the latter, always a warm and delightful friend, made the most memorable of all his youthful pronouncements. 'I may not,' he said, 'at this stage of my career [he was paying super-tax before he was twenty-one] be armed at every point with the equipment of my best contemporaries, but I possess to an extent that none of them can begin to equal this overwhelming desire to express myself. And the tragedy of it all is that I have nothing in the whole wide world to express. I am like an explosion that goes off and leaves the house still standing.' Since then he has retained and developed the urge for, and the gift of, expression. His biography of his father offers him at last a supreme opportunity and an adequate theme. A still more intimate friend, not yet a politician though a Socialist before he left Oxford, was Hugh Gaitskell, whom she used to visit in the rooms of 2 Isis Street which he shared with me and Roger Nickalls. He introduced me to her as told in my last book.

They shared many gay experiences at Oxford, but within a year of leaving he was writing to her from Nottingham, where he was working for the W.E.A., that she was quite right in some ways in thinking he was becoming more serious. He had just paid a flying visit to Oxford.

'After seeing you', he wrote, 'the thing I enjoyed most was talking to Cole about adult education and economics. Oxford seemed just the same and yet this time I felt just faintly bored.' For the moment the old parties and the old conversation had lost their charm. It was not till long afterwards that Oxford recovered his full devotion.

In the same letter he added this about his 'taste'. 'Perhaps it is just a mixture of high-browness and objection to your spending your time with hearties—you see they do have a deteriorating effect on you.'

A stronger cultural influence was Maurice Bowra, since then warden of Wadham. Maurice was, and is, the prophet of the art of learning, justifying and exemplifying it in epigrams and a tone of voice which everyone has copied and no one quite lived up to. John Betjeman, Osbert Lancaster, Stephen Spender, Tom Driberg were sympathetic literary figures. Rosalie Mander, John Sparrow, Christine and Michael Hope and Harry d'Avigdor-Goldsmid were specially close. A little later were to come great friendships with David Cecil and Isaiah

Berlin. David, the most unselfish and creative of conversation-
alists, endlessly kind in later years, like Agnes Headlam-Morley
and Arthur Goodhart, to waves of my children as they poured
through Oxford. Isaiah soon to divide the great thinkers into
foxes and hedgehogs while retaining their composite virtues.
Roy and Billa Harrod came to mean much.

Then, as told elsewhere, came Stoke-on-Trent, the W.E.A.,
her Socialist life story, and then her marriage and her eight
children. It was not until somewhere around 1952, with Kevin
our youngest child by then five years old, that her creative
urge began to turn back to earlier loves. She has indeed written
much since that time.

There have been countless articles, many of them collected
in a book (*Points for Parents*); a party book for children with
contributions from Antonia, Judith, and Rachel, whimsically
described by Bernard Levin as a 'remarkable, helpful, serious,
and *worthy contribution to labour* problems' (my italics). She
edited a substantial book of essays, *Catholic Approaches*,
which somehow failed to arouse attention but which remains a
classical illustration of Catholic subtleties. She has published
a detailed study of the Jameson Raid, reviewed in glowing
terms by almost everyone, including Robert Blake and Alan
Taylor in the *Sunday Times* and the *Observer* respectively.
For the last four years she has been working on a single-volume
life of Queen Victoria based on long independent researches
at Windsor Castle and elsewhere.

I can't suppose that so God-given a talent as hers could ever
have been smothered finally and hopelessly, but in fact the
start of the great outpouring was quite accidental.

Christina Foyle was helping to provide me with some lectures and happened to ask me whether my wife had ever
thought of doing a column. I said, 'No, but now you mention
it, why on earth not?' Christina has friends all over journalism
and before much time had passed Elizabeth was doing three
trial articles on the upbringing of children for Tony Hern,
then features editor of the *Daily Express*. To be candid, I
thought it was about time that Elizabeth began to be paid for
her output of wisdom. As a mother of eight she had long been
a target for newspapers anxious to obtain views on every

conceivable problem of the family. She was endlessly pursued by newspapers high and low to the benefit of them and their readers but without profit to herself. The hour seemed to have come when the labourer should have treatment worthy of her hire.

Just about then we were summoned (on approval perhaps) to spend a night with Lord Beaverbrook at Cherkley. I had never stayed there before, although I had been entertained by him at Cherkley and at Stornaway House a quarter of a century earlier when writing my *Peace by Ordeal*. The place seemed full of historical ghosts. I almost expected Lloyd George, Bonar Law, and Birkenhead to join us in the conversation, though they would hardly have put our host in the shade. Lord Beaverbrook asked about my forthcoming autobiography. In the event it received a grand review in the *Daily Express* and a less encouraging mention in the *Evening Standard*. By and large I have much for which to be grateful for in my treatment by his newspapers. Since then at a grievous moment he showed deep sympathy and understanding. But he was really interested in Elizabeth—his new contributor. As he saw us off on Monday morning he asked who was driving the car. I told him Elizabeth. 'I thought so,' he replied with evident satisfaction.

Incidentally, I obtained an international driver's certificate years ago in order to act as Roger Chetwode's assistant chauffeur on the drive from Le Havre to Florence, taking the Alps in our stride. But it is many years since I have had a driving licence at all and have belonged therefore to a non-driving fraternity which I believe includes Lord Attlee, Victor Gollancz, Dick Crossman, and our friend and neighbour Wolf Mankowitz. When I left the National Bank in February 1963 the staff in England and Ireland with prodigal goodness gave me a Mini car on the understanding that I would learn to drive it. Lessons have been paid for and begun but suspended; the distraction of writing this book was too great. They will now be resumed.

To return to Elizabeth. For two years she wrote a weekly article on children for the *Daily Express*. She became deeply versed in what Lord Beaverbrook called 'the black art'. When that came to an end she led a less exacting life with the *News of the World.* By a curious Freudianism she used always to refer to it as the *Observer*. 'I must do my *Observer* article,' she used to say and I learnt in time that it was best not to make a correction. Then came two years on the *Sunday Times* under the personal tuition of Harry Hodson, the editor. Roy Thomson, when he acquired the paper, showed a benevolent interest. It is expected that she will write for the *Observer* when her life of Queen Victoria is finished. All of these articles and many of the others in various magazines deal with family questions, but as the children grew older Elizabeth's main interest seemed to move from tiny tots to teenagers and more recently to involve her in nineteenth-century political history.

What must seem peculiar at first is the combination of mass-circulation writing for parents with heavy scholarship and research into Jameson, Queen Victoria, and other related topics. It is rare, perhaps, but hardly unique. Cecil Woodham-Smith, a writer Elizabeth much admires and is happy to learn from, told me that she first took a classics degree at Oxford, then went into advertising, and then wrote popular best-sellers under a *nom de plume*. Only then came the famous books of her maturity, *Florence Nightingale*, *The Reason Why*, and *The Great Hunger* (called in America *Ireland's Hunger, England's Fault*). Many have rightly praised her narrative style. This she attributes to the earlier disciplines, cultured and crude. The same may fairly be said of Elizabeth. She has only one fault as an author, a persistent hankering after the discovery and the statement of the full truth. This means in practice that she writes many more words than she wishes to publish. As she is the least verbose of writers and there is no padding likely to be removed, there is much pain and toil in the cutting.

The origin of her book on the Jameson Raid was curious. Joseph Chamberlain was her great-uncle and, as already mentioned, Neville Chamberlain was her mother's cousin. Elizabeth was brought up in a devout Unitarian circle, though she had ceased to be a Unitarian long before she became a Catholic. The magic of Chamberlain's career in his earlier Radical period and his reasons for lapsing into Imperialism fascinated her. So indeed did the whole ethos of that industrial and moral world of Chamberlains, Nettlefolds, Kenricks, and other related Unitarians who built up the modern Birmingham. She threw herself into a biography of Joe. But the old trouble asserted itself. She insisted on exploring every nook and cranny in the life of him and his contemporaries. She roughed out three chapters on a single episode: the Jameson Raid, 1895–6. Clearly if she went on at this rate she would make the Garvin and Amery life look like slim volumes. For once I had a brilliant thought. Why not turn the book into a monograph on the Jameson Raid and leave the life of Joe for another day?

In a trice 30,000 words on Jameson were available. The publishers wanted 80,000. Elizabeth produced almost 180,000 before they could draw up a contract. These were cut down to 140,000 with some agony, which was accepted as the right number. The applause was amply deserved. Robert Blake singled out her chapter on Chamberlain's character and psychology as perhaps the most penetrating we possessed of that statesman. None of his later views arrived at by the time of the Jameson Raid made any appeal to her and yet perhaps the family relationship assisted her to enter into his soul.

Soon afterwards Elizabeth was drawn to the idea of writing about a great Victorian woman, Josephine Butler for example or Beatrice Webb or Virginia Crawford, who figures so luridly in the Dilke story and later founded the Catholic Social Guild. But others had tackled or were tackling them. Finally Graham Watson, of Curtis Brown, suggested Queen Victoria, and of course it was the right answer.

She has often appeared on television. On the whole I prefer her in serious parts, but that is apt to mean on mother-and-child questions in a Catholic role and that may restrict one's appearances as quite a few Catholics have found. When the Brains Trust was first started Elizabeth was one of the original group who seemed to be potentially regulars. All went well till a performance on a Sunday afternoon witnessed on the screen by myself. A question of this kind arose: 'What makes life worth living after forty-five?' Elizabeth testified to the duty of serving God. Julian Huxley beside her gave a great groan, metaphorically at least, and his head went down into his hands. This was the end of Elizabeth on the Brains Trust. If only she had been Teilhard de Chardin the Jesuit, for whose *Phenomenon of Man* he wrote so understanding and affectionate a preface. She was never asked to take part in the Brains Trust again, a revealing fact.

When she began to be used again it was either in quiz-like programmes or in company with Catholic figures like Gilbert Harding, where a clash need not be expected. Not long afterwards Father D'Arcy, S.J., came into sharp conflict with Freddy Ayer. Father D'Arcy, to quote Maurice Richardson, 'came out of his corner swinging punches at all angles'. That was the end of Father D'Arcy on the Brains Trust. Also it was a long time before he was used on television in any way. In some mysterious way he was supposed to have broken the conventions. I know well that Freddy Ayer would be the last person to intervene for this purpose. 'Freddy is always a gentleman,' said Father D'Arcy. He has always been a genuine champion of intellectual freedom whatever the views propounded. Before the war, when we were colleagues at Christ Church, we took a joint seminar in political philosophy. I can remember the almost hypnotic effect of his views on Sorel.

The most telling of all her appearances was in the autumn of 1962 when she was asked to discuss the killing of a thalidomide baby by a Belgian doctor at the request of the mother. The fact that the mother, doctor, and others had been tried for their lives, and their fate had been apparently uncertain, had swung a great deal of sentiment behind them. The issue had tended to become 'Would it be tolerable to execute or punish severely these tragic figures'. The question whether they were right to kill the baby had been overlaid. Elizabeth's opponent was Barbara Wootton, between whom and Elizabeth there is great affection and respect. Robin Day was in the chair. The choice of Barbara to put the case for mercy killing at its most rational was ideal except in one respect. Those who know Barbara are well aware that her opposition to the taking of human life is carried to a point of extreme principle. Long will be remembered her poignant prose poem of horrified indignation after the Home Secretary had refused to reprieve young Forsyth. Others know that she has declined to sit in her magistrates' court when a nuclear disarmer is being tried there.

She seldom, if ever, endures a debate in the House of Lords on defence.

It was to me, and I think to most of her friends, inconceivable that she could ever have had a part in the killing of a helpless baby. And this, I at least felt, was precisely what came out of the debate. Here were two immensely human and civilized women, but Elizabeth spoke out of overwhelming conviction. Barbara said nothing which she did not completely believe, but presented a case that fell short of an all-round certainty. It was suggested to me afterwards that Barbara showed a certain delicacy and leniency towards Elizabeth's religious beliefs. That sensitivity, I'm sure, was present. Speaking admittedly with a double bias, I can only report that Elizabeth seemed to me and to many others to shift the real issue from the circumference to the centre of the question. No one who heard her could avoid asking themselves the crucial question. Could I ever kill or join in the killing of a child in these circumstances? Many would have agreed with her before she spoke and many more after the programme.

4

Principles and Powers

I

'The Honourable Stile of Christian'

I HAVE given endless talks in the last twenty-odd years on 'The Christian in Politics', or (as it has often been) 'The Catholic in Politics'. Sometimes I have gained the impression that I have been of help to others, yet I seem to remember that C. S. Lewis reminds us that one is never an easier prey to the devil than when one has just defended Christianity successfully in public.

After all, when one lectures on 'The Christian in Politics' one is not far from saying: (i) A Christian in politics is a better man than other politicians. (ii) I am a Christian in politics, therefore I am better than, at any rate, most other politicians. (iii) And it may interest you to know in what my special virtue consists. This brings back a memory of Desmond McCarthy in an analogous situation. He tells somewhere of a young man coming to see him and confiding that he wanted to be a good writer. 'How good a writer must you be?' asked Desmond McCarthy. 'Shakespeare?' 'Well, hardly Shakespeare.' 'D. H. Lawrence?' 'Well, I would be satisfied if I fell quite a lot short of Lawrence.' 'Would you be satisfied,' said Desmond McCarthy, who in his own modest words was anxious to 'try him high'—he was after all the most famous literary critic of the day—'Would you be satisfied if you were no better than me?' The young man, as I remember the story—perhaps not quite accurately—blenched and went away sorrowful, for he had the abounding ambitions of the young. In what follows, therefore, I am taking the risk of being told all too bluntly that if Christianity makes as much difference as I claim to a politician it ought to have made more difference to me. But anyone who uses autobiography to propound any values at all is running that kind of risk and must be prepared for the consequences.

One distinction must be drawn at once. The distinction between Christian policies or programmes on the one hand, and the conduct of the individual Christian in politics on the other. The phrase 'Christian political principles' is a shade ambiguous, but expanded into 'Christian political and social principles' is clearly used in reference to policies and programmes rather than conduct. Let me take this part of the matter first. I suppose that if a non-Christian asked a Christian, Catholic or Protestant, where he could find the recent statement of Christian political and social principles, the latter could not do better than point to Pope John XXIII's last encyclical *Pacem in Terris* (Peace on Earth). Published in April 1963, it was at once acclaimed throughout the world, markedly so by the Communists, among others. This was before the special overpowering wave of sympathy which was aroused by the mortal illness of the Pope.

It happens that I read a full text of the encyclical in the *New York Times*, and alongside it the unprecedented approval from so many different quarters. Making every allowance for the impression that the Pope's unique lovability had already effected, I was still interested to discover what there was in the document itself which seemed to reach out across every barrier of group interest or ideology. Reading it for the first time, I found the special novelty where others were finding it. In Part V (that is, near the end) occurs this striking passage:

'It must be borne in mind that neither can false philosophical teachings regarding the nature, origin and destiny of the universe and of man be identified with historical movements that have economic, social, cultural or political ends, not even when these movements have originated from those teachings and have drawn and still draw inspiration therefrom.' No one can

[178]

mistake the reference here to the distinction drawn between Marxism as an atheist philosophy and Communism as a historical movement which animates many millions of men and women. The Pope goes on to say that the teachings—the Marxism, for example—remains the same; but the movement undergoes changes of a profound nature. And he adds these still more striking, still more surprising words: 'Who can deny that those movements, in so far as they conform to the dictates of right reason and are interpreters of the lawful aspirations of the human person, contain elements that are positive and deserving of approval?' In other words, even Communism today, in so far as it is a *human* movement and not just an abstract expression of error, is capable of deserving approval. Whoever thought to hear such language from a Pope of Rome?

Certainly when I lectured almost immediately to a gathering of Catholic seminarists in Birmingham, and just after that to a group of Jesuits from every country under heaven, I found ready agreement with my opinion that this was a momentous passage. It was not difficult to believe that the Communist leaders, already encouraged to look for a new toleration in the Vatican, had found here reassurance beyond their hopes.

But I read the encyclical again on the Saturday when the Pope lay dying, and found a still deeper, more universal message. There is an unmatchable recurring emphasis on the dignity inherent in each one of us by virtue of our human nature. For example he mentions a number of modern tendencies. The working classes have gradually gained ground in economic and public affairs. Women are now taking a part in public life. The division is disappearing between nations that rule and nations subject to them. A charter of fundamental human rights is being everywhere formulated, as is a statement of the relationship between the government and the governed. In all these and similar cases the Pope expresses clear approval of what is taking place, if only because it is a major manifestation of the human spirit. He seems to see in history the working of a beneficent providence.

He is utterly removed from the kind of preacher who considers it his main task to warn his congregation against the evils and increased temptations of the time. 'The tendencies to which we have referred', says the Pope, 'do clearly show that the men of our time have become increasingly conscious of their dignity as human beings.' Later he praises the united declaration of human rights issued by the United Nations Organization in 1948, if only because the dignity of a person is acknowledged to all human beings. And later he makes the same point about those who disagree with Catholic teaching. 'The person', he says, 'who errs is always and above all a human being, and he retains in every case his dignity as a human person. He must be always regarded and treated in accordance with that lofty dignity.'

The word lovable has been used so often about the late Pope as to lose some of its meaning. It almost seems to be treated as a physical quality, without doctrinal significance, yet if I am asked whether Pope John XXIII conquered the hearts of the world by sheer personality, or by personality plus doctrine, I would reply, the latter. And his unlimited love for human beings was inextricably associated with his endless stress on the dignity of every human person.

The question naturally arises, was there anything distinctively Christian in such a social philosophy? Pope John himself said in *Pacem in Terris*: 'The doctrinal principles outlined in this document derive from or are suggested by requirements inherent in human nature itself, and are for the most part dictates of the natural law.' He pointed out that therefore they provided Catholics with a vast field of possible contact, not only with Christians outside the Catholic Church, but with all who are 'endowed with the light of reason, and with a natural and operative honesty'. It is open, therefore, to any modern democrat of liberal temperament but agnostic views to persuade himself that the Pope is only saying what he himself—and for that matter, John Stuart Mill—has said all along, in slightly different words. It is hard to prove such an assertion wrong, and yet no one in a supreme position has ever demonstrated so clearly as the late Pope what could be meant in action by a universal belief in human dignity. And Christians must be allowed to attribute a special dimension of value and significance to words which they believe were uttered under the inspiration of the Holy Spirit.

It is fair to mention the incalculable debt which the liberal thinkers themselves owe to the Christian tradition.

But the question persists: is there anything distinctive about a Christian policy as such; something to make you say about a given social or economic or international programme, that is obviously Christian? Or to put the matter the other way round, should a group of Christians expect to agree, in outline at least, on major policy? Personally I very much doubt it. Christian sociologists and public men can be roughly divided into those who maximize and those who minimize the distinctiveness of the Christian contribution in terms of policy. I would describe myself as a minimizer on the plane of theory and maximizer on that of practice. That may need a little explaining.

Mr. Walter James, in his *Christianity and Politics*, the most thorough recent discussion of the whole question, is a supreme minimizer. Part of his attitude is summarized by a quotation from Troeltsch: 'There is not a trace of social reform in Jesus's teaching.' He goes too far there, in my eyes, but a lot of learned Christians will agree with him, and, recognizing that, I cannot regard Christian political and social principles on paper as providing more than a set of standards against which an actual policy must be judged. Yet I remain unrepentantly convinced that even though the conclusions of the natural law are open to everyone with a brain to think with, the average Christian, with and without supernatural aid, is much more likely than the average non-Christian to try to give effect to them. So that although in theory I agree that any enlightened social policy could be hatched by non-Christians, in practice it is much more likely to emerge from a Christian source, whether or not it can be ascribed to it beyond all possibility of argument.

Are there any spheres, however, where Christian attitudes can be identified quite easily? There are, I would suggest, two:

1. Christian interests may be directly involved. I am thinking of the right to worship and the right to a Christian education. Both these demands, but particularly the latter, may take a denominational form. In England, for example, the most active form of the problem is the question, how much if at all,

a Christian of a particular denomination should pay extra for the education of his children. It would be too much to say, indeed it would be contrary to much historical experience, to argue that over this whole range of topics the Christians have stood together though they are much closer to one another than they were. I mention such topics now because no Christian will come at them unaffected by his Christianity, or indeed his particular brand of it.

2. The other sphere where non-Christians and anti-Christians at least are quick to notice and denounce a Christian approach is often spoken of as though it were one area of thought. But in fact it divides itself into two such areas without any obvious link between them. On the one hand we have what may be called 'the life and death subjects': euthanasia, including the special case of the thalidomide babies; abortion; suicide. On the other we have the 'sex and marriage' subjects: birth control, A.I.D., homosexuality, divorce, etc., to mention only the forms in which these issues tend to come before Parliament. In the one case a right to life and a duty to live are asserted; in the other all sex relations with man or woman outside marriage are denounced as sinful. Catholics and many others go further on behalf of the stability of the family and the purity of the sexual act in rejecting divorce and birth control. If anything ties together what I have called these two distinct areas it is the fact that in each case a Christian tradition asserts a natural law which overrides immediate pleasure and (in the simplest case of all—voluntary euthanasia), immediate relief of suffering. My purpose here is not to argue the rights and wrongs of these intricate matters. I am simply pointing out that a Christian politician will run into controversies on these Christian topics, which are quite unrelated to party politics and his other affiliations.

But they are not the main stuff of his political activities unless he specializes on them. On one occasion in the House of Lords we had three successive issues on the same afternoon where it was my duty to take a special line as a Catholic; a line taken, of course, by many others, Catholic and non-Catholic. If I remember rightly, we had to deal one after another with illegitimacy, denominational education, and birth control.

But that situation was quite exceptional, and is not likely to be reproduced. On the Illegitimacy Bill I found myself in a lobby full of rather right-wing Conservatives, and containing only one member of the Labour Party—a bewildering experience.

Which brings us to the moral conduct of the Christian politician. I am thinking primarily of those who make politics at least a large part of their career, but *mutatis mutandis*, what follows can be applied in a kind of descending scale through local government (in which I myself graduated) to all who play their parts as citizens, however briefly and intermittently. Here again, Mr. Walter James is a minimizer. He seems to fear that Christians cannot raise the standard of political conduct which is likely to be determined by circumstances. If this is his meaning (it is surrounded by many subtle qualifications) I sharply disagree with him. The late Lord Halifax, Sir Stafford Cripps, and Mr. George Lansbury are evidence to the contrary. If individual human beings are ever allowed to have raised the moral standard of their time it must be conceded to these three at least, and to many others of lesser fame.

I may be told that Hugh Gaitskell also raised the moral standard of his time, and he is not on record as a professing Christian. He is not on record, it is true, in a contrary sense. When he became leader of the Labour Party I wrote a letter which I shall mention later. In a lecture on the United Nations he asserted unequivocally the authority of spiritual forces. Not that he was near the Catholic, or any other particular Church, though he was buried according to the rites of the Church of England and his children were baptized and confirmed. I am trying to concede the point, which is surely undeniable, that it is not *only* Christians who have raised moral standards. Which does not interfere with my own conviction that in politics as elsewhere, they are *most* likely to be raised by Christians.

Another point arises here, which is seldom discussed, but in which I have long been interested. Take the best Christians one knows, and the best humanists. Assume for the sake of argument that they are equally good. Will the moral conduct of the Christian be likely to differ from that of the humanist? Will he be stronger at some points and weaker at others? (I must ignore the complication that a high proportion of leading people in England are half Christian, half humanist. They hover uncertainly on the borderline.) We must assume that each is equally unselfish; that in one respect at least the humanist follows the Christian ethic. He seeks to do to others what he would like them to do to himself. Starting from that point, the Christian in my experience is more ready to forgive, to love his enemies, and to admit his own unworthiness. It was no accident, in my mind, that the first voices raised strongly in this country for reconciliation with Germany after the war were those of the Bishop of Chichester; Dick Stokes; the *Catholic Herald*; and Victor Gollancz, who, though a Jew, is imbued with a profound Christianity.

The humanist at his best may benefit (I am trying to be ultra-fair) from being less concerned with his own soul, less hampered by doubts, and therefore more positive in action. Sir Julian Huxley and Lord Russell may be pointed to as bold reformers over a long period, though neither has been, strictly speaking, a politician. If this is so the kind of high-minded Christian we are thinking of is therefore going to approach *any* career with more self-criticism than the non-Christian. He is going to discover a fair crop of dilemmas, whatever profession he undertakes.

But before we become entangled in the intricacies which follow I would stress a particular difficulty in the political life which does not exist on the same scale elsewhere. The politician spends a large part of his time struggling to gain his opportunity. If he does not struggle, and go on struggling, he is hardly likely, in the democratic age, to obtain his chance, or retain it. In other professions—medicine, the Bar, the arts, business, for example—the young man struggles, but once he gets his chance, he is unlucky if he does not spend most of his life exercising his talents. The high-ranking barrister no doubt has to work extremely hard—harder than any politician, except perhaps the Foreign Secretary—but he is working in the exercise of his craft; the politician is much less fortunate. So much of his time and energy is devoted inevitably to gaining the opportunity of rendering service.

Admittedly, there is much variety of experience here. Mr.

Macmillan held no office till he was forty-six, though first elected fifteen years earlier. Mr. Butler became an under-secretary when he was twenty-nine, and with the single interval of the Labour period of 1938–45 has been in office for the whole of the thirty-three years since. And yet even he may feel that it has all been a preparation or search for an oppor-tunity that never comes. Mr. Grimond has never been in office, and perhaps—through no weakness of his own—never will be. Mr. Crossman, at the age of fifty-six, has, again, never been in office, though it is very likely he will be. I myself appeared in Parliament (the House of Lords) when I was thirty-nine, and was at once made a Lord-in-Waiting, the lowest thing in ministerial life. I was Minister for Germany at forty-one (profiled in the *Observer*); Minister of Civil Aviation (nominally a promotion) at forty-two.

We are approaching here what is to my mind the subtlest of the temptations in politics. But I must first say a word about the moral conflicts more often referred to.

In his *Profiles in Courage*, the fruit of searching reflection, President Kennedy defends his fellow politicians on the whole against Mr. Walter Lippmann's charge that with very rare exceptions the successful Democratic politicians are 'insecure intimidated men'. 'In no other occupation except politics', says Mr. Kennedy, 'is it expected that a man will sacrifice honours, privileges, and a chosen career on a single issue.' Mr. Kennedy is primarily concerned with the *courage* required in politics. He quotes with envy Congressman McGroaty of California who wrote to a tiresome constituent: 'One of the countless drawbacks of being in Congress is that I am com-pelled to receive impertinent letters from people such as you. Will you please take two running jumps and go to hell.'

The courage which he has in mind is principally the courage to think out what is right and to do it in the face of terrifying pressures. He on the whole finds this quality well exhibited in American history. When I had the privilege of meeting Presi-dent Kennedy at a reception given by Mr. de Valera on his Irish visit in 1963 I was struck by the rapidity of his responses and his spontaneity. I mentioned my daughter Antonia in the brief moment we were together and he at once recalled with enthusiasm meeting her in Washington. All afternoon I watched him relaxing and at the same time reacting happily to the Irish crowd. He basked visibly and naturally in every aspect of his triumphant homecoming. I said to an American intimate of his that he was obviously a wonderful extrovert. 'That's just what he's not,' was the reply. 'You read *Profiles in Courage*.' I did and saw at once what was meant and how closely the President must have examined his own conscience on many political issues. No practising politician has given me a clearer sense of probing intensively to the bottom of some, though not all, of the deepest moral issues arising.

In 1942 I wrote an article about political morality in the *Political Quarterly* which continues to be quoted occasionally, as by Walter James, for example. I covered much the same ground twelve years later in an essay on 'The Catholic in Politics' which I contributed to my wife's *Catholic Approaches*. On each occasion I dealt among other difficulties besetting the politician with the temptation against *honesty*. It is certainly this which most people have in mind if they refer to politics as 'a dirty business'. How can one, they ask, agree with twenty or so colleagues in the Cabinet, or several hundred M.P.s of one's own Party; or a good many thousand active workers in the Party; or quite a few million who vote for it? And if one doesn't agree, how can one pretend, or even conceal one's disagreement by silence?

These are real questions which will trouble politicians and their critics till the end of time. The politician gets used to living with them, just as the barrister gets used to living with the question, 'How can you defend a prisoner you know to be guilty?' The process, I suppose, by which one's conscience is appeased, is the thought that in politics as at the Bar a code is necessary for the public good; that politics is team-work; and that certain conventions, well understood all round, are indispensable if politics is to be carried on. But almost every politician with any claim to greatness has challenged his Party, and whether a religious man or not, has said to them in effect what Socrates said to his judges, 'Men of Athens I love you dearly, but I love God more.' Or, St. Thomas More said, as he went to the scaffold, 'The King's servant, but God's servant first.'

Sir Winston Churchill changed his Party twice, and for years before the war was in open conflict with the Conservative leadership. Mr. Harold Macmillan at one point before the war rejected the Conservative whip, and during that phase spoke at the Oxford by-election after Munich against the official Conservative candidate, the present Lord Hailsham. Lord Avon, then Mr. Anthony Eden, Duff Cooper, and the present Lord Salisbury all resigned from the Chamberlain Government. In 1951 Aneurin Bevan, Harold Wilson, and John Freeman did the same to the Attlee Government. Three very different men, all of immense political sophistication, were equally ready to sacrifice for what they regarded as a principle their entire political careers.

If anyone supposed that Hugh Gaitskell was far too orthodox, or too conventional a Wykehamist to act with equal boldness, he soon found himself mistaken. It is said that when Hugh Gaitskell went to see Lord Attlee on the morning of his budget speech he informed Clem Attlee that he and Nye Bevan were in complete disagreement about the health charges, and that neither would give way. 'In that case,' said Clem Attlee from his bed of sickness, '—— must go.' 'Certainly,' said Hugh, thinking Attlee said he must go. 'I said he must go,' said Clem Attlee, which put a different complexion on it. The story is here mentioned to show that Hugh Gaitskell was as ready as anyone to resign on a point of principle. Later, when he challenged the Party Conference and called upon his supporters to 'fight, and fight, and fight again' he demonstrated this to the entire world.

Some of my own experiences on this front have been touched on rather gently in an earlier book. I did not mention there how close we came to expulsion in the Oxford City Labour Party at the time of the Popular Front in 1938. We were sure to start with that our principles were higher than those of wicked old Transport House, but we were eventually persuaded that we could toe the line without dishonour. I gave a somewhat muted, though not inaccurate version of the distress I underwent from 1947 to 1951. I felt there was a complete difference of approach to the German problem between myself and the Labour Government of which I was a member. I need not go through the whole recital. When I was made Minister of Civil Aviation in 1948 it might reasonably have been thought by my superiors that honour had been satisfied all round. But I continued to be haunted by conscience, and to make myself a considerable, though ineffective, nuisance.

More than once I wrote to Clem Attlee, the Prime Minister, offering my resignation. He was a veritable magician in dealing with long, emotional screeds of that kind. His answer was always just about the same: 'My dear Frank, I will look into the points you mention. I am hard-pressed just now, but will see you as soon as possible. Yours ever, Clem.' After which nothing much happened, as one kicked one's heels and cooled off, and the situation changed enough to make the original letter slightly obsolete. But there came a moment in 1949 when the British insisted on pursuing the original policy of dismantling a large part of German industry. (A year later the policy of rearming Germany was accepted in principle.) This, I told myself and Elizabeth, was the end. I wrote the strongest of all my letters to the Prime Minister, attaching a time-limit to my resignation, and left home convinced that I would be a sensational outcast by evening. I ate my solitary lunch at the Athenaeum, and walked across the Horse Guards to Number 10. And there Clem Attlee had surpassed his usual artistry, how I shall never know, in preparing the interview. (I remember an earlier resignation, deliberately tendered to him at his room in the House of Commons, which was interrupted scientifically by the division bell at ten o'clock. On his return the resignation lapsed through mutual inanition.)

This time the Cabinet Room, where he usually interviewed Ministers, was in the hands of the decorators. 'Hope you don't mind my seeing you here,' he remarked to me cordially, as he sat me down in the secretary's room, one or two of the secretaries still sitting in the background. The month was August. He had just come up in country clothes from Chequers, and he began with some friendly, well-informed enquiries about Elizabeth, Antonia, and the other children. I brought myself to suggest that in view of the gravity of the topic to be discussed it would be better if we were alone. 'Oh yes,' he said, 'you mean the matter you wrote to me about. Oh, that's quite all right: Ernest Bevin's coming back from Strasbourg tonight, and the whole thing's being looked into afresh.' He then, as far as I can remember, returned to the subject of Elizabeth, Antonia, and the other children.

I shambled from the room, uncertain then, as I am uncertain now, whether I had achieved something quite substantial or been outwitted once again in the kindliest of all possible ways. Events in fact, and American policy, were dictating a steady change in the British attitude. Who shall say whether I did or did not assist them?

I tell that story, which epitomizes a long period of strain and indecision, to prove that I am not unaware of the clash that may arise between loyalty, or, as I have called it earlier, 'the duty of team-work', and one's personal integrity. If one takes some of the individuals who have made the biggest personal impact on public affairs in recent times one finds that some of them would in all circumstances have put integrity before team-work, and been very quick to find a conflict. Dick Stokes, Victor Gollancz, Lord Beveridge, and Lord Russell would all have fallen into this category. Of these only Dick Stokes was a professional politician. He did not receive office till too late. His premature and always-to-be-lamented death was to follow.

Dick Stokes, as I wrote at the time in the *Observer*, to the Catholic masses of this country was a man apart. There was no one of whose censure one was more nervous; no one of whose friendship one was more proud. He was often spoken of as the most popular member of the House of Commons. He had been decorated for valour in the First World War and was a most audacious critic of the Government in the Second. But he told me he had never done anything which required such courage as entering the House of Commons in 1942 to protest against 1,000-bomber raids on Cologne. 'I was almost blown out of the Chamber by sheer anger.' I cherish the dream that he would have brought to the next Labour Cabinet the strength and experience of a successful business man and the moral impulse of an irrepressible Christian.

I return later to a statesman of equal integrity, but one whose synthesis was different, Clem Attlee.

I hope that I shall not seem to have been coarsened by the years if I suggest that dilemmas of the kind arising from what I have called 'temptations against honesty' are not the most fundamental. They may produce a poignant crisis of conscience; I once took a dilemma of mine to a Jesuit priest, an intimate and valued friend, and was told—very wisely—that I really must make up my mind for myself. But in the end the issues are fairly near the surface of life, if only because the conventions are fairly well worked out. One knows, or should know, what is happening to oneself, which may be far from the case with some other temptations.

In both my essays I have mentioned—the one in the *Political Quarterly* and the one in *Catholic Approaches*—I went on to stress the kind of temptation unconnected with courage or honesty. I pointed to temptations against charity, and, still more obviously, against humility. The older I become, the more I find myself dwelling on these. After all, the politician, if he is to do any good at all, must obtain his opportunity. That I have said already, but I now add that he can only obtain it by winning popularity not just for his policies but for himself. A lifelong search for popularity, much of it among complete strangers, that is to say 'the public', who can know very little of what one is like, is an inevitable condition of a political career, a *sine qua non* of achievement. An American President provides perhaps the best example, but every candidate is engaged on the same quest, and a Parliamentary reputation is impossible without some degree of it.

But how can one reconcile a search of this kind for popularity with the teaching of the spiritual books? 'Our whole lives', says St. Francis de Sales, 'should be coloured by the virtues of gentleness, temperance, modesty and humility.' Is it fair to ask how a constituency association would assess the value of a candidate recommended for these qualities, against one who was said to be a tough fighter, full of push and drive? (The two sets of qualities are not exactly opposed, but they suggest two different types of person.) How much store would even a Prime Minister set on gentleness, temperance, modesty, and humility in choosing his Cabinet? It is true that later on St. Francis de Sales makes this concession: 'Everyone indeed may accept and maintain the rank due to him, without losing his humility, so long as he does so without affectation or contention.' But this seems to take us no further than the great noble who starts with a lofty rank, and is allowed to defend it. It does not help us much when each of us has to make his own way for himself, in stern competition, not so much with a political enemy, as with his own political comrades, and, it may well be, his closest friends.

A few years ago a small spiritual book was published called *The Way* by Joseph Escriva. Since then it has sold more than 100,000 copies in various countries and editions. It is full of inspiration and challenge. But suppose a politician, conscious, it may be, of powers beyond the average, tries to follow its guidance? On page 21 (English edition) he is called to arms: 'You a drifter? You one of the herd? You, who were born to be a leader!' And on the next page: 'In that way you will first become master of yourself, and then a guide, a chief, a leader: to compel and to sway and to inspire others with your word, with your example, with your knowledge and with your power.' These are words surely to arouse the legitimate ardour of politicians, young and not-so-young. And yet one feels uneasy, at so to speak setting oneself apart from one's companions, if only in aspiration.

The Way does not neglect the dangers. Read on a little way and you find this: 'You seem incapable of feeling the fraternity of Christ. In those around you, you do not see brothers, you see stepping-stones.' And then, still more clearly, the clue is pointed out: 'You will never be a leader if in the crowd you see a mere footstool to give you height. You will be a leader if you are ambitious for the salvation of all mankind.' To put it in my own contemporary idiom: 'You have got to be on fire with concern for what happens to your fellow men', as Hugh Gaitskell burned with ardour for what he deemed the right outcome in his tremendous speech on the Common Market at Brighton. There, in a short compass, the right steps are surely marked out.

Triumph and disaster have been described as twin impostors,

but to a character predominantly good, the second seems much less disastrous. In an earlier book I described the Miserere Psalm as my favourite and singled out the reference to a broken and contrite heart and the sacrifice of an afflicted spirit. Since my own humiliating departure from the Army it would always have a special meaning for me.

When, a few months after his own immense disaster, I had lunch with Jack Profumo, I asked myself anxiously whether I had not lost sight of the Miserere message, when I found him so overwhelmingly conscience stricken, so gallant, so utterly determined not to blame anyone, even slightly—except himself. I came away with an irresistible conviction. 'Whatever the past and the future may hold for him and me, at this moment,' I felt sure, 'he is nearer to the Kingdom of God than I am.' Nearer, for that matter, than the general run of politicians.

And yet that phrase 'the fraternity of Christ' makes one pause and wonder whether one has even begun to understand what this kind of life would involve. Since I am writing an autobiography I might as well come clean and confess that jealousy is my own worst quality as far as I can judge.

St. Francis de Sales, in the passage just quoted, remarks that 'Charity is patient, is kind; charity feels no envy.' (And at the moment I am not distinguishing between jealousy and envy.) The curious thing is that politicians are on the whole occupationally kind, and on the whole occupationally jealous. If they are introspective they will probably be aware of their jealousy and take some steps to counter it. But it is there, perhaps inevitably there, a great part of the time, and does not in fact exclude a feeling of great affection for the person envied. I am afraid, I think, that this tendency to jealousy is part of the occupational risk of politics. How gravely we are in need of the prayer of Thomas Fuller: 'Lord, I perceive my soul deeply guilty of envy. . . . I had rather thy work be undone than done better by another than myself! . . . Dispossess me, Lord, of this bad spirit, and turn my envy into holy emulation; . . . yea, make other men's gifts to be mine, by making me thankful to thee for them.'

For a number of years in talking about the Christian in politics, I found everything summed up in the text from St.

James's Epistle: 'Religion pure and undefiled is this: to visit the widows and the fatherless in their affliction, and to keep oneself unspotted from the world.' But now that does not seem to me to be more than part of the truth. A politician could be remarkably pure by any ordinary standards, and labour devotedly for the salvation of all mankind, and yet lack the 'fraternity of Christ'. Some years ago, not as long ago as I could wish, I was told that a political colleague had said of me: 'He talks a lot about equality, but he doesn't treat me as an equal.' The man in question was not outstanding in any particular way, and I fear that there may have been all too much truth in his remark. But, of course, in so far as it was true, I was being totally un-Christian, however enlightened my views, however dedicated I might be to human betterment in general.

Jealousy, then, is not the only danger. A certain inward callousness towards those who don't matter; an unconscious treatment of them as 'stepping-stones', is just as vicious and just as likely in politics. Those who follow other professions must testify about the spiritual perils there. To the politician I can only offer this double piece of advice: 'Ask oneself in the first place, and keep on asking oneself, whether one is allowing one's ambitions to interfere with human affections; and, having done so, set oneself to love those particularly that one is most concerned with. And when I say "love" I do not merely mean that one should take care to tolerate them, or forgive them, as one forgives a so-called enemy. But one must really like and appreciate and if possible admire them for what is most personal to them, for what makes them themselves. Not just because one ought to in the abstract. If all goes well, one does become so genuinely fond of them that one greets good news for them as though it benefited oneself, and bad news for them as a personal disaster. The final triumph is when one's least attractive colleague turns to one, and asks in the words of the tiresome nun befriended by St. Teresa of Lisieux, "What is there about me which attracts you so much?" '

The last paragraph is sincere and contains what I know to be helpful advice. But it trembles on the brink of its own arrogance. It reminds me too much of that prayer of Marcus

Aurelius which means much to one of my great friends but which does not appeal to me. 'Say to thyself, Marcus, today I shall run up against the busybody, the ungrateful, the over-bearing, the deceitful, the envious, the self-centred. But I, understanding the nature of the good, can neither be damaged by any of them nor can be angry with my kinsman or estranged from him.'

Raymond Mortimer, reviewing my *Born to Believe*, referred to me as a 'philistine' (which unremittingly rankles), but he also described me as the ideal schoolmaster and went on to pay me the highest and most encouraging compliment that I have ever received. I was, he said, 'one of those who would always find something to like and encourage in the most unattractive and unpopular of boys'. Again I fear most of us politicians require to believe that we are more attractive and less tiresome than the average if we are to operate at all. There is no reason to suppose that we are right as others see us, but even if we were such distinctions would be trivial in face of the super-human tasks which confront the world today and will always confront it. They are most trivial of all in face of common suffering when it comes to us close at home and we realize a little of its meaning. In the sight of God such distinctions are, of course, quite meaningless. One's own striving and experi-ence at times seem almost negligible and yet they are of infinite worth if offered unreservedly as part of the common lot of humanity.

2

'The Hour of the Timid'

M. MAURIAC, equally applauded as a novelist and a Catholic, tells us in *The Stumbling Block* that he has more than once been called Tartuffe, the Impostor. This particular charge, he finds, makes a convenient starting point. I find the same. I have been introduced so often at Catholic functions in recent years as an exemplary Catholic. At one dizzy moment I found myself speaking at Maynooth.

I was one of two Catholics, George Rendel being the other, in the absence of the Duke of Norfolk, Lord Perth, and Douglas Woodruff, who unofficially represented the Church at the Anglican service in memory of Pope John XXIII. The service was a touching act of friendship by the present Archbishop of Canterbury. I am one of half a dozen Catholic Privy Councillors. When a Catholic point of view is expressed in 'The Lords', David Perth, Harry Iddesleigh or I take the lead. I was actually referred to at the end of the debate on birth regulations as 'My Lord Cardinal Longford' by my inimitable friend Lord Brabazon, probably the most popular speaker in either House. ('Old Brab,' said Clem Attlee, 'a little while ago went down the Cresta Run. Not bad for a man in his seventies.')

Within two years I may be standing on some honoured platform, 'a sixty-year-old smiling public man' (as W. B. Yeats described himself), receiving, if not homage, a good measure of respect. I am bound to ask myself, I retain the grace to ask myself quite often, is there not something phoney about the production? Is there not some fundamental contradiction here? I am not referring to religious doubts. These I have been largely spared. If I have difficulties (the personal devil, for instance) they are not such as others seem to take seriously. If I have grave ritualistic limitations (after twenty-two years in the Church I am still unable to serve Mass) they appear to embarrass me more than anyone else, except the priest occasionally deprived of a server. But I never fail to doubt whether the idea of an active Party politician, involved in a career of that kind, and the idea of a human witness to the Catholic spirit are not basically incompatible. For this reason, among others, I feel that Harry Iddesleigh, who moved from the Conservative benches to the cross-benches in protest against Suez, is a more satisfactory spokesman than I am. Incidentally, he is a good example to the Church of one who is not just a good Catholic but a good House of Lords man. Small, intrepid, highly independent in flavour, he is very much to the taste of the House. Yet my own lot seems to be cast as a prominent Catholic and Labour politician in the House of Lords whatever the dubieties attaching. As I said in the House last year on the supposition that I would not be allowed to leave it for the Commons: 'I must abandon myself to the Divine Providence. Like Robert Louis Stevenson, I must salute the romance of destiny.'

Naturally I do not like to think of my Catholic life these last twelve years as centred in the House of Lords. 'I do not think', wrote Evelyn Waugh to Elizabeth when she was received into the Church in 1946, 'that anyone outside the Church can ever understand the meaning of the "household of the Faith", the supernatural unity in love that exists behind the superficial wrangles. It is a fragment of that love that I send to you today.' Elizabeth and I have many times verified the truth of those words since.

I must not begin to recite a list of Catholic friends. And yet among priests I must at least mention my debt to Father Martin D'Arcy and Franciscan priests of the Greyfriars, Oxford, who between them brought me into the Church. And after that Archbishop Mathew, Father Gervase Mathew, who prepared and received Elizabeth, and our own parish priests, Father de Zulueta of the Church of St. Thomas More, Chelsea, and Father Chadwick of Burwash and Hurst Green.

Certainly I have no better friends than those in the Church; Agnes Headlam-Morley, George and Anne Martelli, Bice Fawcett, Marie-Noël Kelly, Frances Phipps, the Burns, the Speaights and the Grisewoods. . . . And Daphne and Arthur Pollen of course. Francis, their son, designed and built, while Arthur adorned, a small octagonal chapel with a lofty tower for our own Catholic community in Hurst Green. Ultra-modern in style, it at first bewildered our local population, but admiration is now, I think, general, and its reputation has spread widely. Built by Mr. Oliver, of Hurst Green, and local labour, much of the money for it has been raised by fêtes which have been opened by Eamonn Andrews, Gilbert Harding, Alec Guiness, and other Catholic stars. With these fêtes non-Catholics have helped enthusiastically. Sir Edward Boyle, our unofficial squire, has spoken for us repeatedly and the Anglican vicar, Mr. Bell, has been a welcome guest. When I said to one of our Anglican helpers that we had set an example in Hurst Green which was now being followed by Rome and Canter-bury he replied with a solemn face, 'Well, we more or less forced them into it, didn't we?' I often reflect on Arthur Pollen's quiet, contemplative, unselfseeking, deeply cultivated Catholicism as a necessary corrective to anything that is over-worldly or frenzied in mine.

The Duke of Norfolk holds the undisputed position as leader of the Catholic laity and performs his part to perfection. There is refinement under his weather-beaten countryman's appearance. He was presiding at the centenary dinner of the Catholic Revival in 1950; the banqueting chamber was full to overflowing with cardinals, archbishops, and bishops. The Duke had to propose the health of Cardinal Griffin. As a Minister of the Crown at that time, I was sitting at the Cardinal's other side. The task seemed one of insuperable difficulty. It was known, and indeed visible, that the Cardinal was very ill. Only supernatural fortitude had brought him to the dinner at all. 'I rise, Your Eminence,' said the Duke, 'to propose your health. Your Eminence, we learn with regret that your health has not been too good lately. Your Eminence, we hope that your health will soon be much improved. Your Eminence, your health.' It was beautifully done and most things that Bernard Norfolk has touched, from the coronation downwards, have the same indefinable instinct.

But he seldom speaks in the Lords, conceiving, I think, that his duties as Earl Marshal restrict his freedom of utterance. The intellectual leadership of the laity in Britain has lain with Douglas Woodruff. He has one of the largest minds of our time, just as Mia Woodruff, ceaselessly aiding the stricken, has one of the largest hearts. Among public men, Bill Carron, George Woodcock, Bob Mellish and Chris Hollis possess the kind of influence and the kind of reputation which I most admire and envy. My son-in-law, Hugh Fraser, is already Secretary of State for Air. It is sometimes said that a Catholic could never be Prime Minister. Can they be so sure?

But I hasten back to my own public activities as a Catholic. They can roughly be divided into services rendered within the Church and services outside. The first has taken the form of many addresses to gatherings large and small, to prize-givings, conferences, etc. They must be passed over with gratitude on my part. They have required some energy when I have been tired, but they have been happy occasions, gratifying to the ego, a source of strength in the cold world outside. Perhaps if I quote a letter it will illustrate how much Catholic action is available without honour or glory. I had been visiting a prisoner (on the hostel scheme already referred to) and spent the night with two complete strangers. They were great friends of Antonia's and Hugh's and I knew they were good Catholics, but they were not concerned with prison work, although the brother of my hostess was a prison visitor. I mentioned my prisoner friend in the hope that my host's brother-in-law would look him up. My friend is a Catholic, though I don't think I said so.

It never occurred to me that my host and hostess would do any more. They are very busy people living some miles from the prison. Some weeks later a letter arrived from my hostess:

'You will be interested to learn that David B . . . [my prisoner friend] is quite one of the family now. He has come out for the last three or four Sundays and we like him very much. Yesterday my husband and he and an old priest went on a long day's pilgrimage to a shrine. We are so glad you put him in touch with us. Do let us know if you have any more protégés.'

I rang up after lunch to thank her. The telephone was answered by David himself. All this will make me feel still more humble when I lecture on Catholic obligation. But it illustrates better than I could what Evelyn meant by 'the household of the Faith'.

I pass to Catholic activities outside the Church. In May 1963 I was greatly honoured to be invited to contribute an article to the *Jewish Chronicle* about Catholic-Jewish understanding. the *Jewish Chronicle* kindly presented me as one who had consistently spoken up as a friend of the Jews. I have mentioned earlier my pleasure at being able to bring David Montagu to the Board of the National Bank. A great occasion for me was a dinner over which I presided in aid of the Jewish Society for the Mentally Handicapped at which about £60,000 was raised. I deputized at the last moment for an intimate friend, Harry Nathan, who again and again assisted my social work. No one who has been as much involved as I have in the study of delinquency can be unaware of the matchless record of the Jews in keeping their community free of crime. But men like the late Basil Henriques have done more than their fair share of prevention. Is the Christian attitude to the Jews an all round touchstone? It has seemed so to David Astor, a delicate and scrupulous judge.

The chances to speak out effectively as a Catholic are not as numerous as might be thought. The number of Catholics allowed to appear on television, and speak as such, is rationed. The authorities try very hard to be fair. We continue to be handicapped. Catholics are much more likely to be invited if it is thought unlikely that they will put on a Catholic act. When I said the few words on television about Stephen Ward I was congratulated by one good Catholic on my skill in bringing in a prayer for him. He thought that the ideal way of 'bringing in' a bit of true religion. But it is just the 'dragging in' of our religion that the newspapers and television producers are out to prevent. That is, apart from the religious programmes in which Elizabeth and I participated on occasion, but where the main Catholic job has been left to the priests who for the most part appear to much advantage.

Archbishop Heenan and Father Agnellus Andrew are television personalities of vast appeal. It is perhaps worth mentioning here that when I did the practice run for the piece on Stephen Ward I asked the producer what he thought. He replied, 'Very good, but since you ask me, I wonder if you would consider leaving out the last sentence referring to prayer.' I said that I thought that that sentence would give pleasure to many, which it appears to have done. I haven't heard of any annoyance it caused. My conscious motive was certainly not one of exploiting the opportunity of working in a bit of religious propaganda.

I remember that some years back a B.B.C. producer of very good standing made quite a strong effort to prevent my 'dragging in' religion when taking part in a programme on the causes of crime. He begged me to remember that only a minority of the audience were Christian, a point I vigorously disputed. I remember how furious Lord Reith was when he heard of it. He was sure it would never have happened in his time. Sir Ian Jacob, the Director General, was kind enough to look into my complaint later on. He reported that I had misunderstood what had been said to me.

If I had a pen like Chesterton or Belloc there would be an outlet in literature for the preaching of the Catholic faith today, and certainly it is in literature that Catholics today are most successful, though they do not use it for direct propaganda. Evelyn Waugh and Graham Greene are, after all, in the world class. For the rest there has been some scope in addresses to university bodies and in university debates. At Oxford, Cambridge, Queen's University, Belfast, and elsewhere my opponents have included A. S. Neill, Margaret Knight, William Empson, and A. L. Rowse, all as sincere as I was.

A surprise defeat at Cambridge by four votes against Leslie Rowse on the motion that 'God made man in His own image and likeness' was the most mortifying. A good majority against Margaret Knight's motion that 'Religion is unnecessary for Morals' was no doubt predictable at Queen's University, Belfast, once the Protestant undergraduates had decided that Catholics were better than agnostics. To be fair, I found the religious atmosphere at Queen's gay and tolerant. A youth who said he was going to join the Orange Order because he believed in religious tolerance was treated as the greatest joke imaginable.

But in practice it must be principally in the House of Lords that a Catholic peer can 'represent' his Church. Our twenty-eight Catholic M.P.s do yeoman work in the Commons. In our House we struggle along with a nominal roll of thirty Catholics and perhaps fifteen available for a division on a serious Catholic issue. The others appear to live in very remote parts of these islands. I am in the peculiar position of being the only Labour peer out of a nominal sixty who is a Catholic. Edwin Plowden, apart from myself, is the only Catholic out of over 200 peers of all kinds created since the war. These last figures do not, I fancy, reveal an anti-Catholic prejudice. We are latecomers into British public life. With the Catholic population increasing rapidly, above all the Catholic professional class, we should see something very different in twenty years—if peers are still being created.

The first duty of a Catholic in politics is to be a good politician, to exhibit the natural virtues, including Party loyalty. Catholics are completely split between the Parties, in the Lords overwhelmingly Conservative and in the Commons evenly divided; outside Parliament, Labour, so it is said. There were some protests from Catholic friends when I spoke against two Catholics at Brighton at the last election. Maybe I wasn't clever about it. I live in Sussex and one of the Labour candidates, Lewis Cohen, was a personal friend. For the most part, therefore, if Catholics are to represent their Church in public work they must do so rather by high moral standards and abnormal zeal and compassion than by support of particular policies. But, as mentioned in the last chapter, there are two spheres where a distinctive course must be followed. The sphere of special Church interest and the sphere of special Church rules.

At some moments, though not lately, foreign policy could raise a whole lot of issues of its own. Education is the most obvious example of a Catholic interest. When the last Bill to relieve the burden on the Churches was going through the Houses, Lord Alexander, our leader, wished to speak, but, as a Baptist, he couldn't represent the Party view. Lord Mac-Donald likewise—he was a Congregationalist. And likewise myself, a Catholic. In the end all these three zealous Christians had 'to speak for themselves only', and the task of representing the Labour Party fell to Lord Silkin—a Jew. He must have laughed inwardly, but is far too kind to show it. On the whole the Catholic peers have been spared the denominational problems of education these last few years through the statesmanship of Bishop Beck, and of certain Conservative Ministers and Labour leaders.

Harold Wilson has taken a lively interest in Catholic and other religious education. He sits for Huyton, one of the most Catholic constituencies in the country, and is on close and friendly terms with the clergy. This I know for myself, having spoken for him these last few elections, and having, on one occasion at least, spent an evening in the presbytery with Harold and the parish priest. And indeed the same story has come back to me in all sorts of ways—always favourable to Harold. 'He does a lot for us. He never lets the Ministry alone. He's a man who follows up words with deeds.' Now, critics of Harold, less vocal today than a little while back, will at this point say: 'Ha, ha, he knows which side his bread is buttered on. He needs their votes, etc.' But this, in my eyes, is a superficial view and indeed an inaccurate one. Harold Wilson is naturally at home in a Catholic presbytery with a Catholic priest whose social origin is the same as his own. He is naturally, and without effort, in sympathy with the struggles and sacrifices of a simple Catholic working-class community in pursuit of a reasonable education. Much more at home, in fact, in such surroundings than in upper-class society.

Harold is a believing Christian, a nonconformist; his wife is the daughter of a nonconformist minister. Today this could assist his relationship with the Catholic masses. The old contentions between Catholics and nonconformists, still reflected perhaps in Wales and in some of my older nonconformist colleagues, are fading out in a mutual discovery of vital moral standards in common, though divergences remain on drinking and betting. Some years ago Herbert Morrison said to me, 'You Catholics have got some tiresome tricks but if you stick to it you might become the nonconformists of the future.' Later I heard Lord Alexander say to Jack Lawson, when a Catholic peer was denouncing our modern Babylon, 'You know, Jack, these Catholics speak more like nonconformist ministers every day.'

Harold Wilson was until recently accused of some deviousness. I have demanded illustrations of this alleged weakness and have never been supplied with any. He used to strike me sometimes as ill at ease and embarrassed, thinking and speaking too quickly for his company, but never like that in Huyton or among the working classes. I know very well that he is an easy man to do business with. A man totally free of malice in spite of being much attacked, a man too careful to form as many friendships as a man should, yet not incapable of forming them, a man whose intellect travels like lightning through a problem presented to it, and a man who has for many years been close to Catholic issues. From such a man the Catholic Church will not seek and expect favours, but they will, I am sure, receive a high degree of understanding.

So much, though it has not been enough, for Catholic interests. Now comes the area of Catholic rules, or the two areas as I have distinguished them. The life and death subjects—euthanasia, suicide, etc.—and the sex and marriage subjects—homosexuality, birth control, divorce, etc. I should now, I suppose, add premarital sexual intercourse (which I prefer to call premarital fornication). Curiously enough, the *Daily Express*, whose views on this subject have coincided with mine, asked me for a statement which they duly published but left out the word 'fornication', though its use greatly strengthened my argument and theirs. An edifying, but here an overdone, squeamishness. In all these cases the Catholic case seems at first sight to be negative, in the sense that we want to stop someone doing something which would appear to lessen immediate suffering and bring immediate pleasure. In the long run the

Church insists not only virtue but happiness will be augmented by its various rules, its stricter code. But in the short run the anti-Church side comes forward with the more obvious seductions.

I faced this issue squarely, and I hope fairly, when I spoke against A.I.D. in the House in 1958. 'There are some of us,' I said, 'whose main interest in public questions derives from a desire to help the weak, the afflicted, the poor, the old, and the lonely. This sentiment,' I went on, 'would seem to place us naturally and easily on the side of the childless couple, but whatever we like to call our ethics, Aristotelian, Kantian, Utilitarian, Humanitarian, or simply Christian, we must all be aware that immediate happiness, while a laudable objective to be promoted by all scientific means, is not the highest value here. Grapes cannot be grown from thorns or figs from thistles. It is literally impossible to help anyone, a childless couple or anybody else, however humane our purpose, by evil means.'

In other words, there are some methods which may be legitimate for the non-Christian, though rejected by many of the best of them, but illegitimate most decidedly so for Catholics. This is what Catholic spokesmen have been trying to say in a more generalized way in a number of debates. Claiming no monopoly of such a well-established tradition, we have felt a special responsibility for seeing that these truths were unremittingly asserted. It may be that the difference between the Christian point of view and the opposite (however the latter is labelled) can be traced to a difference in philosophy proper. Father Eric D'Arcy, who is well versed in modern philosophy of all kinds, writes as follows in his new book: 'For Aquinas some kind of acts are intrinsically evil, for Kant there are some duties of perfect obligation, whereas for Bentham every action whatever is to be approved on the principle of utility.' Father Eric D'Arcy does not add, though I am sure it is so, that of these philosophies, the Benthamite is far the least likely to produce a clear ruling against an act of personal pleasure in a particular case.

It may be that the Church tradition owes as much to revelation as to pure reasoning, though no Catholic intellectual

would be content with a solution that seemed to him to oppose
his reason or there may be a combination of factors. But we
must be clear about the issue. For example the question whether
fornication before marriage itself or outside marriage is wrong
is wont to be wrapped up with two others. (1) Last year a
Ministry of Education medical officer who justified premarital
intercourse between engaged couples on suitable occasions
confused the issue well and truly. He suggested that there could
be a conflict between charity and chastity. He quoted a saying
of our Lord which I have ventured to use myself as mentioned
earlier in this book, 'He that is without sin among you let
him . . .' But the doctor did not add (nor did I, but that was not
relevant to my purpose) that our Lord dismissed the lady with
the words, 'Go, and sin no more.' We Catholics and other
Christians have tried to assert in our speeches the need for
compassion along with the recognition of sin, but that is
totally different from denying that the sin exists or con-
doning it.

(2) Again, we clever ones, Christian and non-Christian, are
also so quick to distinguish between crime and sin, that the
'baby of sin is apt to be got rid of with the bathwater of crime'.
When I moved the adoption of the Wolfenden Report with-
drawing the criminal ban on homosexual behaviour between
consenting adults I insisted, of course, that the sin of homosexual practice, like that of heterosexual irregularity, remained
as heinous as ever. But speaking for myself I would never like
to be dogmatic in advance as to where a Christian should find
himself on a particular measure which did not beyond all
doubt encourage sinfulness.

Examining my conscience over the last few years in the House
I am rather sorry to think that I was not more active in trying
to remove the legal penalties on attempted suicide. I am still not
sure that we Catholics were on the right side of the Illegitimacy
Bill in refusing so firmly to allow a child born in adultery to be
made legitimate later. But I must add something more about
the alleged negation of the Christian rules.

I have been much influenced, indeed swept away, by the
writing of Dr. Kung, the young German theologian.

I had the pleasure of giving lunch to him. He hardly looks his thirty-four years, in some ways reminds me physically of T. E. Lawrence, in a layman's collar and tie, a modest definite personality, hardly less striking than his books. It is, I suppose, his teaching about the need for a new Catholic approach to the other Churches that has carried his name to the ends of the earth. 'If our Church,' said Dr. Kung, 'had been in a better state the Protestants would not have separated themselves from us. It is true the Church is not of this world but she is in this sinful world and this sinful world is in the Church. Catholic reform being renewal is not just a restoration of a former condition but a creative reform of the state of the Church.' His impact has coincided by a master stroke of providence with the brief but cataclysmic reign of Pope John XXIII. But there are other lessons at least as universal to be found in Kung and ones irrespective of the relations between Churches.

He writes, for instance, of a theory of 'mutual encounter' in which rules and obligations are to be subordinated to the law of love. Even before I had read Kung I had stumbled, in Duckett's Bookshop, on *The Primacy of Charity in Moral Theology*, which I sought to digest during a youthful house party of Thomas's at Tullynally. (I am just getting used to that name.) The message can be briefly stated, though capable of endless elaboration. 'Too many textbooks,' says Father Gilleman, s.j., 'keep harping with casuistic bias on minimum obligation and sin. Current textbooks are concerned with strict obligations so that a formulation of natural morality can appear quite sufficient to them. But the supernatural value of moral life comes from its impregnation with charity. Charity is the form of (all) virtues.' There is here no hint of a general revisionism, no suggestion that the rules of sexual morality, for instance, might be relaxed as coming into conflict with charity. What is here preached is a higher, more arduous, morality than that which any of us are accustomed either to preach or to practise. A prospect is opened philosophically to the thoughtful, as it was laid bare by Pope John XXIII for the feeling millions, in which the Christian social creed becomes positive and active. Fraternal love and service and the so-called negative restrictions are seen to be inherent in a communal assent to God.

I had groped after this idea at the end of a debate in the Lords on birth regulation. 'The family ideal must be based on love in the first place and in the second place the conception that there are certain limits beyond which one cannot pass without committing sin. The further we travel along the paths of self-control and sacrifice, the more rapidly we shall learn what it really means to love.' Quintin Hailsham put it, as often, better than any of us. He mentioned 'the instinct which had kept the human race going for 500,000 years', and concluded, 'Nobody can come to peace with himself, and no society can come to peace with itself, until it comes to live with that instinct in terms of self control and of the unusual and peculiar state of mind we call purity.'

During recent years one Lords debate stands out in my memory beyond all others. That on Christian Unity in May 1961. It was entirely initiated by Boofy Arran, who sometimes plays the fool outrageously but has a sharp eager mind, a compelling manner of speech, and a deep underlying seriousness. He was pressing for such a debate when Lord Fisher, then Archbishop of Canterbury, paid his history-making visit to Rome. And surely that was the single act most beneficial to the human race which any individual has taken since the war. To avoid a spirit of holy emulation I except the Pope's original summons of the Vatican Council. It would be less than honest for me to claim that I had expected Archbishop Fisher to take the initiative. I knew that his courage and self-confidence were exceptional. But I hope I may be forgiven for thinking, like many Catholics, that he was one without much love for our Communion. This made us sad, because we all had much respect for him and I admired him for special reasons.

On one occasion he and I were arguing about interdenominational relations in the passage of the House of Lords. He was complaining that the Catholic hierarchy had failed to respond to overtures soon after the war. I thought he had gone too far, and drawing myself up, metaphorically, I said I asked to be excused and rather pompously withdrew. Later I realized that my showing had not been either civil or Christian, particularly in view of our relative positions. I was wondering how to begin a letter of apology when a note arrived from the Archbishop. (I cannot lay my hands on it, but I am sure this is its essence).

[207]

'Please forgive me for being so argumentative this morning. I thought you in the wrong until I remembered that this was the third quarrel I'd had today. I realized that I must have got out of bed the wrong side.' What can you say about an Archbishop of Canterbury who can write at once like that to a slightly impertinent Catholic peer except that it is the true Christian conscience at work? At any rate the memorable visit to the Pope was made. The debate drew near and I prepared, as did Harry Iddesleigh and Peter Lothian, what should be said from the Catholic standpoint.

It became understood that all the speeches, with one exception, would applaud the Archbishop's initiative and speak in favour of at least some form of unity. But the opposition was a mighty one—our leader, Lord Alexander of Hillsborough. It is a simple matter of fact, a very fortunate fact, it seems to me, that the House of Lords these last few years has been led from both Government and Opposition sides by two fervent and articulate Christians in Lord Hailsham and Lord Alexander. Not that other leaders and major figures in the House in recent years have been less firm in their Christianity. But Lord Hailsham, with his academic background of Church history and theology, and Lord Alexander, a lay preacher of native eloquence and vast experience, have commanded both the equipment and the will to create an atmosphere of explicit Christianity which I have found highly congenial.

The bishops have, so to speak, been encouraged, to our great benefit, to spread their wings. Some of the tougher M.P.s from the House of Commons have found it, I'm told, a little hard at first to catch on. It would usually be said, I think not unkindly, that Albert Alexander has strong feelings against the Church of Rome. When I knew him I realized how a devoutly religious man could believe in appalling things about my Church and see her as an enemy to be met and countered at every turn. As President of the Protestant Alliance, he was, and is, well briefed in Catholic peccadillos from Spain to Columbia and reaching far back into history. He seems to labour under the impression that the Vatican and the Kremlin are sufficiently in league to constitute a joint danger.

This being so, and in no way anxious to cause pain to any-

one, he was opposed to the whole idea of a debate in which he
would be compelled to express his convictions. He had led
a deputation of Protestants to the Archbishop of Canterbury
before the latter's visit to Rome and had gained the idea that it
was to be only a courtesy visit. Now to be told it was being
accepted on all sides as changing the course of history! Albert
was, in fact, in a very difficult position. He must speak out in
sharp criticism more of the Archbishop than of my Church.
He owed that to his conscience and to his official leadership
of the Protestant Alliance. But he was too good a leader of
the Opposition to do it from the front bench. When the day
came he repaired to the third bench beneath the gangway
and I followed.

The debate contained its fill of drama. As Albert attacked the
Archbishop's leadership of the Church of England, the latter
rose twelve times to interrupt. At one critical moment the
Archbishop might have defeated a lesser combatant. When
pressed, in effect, to say if he was a Catholic or Protestant it
came as a surprise to many when he replied, 'I happen to be
both a Catholic and Protestant.' But Albert was not easily
defeated. 'It all depends, does it not, on what you mean by a
Catholic—if you are first a Protestant it should be a Protestant
view of a Catholic, should it not?' No subsequent speaker
agreed with Albert, but there was a venerable grandeur about
his Protestant stand which was fine and moving. I myself
spoke for half an hour with the help of a very successful story
supplied by Tom Corbishley, as always the staunchest of
allies. At the end I was still a friend of Albert's in spite of a
brisk exchange. As we came together later in the debate in our
usual places he muttered, 'Honour among thieves.' It was a
remark worthy of Ernie Bevin. The Archbishop speaking near
the end was unfailingly good. Quintin spoke for a long time,
saying very little, and then suddenly gave us a short peroration
of immense force and spiritual import. I have never felt entitled, except on that one day, to say after a debate that the
virtue had gone out of me. I wonder whether others felt the
same.

Lord Beveridge was brought up without religious beliefs
and was not supposed to have acquired any, but no more

effective Christian speech was made than the one he delivered that afternoon, finishing with what to me, his old henchman, was unbearable pathos. He mentioned that in the Bible Jesus is referred to as 'the Merciful, the Deliverer, and the Bright Morning Star'. 'Let us fix our eyes,' he said, 'on the morning star and with the light of it make a new and happy Christian world, even if it does not admit me to it.' I told him later that at Eton, where there was a great demand for places, the boys who could not be put down for any particular house were put down in the general list. I told him I thought he would be first on the general list for heaven. 'Well,' he said, 'put me down on the general list whether at the top of it or the bottom.'

The Bishop of Leicester was all too generous to me. 'There was a unity,' he said, 'which could be felt and does have expression. I have often myself felt it in this House. . . . I have felt it often when the noble Lord Longford has been speaking.' And he went on to mention Lord Hailsham and Lord Alexander for the same purpose. That compliment coming from such a source I accept with unfailing gratitude. I have often felt that I was getting something from the House, sometimes that I was amusing, or holding the House, hardly ever that I was *giving* to it in any remotely creative sense, though I have often been aware that others have been doing so.

But that afternoon I felt that my years of service, such as they were, to the House, the Labour Party, and the Church were fused in a personal giving which was one rather of will than of words.

Out of many causes whose inspiration I would like to describe as Christian in an undenominational sense, I must mention one, that of the mentally handicapped. I hope that the many dedicated people that labour for it without Christian belief will forgive me for this. In summer 1963 I had handed over the Chairmanship of the National Society for the Mentally Handicapped to that friend of all in trouble, Victor Stonham, remaining myself a Vice Chairman.

I had been Chairman for four years since being approached in 1959 by George Lee, their indefatigable secretary. I have helped to found various societies. For example the New Bridge, already mentioned, and the Anglo-German Association, though Fred Bellenger, George Catlin and, above all, dedicated Julian Piggott, have done much more for the latter than I have done. But the National Society for the Mentally Handicapped already had twenty thousand members and over two hundred branches when I joined them. This although we were a post-war growth. The founders were two parents of mentally handicapped children, Mrs. Drown and Mrs. Frydd. We were a kind of irresistible outburst of feeling among parents of the mentally handicapped. We were at the same time a form of solemn protest at the reluctance of society, apart from a small band of doctors and social workers, to know anything about afflicted children. It was a problem which too many people push out of sight. Looking back, I see that I failed to see enough of the children. Not that the task of getting to know them is easy. Unlike the mentally ill or, for that matter, delinquents, they are unable at any stage of their lives to speak for themselves, to tell us what it is like.

The Queen Mother, our Royal Patron, communicates delightfully with anyone she meets. I have never seen anyone take so much trouble to turn an official visit into a series of personal encounters. Even *she* could not converse with our children when she opened the Slough project. But I did make friends with many of their parents and felt that I could understand a small part of their feelings. I presided regularly over the meetings of the National Executive who came together from all over the country. It is work which in the long run I shall be particularly proud to be connected with, if only because it has been so disgracefully neglected for so long.

The mother of a mentally handicapped child wrote a fine book, *Bartje, My Son*, which describes her efforts and his towards a reasonable life for him. 'Every day,' she ends, 'is a step nearer and the whole world is our friend.' It could be so if the problem were better understood but the difficulty lies there. Even when vastly more is done than at present to train the handicapped children for their own good and for that of society, there are values still to learn. The boundless possibilities of love in each individual, quite apart from his social performance, his infinite worth as a human being, can never be grasped more perfectly than at a National Convention of the Mentally Handicapped. One sees a well-dressed handicapped man sitting in his place and suddenly he falls asleep on his mother's shoulder. He wakes up and one sees him give her a beatific smile.

I would like to mention in particular one big rally last summer. Valerie Hobson has worked hard for the Society for years. This was her first public appearance since her crushing blow. I sat beside her while the Press and television cameras concentrated their batteries. She turned and murmured quietly, 'If I smile, they'll say I'm heartless; if I look depressed, they'll say I've lost my courage.' When the time came she was magnificent. The Mayor of New Romney was able to mention that twelve years before he had called his daughter after her. I could pay unaffected tribute to the esteem in which she was held. The agreement of the crowd was heartfelt.

5

The Ante-Rooms of State

I

The Last Year with Hugh

I T WAS the spring of 1962. I had been chairman of the
National Bank for over seven years, though the best, in
the sense of the year just beginning, was yet to be. Success
was beginning to be generally recognized. I already felt that
I could have looked Mr. Cooke in the face. His son Michael
was going strong with us.

As often in my life, and this seems to be true of many people,
the occasion for a big change seems rather artificial and slender
in retrospect. Which means, I suppose, that subconscious
processes had been at work. A Select Committee of Parliament was examining the possibility of peers renouncing their
titles. Those like Tony Wedgwood-Benn, the one hero of
the struggle, who had refused to take their seats in the Lords,
seemed certain to be allowed to opt out. Those like Lord
Home and Lord Hailsham who had taken their hereditary
seats seemed to have a good chance of escape if they wished
to use it. Quintin Hailsham, but not Alec Home, had originally
protested at the fate which drove him to the Lords. The prospects of 'First Creations', that is, of those who had accepted
newly created titles, seemed much more doubtful.

I seemed to be alone with Lord Trefethin and Oaksey, who
presided at Nuremberg, in belonging to both the last two
categories. When my brother died in 1961 I inherited the
Irish earldom of Longford, and also the English barony of

Silchester. The latter gave a seat in the House of Lords. My brother inherited from my father, killed at Gallipoli, when he was a minor, and could have taken his seat on coming of age in 1923. In fact, as has been seen, he never took it, dedicating himself to Ireland, and hardly ever coming to England. When I inherited his titles one of the attendants at the House of Lords told me that he had moved my hat and coat to my brother's peg. I expressed surprise that a peg had been kept for him all these years, as he had never taken his seat at any time. 'He never applied for leave of absence,' I was told firmly and a shade reprovingly. Later I investigated pegs unused. They were and are 'crowned', so to speak, by that of the Duke of Windsor. That, however, by the way.

On the strength of my brother's title of Silchester, Longford was irrelevant. I would fall into the Home-Hailsham category with a strong chance of liberation, but by accepting the title of Pakenham of Cowley (1945) at the time I became a Labour Lord-in-Waiting, I had put myself in the category of 'First Creations', and might have tied my hands or feet irrevocably. Which has since proved to be the case.

The speculation and discussion in Press and Parliament, though no one seemed aware of my possible interest, set me thinking. If the chance came of standing for the House of Commons would I wish to take advantage of it? It was something I had never contemplated: an unforeseen and unforeseeable factor in my plan of life. But as soon as I gave my mind to it the attractions mounted. Elizabeth had always reproached herself, though it was no possible fault of hers, for agreeing to my acceptance of a peerage. She often said, I am sure truly, that she would not conceivably have agreed if I had not already been booked for the Lords as the heir to a peerage. Now it seemed that if I were still bold and vigorous enough that the error could be wiped out and a new start possibly made.

But what of the bank? and my heavy responsibilities there? Obviously, I could not continue as chairman of a clearing bank and at the same time be an M.P. Worse still, a candidate for Parliament: worst of all, a candidate for a candidature for Parliament. If the chance came my way, and I did decide to opt out of the Lords, and to aim at the Commons, it meant opting out of the bank as well. Of that I never had a moment's doubt.

And would that be fair to the bank? Provided that the right chairman could be found, and the Anglo-Irish requirement made the field a small one, I believed that the bank would actually benefit. Seven years is a long time, usually an excessive time, to preside over anything. I had the feeling that if I stayed much longer at the bank I should have shot my bolt. I felt that my most valuable contribution (and I did not rate it too modestly) had been made already. It was not a question of the heart—my personal attachment to colleagues and staff grew ever stronger with the years—but the bank no longer absorbed as large a part of my thought as earlier. I had myself appointed eleven out of the thirteen directors, including all those in Ireland. We were going forward on well-articulated lines, with every sign of progess. If not exactly in a groove, I was not far off one. There was a lot to be said for a new and vigorous mind in place of me.

About this time I discovered that Ivone Kirkpatrick, a member of the board since 1960, would be available for the chairmanship. It seemed providential. From that moment I felt sure that the bank could not possibly lose by my departure. Once again we had been remembered by our guardian angel.

But what would Hugh say about this idea of opting for the Commons? Clearly no step of that sort could be taken without his advice and consent. On a material plane, the hope of a seat in the House of Commons, let alone a further prospect, would be complete foolishness if he were strongly opposed. But in a purer sense I was eager and willing to fit in with his ideas of how I could be most useful.

Yet I approached the interview in doubt and worry. This, though it was not long since he had referred to me at a large party as 'his oldest friend'; this, though that very day, when I was to see him, I had been given lunch alone by Dora Gaitskell at their house in Frognal Gardens. I was advising her on penal reform, into which she was preparing to throw herself. A long retracing of steps is necessary to understand my contradictions of mood. Hugh Gaitskell was a highly promising member of his generation in the thirties and war period, but

as late as 1945 it would not have occurred as in any way likely
that he would surpass us all and emerge as a world figure while
still in his middle fifties. Evan Durbin, a devoted but discerning
friend, told me of the marked success of his maiden speech,
and the Parliamentary promise exhibited. I was pleased, but
did not guess what was coming. Hugh never had a friend who
meant as much to him as Evan; and Evan cared for him equally
and understood him better than any of us. Hugh could say of
him what Morley said of Chamberlain, 'We lived the life of
brothers.' And so could I. Douglas Jay, very close to Hugh, and
to all concerned in the Treasury, tells me that Hugh demonstrated his clear superiority to any other possible Chancellor
during the devaluation crisis and Stafford Cripps's illness in
1949–50. I knew he was doing well, but quite how well I
did not realize.

In a worldly sense he shot right ahead of all his contemporaries, and almost all his Socialist seniors, when he became
Chancellor of the Exchequer late in 1950, at the age of forty-
four. He then resolved afresh, as I know well, that no eminence, however great, no responsibilities, however arduous,
should impair or attenuate his personal friendships in the
slightest degree. And this he kept to, unswervingly, to the day
of his death, and none of his friends ever questioned his intense
fidelity in private friendship, which equalled (nothing could
surpass) Evan Durbin's own.

This perfect achievement does not in itself contradict
Lloyd George's famous saying, 'There's no friendship at the
top'. Hugh Gaitskell's friends were not quite at the top,
though some were close to it. Yet if some of them had become
his real top-level colleagues later on he would have found a
way to disprove the absolute veracity of the Lloyd George
dictum.

But there is an inevitable snag, too little studied, in the
friendship of leaders. Complete friendship involves complete
equality, but a leader cannot be equal with his followers or
'colleagues', and in one particular way he is specially cut off
from them. He more than anyone else alive is in a position
to influence their fortunes, and they and their wives would not
be human if those fortunes were not their active concern. The

friends of the leader may be the most altruistic of men, yet it would be so much easier to plan their lives effectively, and maximize their contribution, if only they knew what he thought about them, and intended for them. Yet the burning topic cannot be discussed.

And the more high-minded the leaders, the more anxious he be to say no word to cause discouragement, nor yet to encourage unduly, the more rigid at one point the barrier, and at certain moments—recurring perhaps only at long intervals—the more acute the tension.

I remember most if not all of the occasions when Hugh discussed my future with Elizabeth or myself, either on his initiative or mine. At the time of the Prestwick crash, and the cry 'Pakenham must go', he rang up Elizabeth in my absence to beg her to persuade me on no account to resign. In 1951, when he understood from Clem Attlee, the Prime Minister, that I was doubtful about becoming First Lord of the Admiralty, he promptly gave me lunch, and urged me to accept the offer. He knew that I thought I was out of favour because of my pro-German views. He stressed the brightness of my future, in the Lords and elsewhere, if only I did not turn down this chance. Later that year he flattered and embarrassed me by asking me to undertake an important assignment in the field of Western Defence, remaining, of course, First Lord. I explained that I was not well enough at the time, which surprised him, and did not I think convince him. He never alluded to the matter afterwards.

In summer 1954, as already mentioned, I consulted Clem Attlee about becoming chairman of the National Bank, and was advised to have a word with Hugh. Hugh lunched with me at the House of Lords, and soon made it plain that he was not in favour. He doubted if I would learn much—he cited another bank chairman, who was said to be learning little about what was really intricate in national policy—the working of the exchanges and suchlike. He had hoped (still hoped —this was 1954) that if Labour won next time I would be either leader or deputy leader in the Lords. Apart from the Lord Chancellor, those would probably be the only two peers in the Cabinet. He couldn't see the House of Commons

agreeing to any of the departmental posts going to the Lords.
If I withdrew into banking he couldn't be at all sure what if
anything would come my way in a future Labour Government,
and he was as anxious as in 1949 and 1951 that the most should
be made of me, and that I should make the most of myself.

Nevertheless, if it was necessary for financial reasons (Hugh
always seemed to think of me as better off than I was, or to
underestimate my financial responsibilities) I must, of course,
think of my family. He would speak to Clem Attlee in that
sense. Neither of them in the event restrained me. Clem Attlee,
though certainly not Hugh, seemed to think that it was one
up to Labour, as showing that the Tories were not the only
people who were capable of running a bank.

In the same conversation with Hugh I remember expressing
great confidence in him as likely to be the next leader. 'It
doesn't matter,' he replied, 'whether it's me or one of several
others mentioned' (Frank Soskice among them), 'but what is
important is that it should be someone with our kind of
ideas.'

A year and a half later (late 1955) he was indeed leader of
the Party, and I was writing to express my wish, my rather
helpless wish, that I could do something for *him*. I finished
by saying: 'I hope you do not mind if I tell you that I shall
pray for you constantly.' He replied: 'Of course I shan't mind,
Frank, if you pray for me.' I think he said he would like it.
And he added this: 'I expect I am closer to you in those matters
than you suppose.' Religion had always been and, alas remained, a silent subject between us, but I treasure that last
sentence as truer still by the time of his death.

In the next six years he never hesitated when occasion offered
(as at an Anglo-German Association dinner or a City luncheon)
to demonstrate his esteem and friendship. But only twice did
the delicate topic come up of my political future, and then
more or less unavoidably. Twice fairly early in the day I was
invited to join syndicates that were putting in for Independent
Television contracts. Each time he discouraged me, on the
grounds that I might be prominent in a future Labour Government, which must be free to consider the whole issue afresh.
But though our paths crossed during the 1959 election

campaign, I never gained the faintest indication as to what, if anything, he had in store for me if victory came our way.

Somewhere about that time I gained the impression that I had disappointed him quite a lot by failing to produce an economic report which he had asked me, and another leading Socialist, to undertake. There must have been a genuine mis-understanding all round. The original request was very in-formal. I did not realize that Hugh was taking it seriously. I came to assume that he was already receiving more valuable advice than I could offer from the 'third man' whom he saw as often as he wished in the House of Commons, and to whom he was rightly devoted.

I mention all this at the risk of the impression that I was much more concerned with advancement and much less with friendship than I was. But this background, or lack of it, provided on my side, and perhaps on his, a certain element of shyness in our relationship which may have been entirely my fault, except in the sense that Hugh was undeniably shy.

It is hard to define shyness, but one example of it is sufficient. The only service that I am conscious of rendering him (and he rendered me a number) was at the Labour Party Conference in 1959. He was indeed up against it that day. He made an unsuccessful opening speech. It was immensely thoughtful, but coming too soon after the election defeat he had no chance, as he had at Scarborough the following year, to reply to his many savage critics. On the second morning his friends fought strenuously to catch the speaker's eye. I am proud to have been numbered, along with Charlie Pannell, Denis Healey, and Shirley Williams, among those who helped to turn the tide. When I met Hugh in the hotel afterwards he gave me a look of unspeakable gratitude. But he could find virtually no words. A few weeks later he told Archbishop O'Hara, the Apostolic Delegate, that I had made a brilliant speech in his defence, and reported verbatim the best of my jokes—as it happened, a Catholic one.

In 1960 at conference time I had written articles for the *Guardian* and *Observer* and in 1961 for the *Observer* which discussed his leadership with considerable frankness. He told me at the beginning of the 1960 Conference at Scarborough that he liked the *Guardian* article. I gathered that those in the *Observer* were far from acceptable. In the first *Observer* article in October 1960 I described myself as 'a soft Gaitskellite' with the slogan 'Gaitskell for peace in the Party'. Just after his narrow defeat at the Scarborough Conference this may have seemed weak-kneed support. On the other hand, I was gratified by the approval both of Rita Hinden of *Socialist Commentary*, a firm and candid friend of Hugh's, and of Tony Greenwood, a Christian Socialist, and main champion of the Left. In the long run I felt sure I was helping Hugh, but I doubt if it appeared that way to him. A year later, also in the *Observer*, I was pleading for a closer relationship between him and Frank Cousins. Again, this was not quite the line of his closest friends, or mine. Yet I was sure that basically we meant the same thing. He stood for the highest principles in international affairs, for the older League of Nations brought up to date and developed. And so did I.

An Atlantic Alliance was an indispensable condition of peace. But it was only part of a policy. While national sovereignty remained unqualified there was no way round the torturing dilemma. How could a Labour Government ever opt out of an Atlantic Alliance which must retain the deterrent so long as the Communists possessed it? Yet how could any Christian or ethical humanist press the button of the bomb in any circumstances whatever and produce the unspeakable suffering involved? My own thoughts, following those of Clem Attlee and some of the best theologians, had turned more and more to a World Government equipped with an international peace force not just as the ultimate answer but as one which must be pursued as rapidly as possible. I felt that deep down there was an identity of conviction here between Hugh and myself. He had begun to mention World Government at Scarborough. By the time of his death he was beginning to give a powerful lead in that direction.

It follows from the above that the one topic I would never have raised with Hugh in the ordinary way was my own political future. Yet I had a clear duty, as I knew he would appreciate, to discover his reaction to the idea of my opting for the Commons. He would certainly expect to be informed that this was in my mind, and, of course, a strong attitude on his part might—not certainly but possibly—have no little effect on the final decision of Parliament as to what was to be possible for me.

I was received inevitably in the ghastly Shadow Cabinet chamber, in which the leader of the Opposition is doomed to interview his visitors, be they his oldest friends or his most unwelcome acquaintances. He may have met me at the door —Hugh often did, particularly if he was seeing out a predecessor—and would always have done so if he thought it would reassure a guest. But in any case one had to thread one's way past the long Shadow Cabinet table with the empty chairs, to the desk at the far end. A situation from which all possibility of intimacy had long been banished. One day a leader of the Opposition, if still encumbered with that room, will drop a partition and reserve a private cubbyhole for himself. Till then there is neither the dignity of a reception at Number 10 nor the warmth available in a private office, let alone Hugh's special charm which irradiated his own home. Just a journey across an empty waiting-room, with the station master unexpectedly awaiting to enquire one's business. But Hugh was not at all like a station master. Apart from the anxieties inherent in the problem, he was only frightening because his mind was so completely in order, and most of us on this sort of occasion are just a little bit confused.

When I told him that I thought of opting for the Commons, if allowed to do so, it was obviously quite unexpected. He was not incredulous, upset, or exhilarated. He just hadn't thought of such a contingency. He had understood that I wanted to discuss House of Lords Reform generally, in view of a coming debate. 'But do you mean that you wouldn't mind giving up your title?' he asked me. I told him that I wouldn't mind at all. I honestly think that that surprised and pleased him. He seemed to have thought that it would have seemed a real sacrifice; that that kind of honour mattered to me, perhaps for family reasons. He himself, when my brother died, had written a touching letter, saying that he knew how strong were the family ties in my family, and he was writing as one (and no one was more entitled to do so) to whom they mattered enormously.

He persisted in testing me, 'But Labour may not even win the election.' (At that time the great anti-Tory slide had not got under way.) 'I daresay you could get on to the front bench as a spokesman, but it isn't certain.'

'I know,' I replied, without I hope mock-heroics. 'I daresay it would be best to start on the back benches for the first year.'

His mind began to work on the problem, and before I left he seemed to be favouring the adventure.

'You know,' he said, 'I have been looking to you to shoulder heavier responsibilities in the Lords. You know *that*,' he said with emphasis.

I was grateful, but a shade mystified. Was this a reference to the luncheon conversation of 1954, or to the telephone conversations long before the 1959 election, about not joining an ITV syndicate?

'However,' he went on, 'the problem will be less acute now that we are so much stronger in the Lords.'

I muttered something noncommittal, and ventured to mention one or two possibilities in the Commons.

His mouth closed abruptly, and with extreme firmness. 'You won't expect me,' he said, 'to comment on that.'

Later I gathered from Dora, as did Elizabeth from Hugh, that he would quite definitely like me in the Commons if it could be managed.

As the year passed he seemed to become increasingly keen, though he remained aware of the difficulties. When Thomas saw him in the London Library in the late summer, preparing for his lectures in Poland, Hugh warned him that I 'wasn't free yet'. When we had dinner with him and Dora in December a few days before he went to hospital for the first time (and after the Select Committee on House of Lords Reform had reported) he still didn't see why we shouldn't pull it off by an amendment to the Bill, or otherwise.

But whether I was liberated or not soon ceased after that first interview to matter all that much to me. The great thing, the new thing, that year was that Hugh had once again begun to treat me not only as someone whom he could trust but as someone who could help. Not just an old friend—there were other old friends: Maurice Bowra, John Betjeman, John Sparrow; and newer ones like Isaiah and Aline Berlin—for whom his affection was profound, and whom he loved being with, but one who was right in the middle of the political battle. And me, not just an old reliable, whose support was welcome, but who was not really 'with it' in the one sense that counted politically for him.

Two great friends of his and mine left the Labour Party in these years: Hartley Shawcross and Aidan Crawley. These were serious blows. Both if all had gone well would have held high office in a Labour administration. Hartley has that indefinable quality of national standing which would have been of special value to a Party so long out of office. Aidan had been one of my closest friends since Oxford days when I had followed him, anxiously pursuing, out hunting and admired his centuries in the Parks. When he went Labour I had helped him secure a constituency in 1938 and in his last election we had spoken together at his eve-of-the-poll meeting in Buckingham, I on religion and politics, he on greater sacrifices and greater production. He lost by fifty-four votes. A more seductive appeal might have pulled him through. He remains a perfectionist, unlikely, I think, to be satisfied by any Party. Virginia remains perfection.

When one leaves a political Party, as I know from personal experience, one's friends are anxious to discover any reason but the right one for the apparent desertion. If anyone asks how much influence Virginia exerted on Aidan's departure from the Labour Party I would suggest that it was as great or as little as Elizabeth exercised on my departure from the Conservative Party. To understand all is to forgive all. Hugh, a much more integrated character than I am, found it harder to understand than I did. Perhaps I could compensate a little for what Hugh had lost in Hartley and Aidan.

Somehow, unknowingly, I had dropped out when I went into banking—or was it still earlier, and more fundamental, when I went into the House of Lords? For that institution Hugh had remarkably little sympathy, even for a Labour leader. I suppose he might have come there one day himself, in extreme old age; but somehow I can never imagine it. Now I had the sense of being back in the team, and just in time for the championship.

It was not long after the interview recorded that I was asked to see Hugh again. He started diffidently, as always, on the rare occasions when he was asking a favour. No doubt, he said, I knew of the violent and well-justified hostility of the L.C.C. and many other enlightened organizations and individuals to the Government's plans for the so-called reorganization of London. A powerful movement was taking shape to found a non-Party organization to wage a prolonged campaign against the proposed calamity. Those most concerned were very anxious that I should lead the struggle as chairman of the new body. He did so much hope that I would agree. Was I willing?

I asked for a day or two to consider it; to make sure beyond all doubt that I was whole-heartedly in sympathy with the resistance. But I had little doubt that I would accept. I told him candidly that this invitation from him meant far more to me than he would suppose. I reflected, though I did not say, that this was the first time he had asked me to do anything for him or the Party, unless I were to count the episode of the 1951 mission and the abortive economic enquiry. I was overjoyed, then and there, but still more so when I studied the London case against the Government, and realized that it was one after my own heart, and one ideally suited to me. No one could accuse me of having a vested interest in the L.C.C., but I had plenty of experience of local government in Oxford and the social services as a whole. All this Hugh had carefully thought out, but, as was his way in personal matters, he said very little about it.

After Hugh died, and after I had come to achieve new friendships with the L.C.C. leaders, Peggy Jay was talking to one of the most prominent at a dinner at which I spoke. 'We are so lucky,' he said, 'to have got Lord Longford. Hugh pressed him on us so strongly that we agreed. We were rather doubtful at the time, but he has turned out trumps.' This anecdote is not without its significance as a revelation of Hugh's altruism and modesty, of the strength and limitation involved. Hugh couldn't bear to appear to be conferring a favour, and the more intimate the friend, the less likely he was to receive a compliment to his face, except of a routine kind. He probably thought, though this is not the whole explanation, that a real friend didn't need compliments; but I am afraid most of us are of weaker stuff, and if ever Hugh brought himself to pay one we treasured it as from no other source.

2

Mr. Valiant for Truth

WHEN Hugh died I wrote a full-length article in the *Observer*, and never mentioned the Common Market. The omission was not deliberate, nor yet an oversight. It aroused, as far as I am aware, no comments, though the article brought many. Against the whole background of his life and character, the Common Market barely figured. And in any case, by the time of his death, the British chance of admission was beginning to fade.

Yet his own anxieties on the subject had remained acute. Between his first and final visits to the hospital, and when already very ill, he had written about Christmas time a very long letter to President Kennedy seeking to clarify his position. I know nothing of this letter's reception. The President's statement when Hugh died was a remarkable and unqualified tribute.

And it was not long since Hugh Gaitskell and the Common Market had been on everyone's lips together. It was only three months earlier that Hugh had delivered at Brighton a speech about the Common Market which may well rank with Ernest Bevin's tremendous championship of collective security and Hugh's 'Fight and Fight Again' at Scarborough as the most powerful oration ever delivered at a Party conference.

Furthermore, Hugh's Brighton speech was unique in my recollection for a peculiar reason—the distribution of its appeal. It had a colossal overall emotional impact. It took nearly an hour and a half to deliver, and the interest increased rather than diminished throughout. The ovation at the end may have been paralled at a conference, but, outside Russia, it can seldom, if ever, have been surpassed.

Yet the applause, curiously enough, was most delirious from those who for years had been Hugh's principal opponents, and most half-hearted from a number of his devout supporters. I met Michael Foot an hour or two later, and, stupidly forgetting that he had been excluded for the time from the Parliamentary Party, I asked him whether he was going to speak at the Conference. 'Oh no,' replied Michael, 'no one who really agrees with the leader is allowed into the Conference nowadays.' Michael's probity was as unchallenged as Hugh's. His hostility was devoid of all malice, but I had always regarded him as irreconcilable, as standing for a Socialism different from Hugh's, not in degree but in kind. On the other hand, I had never seen any reason why Frank Cousins and Hugh should not hit it off. Frank's background was, of course, totally different from Hugh's, his thought processes might at times bewilder Hugh, or me for that matter. But not only was he a powerful personality, whom it was prudent to get on with, his mind was large and active, one-sided on occasion, but capable of generosity, passionately absorbed in real issues. I take Africa as an example of one of these.

Nance Cousins had said to me a year earlier: 'I could love Dora if she'd let me. She is so warm.' I had argued in the *Observer* for a *rapprochement* when the chances seemed not too good. Yet at the Conference I am describing now, 1962, Frank Cousins rose after Hugh's speech and offered, on behalf of his union, to pay for its publication. Before the year ended he told me he and Nance had been to dinner with Hugh and Dora alone and had been very happy. We reminded each other that it was I who had suggested their coming together and I was the one out of it now.

Hugh's speech horrified the majority of his most militant adherents, in some cases almost to tears. This would be hard to demonstrate statistically. At least two-thirds of the Parliamentary Party had been his convinced supporters for several years and of these no more than fifty, or less than a third, could be described as 'Europeans' or 'Common Marketeers'. But these fifty or so were in most cases not only passionate Europeans but also passionate Gaitskellites. They included inside and outside Parliament the young men who had fought his battle with special zeal in the defence controversy. They were led by Roy Jenkins, who was probably closer to Hugh in this period than any other Member of Parliament in the way that a statesman sometimes finds his most intimate confidant in a member of the younger generation. Gladstone's friendship with Morley will not, I hope, seem too pretentious a comparison.

Born of mining stock, Roy is free of the inhibitions which are apt to assail some of us Socialist intellectuals in coping with a working-class movement. His firmness of character belies a gentle, languid exterior, and, on his record, seems likely to exceed anything that John Morley exhibited in action. He is ideally equipped to write the official biography of Hugh. There is no reason why he should not equal Morley as a political, if not a literary, biographer.

Hugh's feeling for Roy was equalled by that for Tony Crosland, the one perhaps his political, the other his sociological, adviser. When he died he appointed these two as his literary executors. Tony Crosland, whose rare brilliance was matched by a formidable astringency, was a strong European, though other causes seemed to him more urgent. Neither he nor Roy hesitated to 'stand up' to Hugh, though Tony did so more brusquely. To differ from them caused Hugh undoubted pain. But nothing could alter his affection.

It is true that Douglas Jay was strongly 'anti-Market'. Douglas was the oldest of all Hugh's comrades in arms. He had been at Winchester and New College with Hugh. But he did not get to know Hugh well till the early thirties, attracted by an article Hugh had written on social credit—of all extraordinary bonds. An old don, like the present writer, will extend the word brilliant to Douglas Jay and to Tony Crosland as to few others in the House of Commons. Douglas's 'loyalty' to Hugh could be described as calmly fanatical. I have never heard him suggest a defect or error on Hugh's part, however slight.

But his own brain works powerfully and independently, as shown in his *Socialism in the New Society*. It stands with Tony Crosland's *The Future of Socialism* as the most important expression of Socialist thought since the war. But Tony, belonging to a later generation, had the advantage of making a fresh start.

A reputation for practical jokes clung to Douglas in his youth, but no one today can doubt his complete seriousness. In all I say on economics I owe much to his speeches in the House of Commons. After the 1959 election he wrote an article in *Forward* which became all too famous but has since been well lived down. He outlined its contents to me while I was waiting to receive the guests at a dinner party and my mind was elsewhere. I am never quite sure whether I must share the responsibility. Peggy Jay has done splendid work for the education and care of children in London. Patrick Gordon-Walker and Denis Healey, brave and expert, were also against the Market.

I have mentioned the Gaitskellite M.P.s. Bill Rodgers, chairman of the Campaign for Democratic Socialism, most active and effective of all his younger zealots, remained seated when the whole hall rose to him at the finish. The right-wing Trades Union leaders—the majority that is, of the T.U.C.—made no secret of their unhappiness. I spoke for many devoted friends and admirers of Hugh when I wrote a few days later in an article blazoned across the front page of the *Sunday Pictorial*: 'Never had Hugh Gaitskell risen to such oratorical heights. But for many of us who listened it was a heart-breaking experience.'

What had he *said* that created such a pulverizing sensation? At the Conservative Conference a few weeks later Mr. Heath was asked on television whether Mr. Gaitskell's opposition to the Common Market was likely to make his task harder. 'I am not aware,' he replied prudently, 'that Mr. Gaitskell has definitely opposed it. It seems to have been the manner of his delivery that created that impression.' And no doubt there was an element of truth in that.

Hugh had said in his speech that on certain terms he was ready to lead the Party into Europe, but it seemed plain to his audience—plainer perhaps than he intended—that he neither expected those terms to be obtained, nor in his heart wanted them to be obtained. In the House of Lords Lord Attlee had taken a solitary stand in saying bluntly that he didn't want to go into Europe on any terms. Hugh didn't say that at Brighton, but he left an overpowering impression that emotionally his attitude towards the Common Market was the same as Clem Attlee's.

Two days after the mighty speech the Conference was breaking up and I was having lunch with Hugh and Dora Gaitskell in the almost deserted dining-room of the Grand Hotel. They had asked me to join them at lunch as we met in the foyer, and also Randolph Churchill, who was with me. Conversation was a little strained, in spite of Dora's unfailing warmth. I somehow came to say that at the official reception during the recent Commonwealth Premiers' Conference I had found myself standing by Harold Macmillan, and remarked politely, 'I hope you're going to get us into Europe, Prime Minister.' (He had been hammered all day by the Premiers.)

'A good Party line,' put in Randolph, ironically and gleefully, thoroughly enjoying himself.

'Exactly,' said Dora quickly and tactfully, 'on the right terms. That is the Party line.'

Hugh smiled faintly. Such terms as had been published at the beginning of August had convinced him that no acceptable terms were remotely possible. And the final turn-down by de Gaulle—not perhaps the actual outcome he thought most likely—must be held to endorse his conviction that nothing could emerge which the British and the French governments could both accept.

It is a historical curiosity that his real sentiment was so long misunderstood. For there was never a more candid politician. I have heard Hugh more than once distinguish briefly the rival spheres of reason and emotion in politics, but he was seldom interested in carrying that kind of abstract discussion very far. I was never fortunate enough to hear him develop the argument.

When we were at New College he and I were tutored in

economics by a Scot called Harold Salvesen, since then for
many years a whaling magnate of world position. His per-
ceptions went deep rather than wide, but his judgements were
then, and have remained, original and piercing. When Hugh
died he wrote to me: 'It was always obvious that he had first-
rate ability, but I was afraid that his heart might rule his
head. That was his only danger.'

Hugh was Elizabeth's great friend at Oxford before, at my
last Commem, he brought her into my life. He used a never-
forgotten phrase to her more than once: 'Don't let's dramatize
the situation.' (Strange how much drama came to him later;
or did he come to it?) Certainly he referred to himself on occasion in later years as 'a rationalist', but not meaning in that
context an agnostic, but a man who tries to reach conclusions
by the light of reason. On the other hand, the famous reference
to a 'desiccated calculating machine', widely thought to apply
to Hugh, was rightly regarded as very unfair, and would today
seem fantastic.

Many still recall how he broke down and wept at a miners'
gala. The strength of his family life and personal friendships
were recognized by all, the latter sometimes exciting rather
stupid criticism. As his powerful platform technique developed,
as he learnt to let himself go in front of large crowds, matching
and stimulating their emotion with his own, he even began to
be accused of demagogy. If there was any contradiction here
it was one over which he exercised a conscious vigilance.

The day before his great speech at Brighton he was entertained at tea by Socialist Commentary, a group which revered
him much, and to which he owed not a little in the last few
years. They and their friends were overwhelmingly pro-
Common Market, and Hugh had already said enough in recent
weeks to reveal an attitude very different from theirs, though his
full vehemence was yet to be disclosed, and was far from anticipated. Nothing could have been more graceful, and at the same
time more pointed, than Rita Hinden's admonition from the
chair, 'We hope and believe, Hugh, that our ways need not
diverge for long.' Hugh was fully equal to the delicate situation. The difference, if there was one, lay in the sphere of
means, and not of ends. It was always quite wrong to become

emotional about means. They must be selected in the light of cold reason. There was certainly no danger of a dispute about means disturbing the friendship and mutual esteem such as existed between himself and the members of Socialist Commentary. It was beautifully done, all the more so because everyone present, and the Press of the world, were vastly more interested in what he was going to say next day, and of that, without the slightest discourtesy, he gave no foretaste at all.

As we all trooped out, I thought I must say something to Hugh about my own attitude, though I supposed he knew it. 'I am afraid I agree with Roy about all this,' I said, a little meanly perhaps, but it was the shortest way of saying it, and it kept the disagreement, so to speak, between friends.

'I know you do,' he replied.

I said something mild about the issue being enormously complicated.

He agreed, repeated what he had just said at the tea: 'It's a dispute about means. There is no need for emotional differences, luckily.'

We both had in mind the terrific defence battle. There, he would have said, was a difference about ends. Violent emotional differences were there presumably inevitable. They had certainly emerged and continued. As we parted I expected that the next day would be painful. Just how painful I did not guess.

Hugh went home to write his speech after an evening meeting, fell asleep over it, woke up after a few hours, and wrote the rest of it before breakfast. Possibly more time would have led to some adjustment of balance, but I am doubtful. The speech when it came expressed his real feelings, and developed his argument in a manner that, given his attitude, could hardly have been improved on. It was superbly powerful in a double sense, as an intellectual piece of advocacy, and in the emotional force with which every economic and political argument was presented.

After he had been expounding the economic arguments against going into Europe for, say, fifteen minutes, Chris Mayhew, one of Hugh's best friends of the next generation to ours, and someone generally in agreement with him on the Common Market, turned to me and said, 'Now we shall have fifteen minutes of the arguments in favour.' But those arguments were omitted, or, if mentioned, were glossed over so rapidly as to pass without notice. Michael Stewart, sitting next to me, had said beforehand that his view on the Common Market was about the same as Hugh's. Like Chris, he was an excellent speaker and judge of speeches. He was apparently making notes for some other address when Hugh rose. Keeping one ear open, he proceeded with his note-making unruffled and detached. At the end he joined politely and perfunctorily in the applause. I asked him what he thought about the speech and he replied, in his usual kindly, tolerant fashion, 'I thought he rather overstated the cast.'

George Thomas, M.P., pacifist, friend to all the world, but no friend to the Common Market, was sitting just in front of me. As Hugh proceeded, his generous nature was carried away. His delight knew no bounds. When Hugh referred to Canadian sacrifices at Vimy Ridge in the First World War, George was kept in his seat with difficulty.

'But, George,' we protested, 'you're a pacifist. You can't applaud these war heroics.'

'I don't care,' said George, applauding louder than ever. 'I'm enjoying it so much and I'm jolly well going to show it.'

The overwhelming success of the speech stemmed partly from the acceptability of the views, partly from profound admiration for the man, partly from the sheer virtuosity of the performance. There were those who didn't like the views, particularly, of course, the pro-Marketeers, but they particularly revered the man. Some of the Left Wing were qualified, to say the least, in their regard for Hugh and his leadership, but these latest views were enormously to their taste. All were at one in recognizing and responding to the oratorical triumph.

The voice and delivery were splendidly appropriate. The argument was brilliantly worked out, with never a word wasted, for all the last-minute throwing together of the speech. The phrasing was always adequate, though not remarkable, taken sentence by sentence. As John Harris, his intimate adjutant, pointed out to me, 'It's the architecture of Hugh's speeches which is the strongest point of all.' When Hugh cried out that he was sick and tired of hearing the Common Market arguments overstated he lifted the roof off. There was nothing striking in the phrase, but the way he led up to it, 'the art that concealed art', was superb.

For me the supreme quality—one, incidentally, pointed out by Chris Mayhew—was the passion with which, throughout an hour and a half of close reasoning, he clothed each individual argument. Each one seemed, in a sense, to emerge from his deepest being. All the limitless concern of a great university don for the truth; and of a great social reformer for human betterment; and indeed of a great Englishman for his country, seemed to be fused in him that day. After he died Marjorie Durbin told me he used to make her weep with sympathy thirty-five years earlier when as a young don at University College, London, he used to describe the sufferings of the working class during the Industrial Revolution. For most of the intervening years his latent genius of human communication had been half suppressed in all the admirable Parliamentary and platform performances. Since Scarborough, or perhaps a little earlier, it had begun to raise its head. And here it was revealed as a primitive force, which even its possessor had hardly come to terms with yet.

Eventually it was over, and so was most of the morning. The Europeans were speechless with anger and resentment. They had known that he differed from them before, but they had never felt till now how much he was emotionally against it. They had hoped in any case that he would show some respect for their point of view. They felt that he had in fact shown none; and if this sounds a little hysterical, the almost incredulous glee of their old antagonists of the Left, including those on the platform, was there to justify their stand-point. Harry Waltston, the ideal companion for this kind of occasion, was grim. Tony Howard counselled prudence.

One Trades Union M.P., who had championed Hugh when he needed champions most, spoke to me bluntly: 'There's a time when a boxer's had so much punishment he can't take any more. Hugh's a grand fellow, but he's fought this conference once. It's more than flesh and blood could manage to take them on a second time.' And the idea, quite erroneous, was being widely circulated that he had judged it politic to conciliate the Left of the Party against his real convictions.

My own role was humiliating enough. All afternoon I strove unsuccessfully, like many M.P.s, including Patrick Gordon Walker, to catch the chairman's eye. As I left the hall, madly frustrated, Ellis Birk, high in the councils of the *Daily Mirror* Group, approached me. 'Hugh Cudlipp saw you failing to get in. Would you like to do an article for the *Pictorial* on Sunday?' After a moment's hesitation—was it disloyal to Hugh?—I said I would try.

Some of my best friends, to adapt the notorious phrase, are journalists, even editors. Apart from others mentioned here, Maurice Green, Oliver Woods; in the younger generation, Kenneth Rose, Paul Johnson. More recently, William Haley, Godfrey Winn, Lena Jeger, for example, are among them. My relations with the *Mirror* Group were good. Cecil King, ruthless, honest, hard to please, shy in the extreme, had seemed to like me. I liked him and his gay idealistic wife Ruth. I liked him most of all when taking a long walk with Cecil and Malcolm Muggeridge in the country. Malcolm was under the mistaken impression that Cecil was fond of walking. This apparently belonged to some earlier phase in Aberdeen, but Cecil's good nature shone through. He is a very tall and very large man, dwarfing a six-foot person like myself. By the time that he and Malcolm had reviewed the whole future of the profession of journalism without undue optimism we had covered many miles and he warned us that we might have to carry him the last part of the way. It was reassuring to learn that his weight had recently come down from twenty to sixteen stone.

Hugh Cudlipp is an elemental force of nature, a man perpetually on fire on behalf of various causes. His background and approach to life are widely different from mine, yet our Socialist impulse seems to be curiously similar. 'We all went down together, we all went down together,' he chanted after a dinner party at our house after the 1959 election, to the slight annoyance of some Socialist leaders. I should like to think that we have all come up together since then.

I had to dash off to a banker's dinner at the Mansion House. Somehow the speaking there seemed tame after Brighton. What would Hugh not have made of Reginald Maudling's chance? Certainly more than a good Chancellor, friendly, relaxed, unconcerned. Then to the bank the next morning. The newspapers hailing Hugh's speech as a biting criticism, for good or for ill, of the whole Common Market project. Then back to Brighton in time for dinner with John Beavan of the *Mirror* Group, and other friends.

At one end of the table Sam Watson, wisest and most inno-cent-looking of the Trades Union leaders, told me of the dead-lock of the Executive Drafting Committee on the Common Market till he suggested that Dick Crossman, declared foe of the Market, should draft the pro-Common Market amend-ments. Dick, he had guilelessly remarked, is our only first-class draftsman, and the result had been that some very good stuff in favour of the Common Market had found its way into the document. At the other end Dick was soon telling me what a fine chap Sam Watson was. 'The joke was,' he said, 'that none of the pro-Common Marketeers on the Committee could draft their own amendments. I had to do it for them.' Blessed are the simple. All the more so if they look simple as well.

Next morning I reported at the Norfolk Hotel, the base of the *Mirror* Group, to work out an article with John Beavan. He gave me more than a little help, above all in striking the right initial note of admiration before criticism which alone could make the article more morally acceptable, or give it much chance of influence. He went off to the Conference leaving me to finish it, and suddenly a great wave of nausea swept over me. Doing the *Pictorial* much less than justice, I felt as though they and I between us were setting out to exploit a precious something in my life which was not only long-standing, but clean and good. I seemed to see the banner headlines: 'Hugh Gaitskell's oldest friend repudiates him.' Could I imagine Hugh doing such a thing in my place? Frankly I couldn't. I rushed after John Beavan to say that this was where I drew the line.

I caught him up in the foyer of the Conference hall and distressfully asked to be released. His demeanour was calm and altogether perfect. He might almost have expected this development. I cannot remember exactly what I said, but somehow I talked myself out under his therapeutic gaze, and soon I was hurrying back to the hotel to complete the article. We had agreed that the least I could do was to finish it before reaching a decision. When it was done I felt better. Hugh might not like it, but he couldn't overlook the affection. John Beavan returned. I agreed to let it go forward and in the sequel was very glad I did so. I made only one stipulation. I must on no account be referred to as 'Hugh Gaitskell's Oldest Friend'. He had described me not so long before in that way himself, to my great pride. But to use his loyal words for his own discomfiture was going too far. One of his oldest friends perhaps—yes, that was a matter of public observation. But 'oldest'—that was between him and me.

It was now lunchtime on this day (Friday). As I entered the Grand (my own hotel) I ran into Hugh and Dora. I muttered something about the marvellous oratory of Hugh's speech— genuine praise in all conscience, but coupled with a remark about my own disagreement. Dora said in the most natural way imaginable: 'Oh yes, I'm sure you do. Most of our friends disagree with us.'

I mentioned my coming article in the *Pictorial*. 'After all,' I said to Hugh, 'you had an hour and a half to let off your feelings. I haven't yet had five minutes. You can imagine I'm bottled up to bursting point.'

Hugh laughed comprehendingly. 'Yes,' he said, 'now I can understand.'

He and Dora both said they felt sure that no article of mine would ever be hurtful. I knew that was true as regards the intention, but how would the result appear?

We went into lunch with Randolph Churchill. As mentioned earlier, I described my recent meeting with Harold Macmillan at the Commonwealth Premiers' soirée. I went on to tell them that the Prime Minister had thrown up his hands dramatically and cried, 'We must play it high; we must play it high!' Some discussion followed about (i) the gambling and (ii) the histrionic propensities of various Prime Ministers. Randolph was particularly at home on this level, clearly counting Hugh for this purpose as a certain member-to-be of the Number 10 fraternity. I was happy to find Hugh and Dora so determined that Common Market differences should have no effect on old friendships, and so anxious to take positive steps to that end.

The article appeared on Sunday. There was the odd compliment, but otherwise silence reigned. A few days later Elizabeth and I were asked to dinner by Desmond Hirshfield, financial adviser to the T.U.C., and a driving force behind the Trades Union Unit Trust of which I am chairman. Bill Carron, President of the A.E.U., was coming. Suddenly things began to take a new turn. Hugh Gaitskell was coming. I never quite understood how this arose, but he knew that Bill Carron and I would be at the party. It might be assumed that it was Bill Carron (probably his most influential single supporter, and, incidentally, perhaps the most influential Catholic layman in the country) he wanted to see. But he appeared glad to have run into me as well.

As soon as we met two things were clear. Nothing was going to make Hugh alter his line on the Common Market by an iota. But, short of that, he would do everything within his power to remove any pain that his Brighton speech might have caused. We did not discuss the Common Market for the first two hours. It seemed likely to remain a forbidden subject. But Hugh said as soon as we met, 'I think you'll like my next speech better than the last one.' And he took us rapidly into a discussion of what he might say on World Government, on which he hoped to make a big pronouncement in the near future in Paris. He consulted me about possible amendments or additions, treating this as one of my special causes and disconcerting me a little, inadvertently by knowing some aspects of it better than I did. We all settled down to the most carefree of evenings. Somehow or other we got round to the perilous topic. Perhaps Elizabeth raised it. She is always far bolder than I am, and in a trice we were all at Hugh hammer and tongs. As soon as one of us stopped, another would take up the tale on behalf of Europe. Desmond and the rest of us deserve some credit perhaps for letting Hugh feel throughout that he was among warm and admiring friends, but it was he who shone. His demeanour, in its patience and forbearance, was almost saint-like, as we all agreed when he left and subsequently.

One saying of his stands out particularly. 'I suppose that I have been all along more against the Common Market emotionally than I realized.' There was something very modest and at the same time very revealing in that. There was one important factor on the developing situation which he had not taken into account—his own emotions. He implied that he might well have spoken with more emotion against the Common Market than the strict logic of the case warranted. And this, if one recalls his warning against emotion at the Socialist Commentary tea, was something that he surely regretted. This would be so on general grounds, but he seemed to realize now that his emotions might have led him to appear to underestimate the case against his view. He did not actually say, but this too he surely implied, that he had done some of his truest friends less than justice. If he was now trying to make it up it was not just for prudent reasons but because he thought his friends were entitled to a moral gesture from his side. Alice Bacon, a true comrade, whom he had gone from London to visit in Leeds when she was seriously ill, had said to him at Brighton, 'A wonderful speech, Hugh—but somehow I liked the one at Scarborough better.'

'So did I,' he replied to her.

From the way he told this to me I could see that the exchange had meant a lot to him.

No doubt many calculations came in. The T.U.C. were likely to need careful treatment. But for me the evening provided yet one more example of Hugh's astonishing capacity for personal growth. I do not believe that two years earlier he would have found a way to hold out a hand like this to the defeated. For, after all, the *Observer*, for example, was saying at this time that for all the influence Roy Jenkins and his circle could now exercise before the election they might as well join the Liberals. Elizabeth and I came away feeling that he had exhibited a new depth of understanding.

He came to dinner with us a little later and showed in conversation with David Astor that his criticisms of British entry into the Common Market on any likely terms were fierce and unabated. We went to dinner with him a few days before he went into hospital, Cecil and Ruth King being what might be called the principal guests. On that occasion the Common Market was not, in my hearing, discussed. After he died I wrote of that last evening together that 'Elizabeth and I were so happy as we went home that the man of all our generation who was shouldering the heaviest responsibilities, soon perhaps heavier still, was the fittest of us all, physically, psychologically and morally'. I said I found him as vigorous as ever, but encountered a new measure of calm. I wrote those words in haste and under some emotion, but would not wish to unsay them now. He mentioned, it is true, that he had to be careful with his diet that evening as he had picked up something in Paris. Perhaps he was rather quieter and did less talking than usual. But I shall always feel a heartfelt gratitude that on this last occasion our friendship should seem as close as thirty-five years earlier in Isis Street, and that he himself should have attained such a zenith as a human being.

We must await his official biography for a considered estimate of his whole attitude to the Common Market and the part he played in regard to it. I remember a casual saying of his at dinner with Norman St. John Stevas in summer 1961 before the Government decided to make public application for membership. Norman, learned and lucid as usual, pressed him about the Common Market. He half jokingly replied, 'I am probably as much in favour of it as Macmillan.' But too much should not be read into that. He was still trying dispassionately to sum up the economic benefits, and ready to suppose that they might be considerable.

But later he concluded, and said repeatedly during and after his period on the fence, that from the purely economic point of view 'there is nothing in it'. At Brighton he told me that if I read (Professor) James Meade I would find 'that James agreed with him'. When I did read James Meade I realized that Hugh might draw support for his standpoint, but so could others for one precisely opposite. Harking back to the dinner with Desmond Hirshfield, I remember stressing the support for the Common Market of his friends Edwin Plowden and Robert

Hall. He agreed that they were the two best names I could have quoted.

It would have gone horribly against Hugh's grain to oppose a policy on any grounds whatever if the economic benefits were manifest. With one part of his nature he never ceased to be a professional economist. But, once convinced that the economics cancelled out, he became increasingly sceptical about the whole adventure on grounds which were a blend of patriotism, socialism, and native caution. At that point, as a party leader, he was not only entitled but obliged to consider the electoral implications and the unity of his own followers. The more he considered it from that angle, the more he recognized that it would be madness to give the Government anything like a blank cheque. And once the terms of August became known, every instinct told him that his Party would be more advantageously placed on the unfavourable side of the fence. The circumstances of Brighton, the craving of the Party —as of all Parties at their annual conferences—for an act of dramatic defiance of the Party enemy may have led him a little further than he intended. Whether that was so or not, he recognized that the pain he had caused many of his best friends at home and abroad was more serious than he had contemplated. He sought immediately, and with much success, to allay it. He left the Party more united than at any time since 1945-7, poised and prepared for victory, a Moses on the verge of the promised land.

Intrinsically he never saw or felt what some of us would call the European vision. He would recognize that there were serious arguments for a Common Market policy, and he was certainly not against the European countries. On occasion his speeches were magnificently received there, for example among German students. But as a Socialist I don't think that he ever quite understood what all the fuss was about. The whole project seemed to him relatively narrow and limited against the world background.

His belief in the United Nations was revealed at the time of Suez as equalled by few Englishmen and surpassed by none. At times it approached extremism. He did not change his ideals or acquire new ones with any facility. If he had lived I am sure that he would have exercised a world influence, not only because of his pre-eminent gifts but because of his world-wide outlook. It is there, on the world stage, that this supreme Englishman would have made his most lasting contribution. It is there inevitably, though the potential benefits can never be measured, that the greatest loss has occurred.

But having said that, one is bound to ask, 'How can one measure loss?' As time passes, his friends are finding that they miss him more rather than less, and the closer the friendship the more poignant the pain. And his life within his family was something still more intimate. It was indeed sacred to him. He would in any case have been a good man; it needed Dora to make him a great one. She, and Julia and Cressida, provided a background 'for all his battles' of love, security, and peace. And Dora did not only help him to bring out what lay deep within himself, in thought, and feelings, and character. She made her own inestimable addition through her own brilliance of intuition, her indomitable convictions, her warmth and width of human affection, and her power of arousing it in return.

3

From Each According to
His Ability . . .

LORD ATTLEE

MANY of his qualities are part of world history and world knowledge. In spite of his economy of words he seemed a very personal leader and he has remained, with Vi, a personal friend. I have sometimes felt, it may be my imagination, that my father's death at Gallipoli, where Clem served so bravely, was a bond. But to me he was a fascinating combination of a technical political virtuoso and a sensitive, even pernickity, moralist. He demanded efficiency and disliked its opposite, whether speaking in Parliament, in administration, or in the Party. His leadership was inextricably interwoven with the party in sentiment and thought. Sometimes, indeed, he appeared to be taking his politics from others. Yet there was concealed in him another voice which one might call his pre-political voice: the voice which he grew up listening to before he became a Socialist, and which inspired him to become a Socialist. It was interesting that his deepest ethical thoughts brought him closest to Socialists with totally different upbringings. Miners, for example George Hall, Jack Lawson or Arthur Jenkins or a man like Arthur Moyle. In the end he and the Party went forward in mutual confidence, they in the conviction that he would follow his conscience (the extreme case being over the Lynsky Tribunal, perhaps, or some vital issue of defence), he assured that they would trust him to act when his information was so much better than theirs could be.

More than once as a Minister I earned his technical

disapproval, as over Germany or the Prestwick crash in 1949. He might have sacked me if things had got much worse, but only once (that I am aware of) did I encounter his moral disapproval. We were arguing about the possibility that German rearmament might increase the risk of war. I remarked stolidly, 'I think it's inevitable anyway,' meaning German rearmament.

He thought that I meant that war was inevitable. 'Well, I don't,' he flashed back with real indignation and contempt.

I explained the thing away, but for a moment a veil had been lifted and I had caught a glimpse of the colossal responsibility he felt for saving the peace. I realized that in his eyes to despair of saving it was the one unspeakable offence.

VICTOR GOLLANCZ

I leave out of comparison the clergy, my relatives, and my teachers. I can then say that there is no individual in this country who has influenced my thought as much as Victor. And this though my disgreements with him have been, and are, considerable. To celebrate his seventieth birthday a large dinner party of his closest friends and closest admirers was organized by Rupert Hart-Davis. It fell to my lot (as H. A. L. Fisher used to say) to propose his health, a task performed *con amore*. These elaborate eulogies can become painful, but I had no need to exaggerate. 'What,' I asked, 'has Victor got that we haven't got?' I could answer that with, 'A tongue of truer natural eloquence, a heart at once more tender and more bold'. I added that Norman Collins had recently compared Victor's energy with that of an all-in wrestler.

When I opened the newspapers one morning and saw pictures of Sir Oswald Moseley trampled in the mud with the gloating headlines 'Moseley mobbed', I turned at once to Victor. I felt instinctively that Victor would be as horrified as I was and much more effective in expression. The result was a joint letter of protest, drafted by Victor, which appeared next morning at the head of *The Times* correspondence column. The boldness in the case of Victor, a Jew, was much more obvious than mine.

Victor's booklet on the case of Adolf Eichmann and my

small book on *The Idea of Punishment* appeared independently about the same time. Mine was in no way concerned with Eichmann, but there were theoretical issues common to both. The special interest of my book was sometimes said to lie in my having restated the case for the retributive element in punishment. Victor insisted that the whole idea of a compensatory, or retributive, justice is not only false, it is based on the ultimate lie. On the theory of punishment we cannot be said, therefore, to be *ad idem*.

I have followed Victor or worked with him in many connections: in his pre-war crusade against Fascism, in his subsequent exposure of the irrevocable clash between social democracy and Communism, in his campaign for feeding starving Germans and for treating our defeated enemies as fellow human beings. It goes without saying that we have been entirely at one in fighting for the abolition of capital punishment, where he has given the lead again and again.

I was for a time chairman of the somewhat turbulent Defence and Aid Fund to Africa in which Victor strove vociferously for peace. Other members included Violet Bonham-Carter, Gerald Gardiner, Oliver Poole, Dennis Hemingford, John Collins, and Michael Scott. The last-named, whether or not one always agrees with him, is cast in the heroic mould. But I have not followed him, or co-operated with him, in the Campaign for Nuclear Disarmament and the demand for unilateral disarmament forthwith. On the strictly religious side his anthologies are treasuries of noble things, including some of Victor's own disguised as 'Contemporary Hebrew'. But he is somewhat too eclectic, or shall I say broadminded, to be my religious pastor.

What, then, is my reason for such extreme acknowledgements as those made earlier? I owe to him clearly the urge to greater zeal and activity which comes from a long and inspiring friendship with him and Ruth. But what is the further debt in the realm of thought I referred to? Strictly it arises where thought and feeling come together; it springs from the meaning that Victor, alone among laymen, manages to give to the concept of the infinite worth of each individual human person.

This is a phrase often used by me in Christian or Socialist orations, but by him given much more powerful and fruitful content. He has the imagination to conceive of the horrors of a world annihilated by nuclear bombs, but to him this is no greater tragedy than the extinction of a single human life by the judicial murder of hanging. Where, if anywhere, do I detect a limitation? To insinuate that he was not accustomed to bearing responsibility would be absurd. Starting from scratch, he has succeeded greatly in the fierce competition of publishing. But what he has not been granted, more's the pity—and, I suppose, has never sought—is the still wider overall responsibility of a Minister or high official. If that came about he might recognize the element of dilemma which haunts me continually when we try to give political effect to abstract values.

DICK CROSSMAN

Elizabeth received many letters after her book on the Jameson Raid. That from Dick Crossman gave her most pleasure of all. Dick had always taken a special interest in Chamberlain since he discovered him in his pre-war development. Dick was then teaching philosophy, particularly the philosophy of Plato, at New College but he was already more than half absorbed in the modern world. 'Dick Crossman,' said H. A. L. Fisher, warden of New College, 'a fine bustling fellow—tells me that he has just discovered Bismarck.' Fisher spoke ironically but fondly. He was very proud of Dick. To Dick, Joe Chamberlain was among other things the first modern orator because the first master of the short sentence, in contrast with the nineteenth-century classical performers. In this respect Chamberlain was followed by Lloyd George and later by Dick himself. Even while still a young man, in popular lectures on Germany, for instance, he could take possession of large audiences, educated and uneducated. He seized them, as it were, by the throat, arguing them to a standstill, one short dialectical sentence succeeding another with tremendous rhetorical effect. He had been reading Simone de Beauvoir just before Jameson and wrote to Elizabeth:

'Now I have two politicians whom I really admire. It is

the book which had made more argument between myself and Anne more than any other book since Roy's *Dilke*—partly no doubt since each of you has had the wisdom to select a really superb story to retell and the skill to obtain new documentation as well as new insight but partly also because you too write about politics as they really happen and as you know they really happen.'

There was a time before the war when Dick was ceaselessly discussed at Oxford. Indeed, the argument about him had never come to an end. Such wonderful powers and such apparent misuse of them so often, though never on any fair-minded view, for personal gain. In the old days he was, or could be, unduly aggressive. There was an occasion when he forced a sensitive don to break into tears and he has publicly described, though it is hard to accept it literally, his harsh treatment of his father when he was still a schoolboy. The one thing I am sure of is that he would treat his father quite differently if he were alive today, though he has insisted on the opposite.

Zita's death was a shattering blow, but Anne has brought him a new tranquillity and comparatively late in life the additional happiness of children. Today he remains, and is likely to remain, a controversial figure, unpredictable, occasionally impossible. His open assault on Hugh Gaitskell's leadership while himself chairman of the Party was barely defensible. But I should doubt if in these latter days he has an enemy or harsh critic whom he cannot placate if he wishes to. His humour, not his strongest point in the old days, is now unsurpassed among politicians. So is his friendliness and his own particular brand of generous, gratuitous enthusiasm. This last quality come out clearly in the long, thoughtful, argumentative letter which he wrote to Elizabeth about her book which I have briefly quoted.

He is often credited, and rightly, with an animal dynamism, but I believe him to possess a much rarer quality, a power of natural leadership—not as common among politicians as one might think and not necessarily associated with the gift of public speech. When I captained Aylesbury at rugby soon after my marriage, Dick and Patrick Gordon Walker used

to come over from Oxford to play for us. They had both
been Greyhounds at the university (second fifteen, which
had been much above my level). I took the game up more
strenuously after going down, but never got higher than an
invitation to play for Buckinghamshire. Frank Owen, a
Welsh Trial cap, but by that time deeply involved in Fleet
Street, came down once and scored a celebrated try in spite
of some discomfort. Dick and I used to pack together in the
second row. Sometimes when I was 'blown' I used to ask him
to take on the leadership of the forwards. 'Come on, chaps,'
he would say, clapping his hands. The effect was always
instantaneous. Partly through circumstances, partly through
his own uncertainty, Dick has been given little scope so far
for the exercise of this rare attribute, but it was recognized
easily enough by Oxford and Cambridge audiences on his
Union visits. On one occasion they turned up in force to give
him breakfast the next morning and then saw him off from
the station like the Pied Piper of Hamelin.

PATRICK GORDON WALKER

In the event of a Labour Government Patrick Gordon Walker
seems certain to be Foreign Secretary. His friendly, solid,
well-carved face has often been seen on television. Yet I
doubt if he personally is as well known to the masses. He has
lacked hitherto what Hugh Gaitskell lacked in earlier years
but acquired convincingly, *the power to communicate with the
general public*—that is, the millions who don't know him
and never will personally. That is the power which Reginald
Maudling, for all his fine abilities, has hitherto lacked and which
Quintin Hailsham so significantly possesses.

But in moral fibre Patrick is the equal of anyone in public
life. He is a rock, a bulwark, a support, a man whose personal
character lends authority to his political line, a priceless asset
in a Foreign Secretary, as Lord Grey proved in 1914, for
instance. If I say that my last anxieties about the Harold
Wilson leadership were removed when I heard Patrick was his
Foreign Secretary I am bringing in the thought that Patrick's
views on foreign policy were always close to those of Hugh

Gaitskell though worked out on his own. I was quite wrong and delighted to be proved wrong in doubting when Hugh died whether full continuity would be maintained.

I first met Patrick when he was tutoring or working with Freddy Birkenhead at Charlton in the Oxford long vacation. He was excellent at games and was a favourite with the whole tribe of Birkenhead-Smiths, Camrose-Berrys with whom so much of my own private happiness was then and still remains tied up. Michael Berry was one of my first and one of my ablest pupils. Freddy Birkenhead has long been recognized as a lover and patron of literature. Today he is taking his place as an outstanding biographer. Pam Berry is a political hostess renowned on both sides of the Atlantic, Sheila Birkenhead is a graceful writer, in no way behind her in sparkle.

Patrick was awarded a studentship (fellowship) at Christ Church on the strength not only of his admirable scholarship but as a reliable games-playing Old Wellingtonian. He was expected to exert a healthy influence on the young men, some of whom were sprouting some rather odd ideas. Soon, very soon, he went socialist and I was brought in. An Old Etonian, member of the Carlton Club, etc. Surely this couldn't go wrong, but, horror of horrors, it went wrong, and I turned socialist also. However, Christ Church has gone on from strength to strength in spite of me.

Patrick fought Oxford for Labour in 1935, a hopeless task at that time. Then came a dark day in autumn 1938 when he was induced, much against his will, to step down from his candidature at the by-election following Munich. Quintin Hogg was opposed by an Independent Progressive candidate, the Master of Balliol. Quintin, or Munich, triumphed over all. Not long after I became the Labour candidate for Oxford— not a sequence of events for me to be proud of, and one for which I have done penance elsewhere. By 1946 Patrick was in the House of Commons with a safe seat. By 1950 he was Secretary of State for Commonwealth Relations. At forty-two he was the youngest member of the Cabinet, bar Harold Wilson; indeed Patrick and Harold are the only remaining members of that Cabinet in the Shadow Cabinet today. But then disaster again intervened.

Patrick was the Minister officially responsible for the expulsion of Seretse Khama, a policy virtually decided upon before he 'took over'. He showed an obstinacy which is perhaps the converse of his rare moral courage. He stuck to his guns, forfeiting much popularity in the Party. Then and later he suffered the kind of eclipse which would have destroyed a weaker character or one less dedicated to Socialism. He has lived through the shadows and emerged stronger than ever, and now his hour is sounding.

What sort of Foreign Minister will he make? He will always be far better informed than most of his colleagues. He used sometimes to be called Mr. Knowall in the old days at Charlton. His French and German are really excellent. He thinks out everything for himself and takes an almost professorial interest in the skills of politics, in all he does he will be on the cautious side, but he will be edging forward. He does not go in for verbal wit, but he has a rich vein of sophisticated humour, enjoying other people's jokes even more than his own. He does not give an impression at first sight of unusual speed or sharpness, but when he takes up a subject it does not take him long to master it, as I saw in a recent discussion with American experts. He is always ready to believe, he has once or twice been almost too ready to believe, that the unpopular course may be the path of duty.

Away from the House of Commons his hospitality is relaxed and informal. His wife Audrey and his children are a source of undiluted strength. Audrey Gordon Walker has always been described as attractive and could now be described as beautiful. Harold Wilson is a lucky man to have Patrick at his elbow and says so freely. Sir Frank Lee, the most powerful Civil Servant of the last few years and some assert the ablest, said to me recently, 'I think it's possible that Patrick Gordon Walker will turn out a great Foreign Secretary.' I think so too.

HAROLD WILSON

I have already spoken of Harold Wilson in a Catholic connection. In adding a few general comments now I shall try to keep to first-hand impressions and avoid the best-known things. When George Brown defeated Harold Wilson for the deputy leadership of the Party I went up to Harold Wilson in the Harcourt Room of the House of Commons and said I was sorry. 'You don't mean that,' said Bill Blyton, M.P., who was sitting beside him. He was a firm ally of Harold's and an equally firm opponent of the Common Market. 'You know you are not sorry at all,' he went on. He meant that George Brown and I (and he knew that I admired George) were supposed to favour the Common Market, and Harold Wilson, in emphasis at least, to be on the other side.

'Oh yes,' I could honestly say, 'I am genuinely sorry on personal grounds. You see, I am fond of Harold.'

'I know that,' Harold Wilson replied, and clearly meant it.

In fact my feelings went a long way back, though strengthened latterly, as already explained, by my visits to his constituency.

I more or less followed him as William Beveridge's personal assistant in the war, though his work must have been much more statistical and much less political than mine. He appears to have started work with William Beveridge at six. I never began till ten, but the lunches and dinners we attended (though William Beveridge declined to stay up late), may have redressed the balance a little. For three years (1947–50) Elizabeth and I lived within a stone's throw of Harold Wilson in Hampstead Garden Suburb. Our children went to parties at their house and their children came to us. Relations were excellent when we met on political occasions. Elizabeth was an early connoisseur of Harold's public speaking, already fierce and witty, and I responded to Mary Wilson's charm. But we did not see a great deal of them. And this was also true of other Socialist families in Hampstead, like the Gordon Walkers, Jays, and Gaitskells. There was more than one reason.

In the first place Harold was ten years or so younger than others of us, and yet he was in the Cabinet, aged thirty-one, in 1947, two and a half years before Patrick Gordon Walker and three years before Hugh Gaitskell. He was very much our junior, yet could not be treated as such. But also, as is now well known, his views on social intercourse are so unusual among the professional classes as to seem positively eccentric. His passion for filling 'the unforgiving minute with duty done' is unrivalled in my experience. A dinner party without an object, or an evening of merely sociable gossip, must seem to him a waste of time or a sin of omission.

This withdrawal from the pleasures of ordinary social life among colleagues and fellow politicians does not, I am sure, spring from any alleged coldness or lack of communal feeling. It springs from the urge to do something useful all the time. But in the result it inhibits the development of friendships and the warmer kind of relationships with other politicians. By chance, I know two intimate friends of Harold Wilson who are much attached to him while probably agreeing with what I have just written. But neither of them is a Member of Parliament. Now that he is leader, his social practice is being rationalized and expounded as a virtue. His freedom from what religious orders call 'particular friendships' is being treated as a strength. There is some force in that, but I hope and believe that he himself will not regard it as the last word on the subject.

Much surprise has been felt that Harold Wilson should have unified the Party so effectively since his election, or, at least, have completed the unifying work of Hugh Gaitskell. There is no surprise in this for me at all. Harold Wilson is naturally a unifying influence on the Labour Party, just as Clem Attlee was—and for the same reason. His whole thought and character have been built up in their maturity within a Labour Party framework, in spite of a short Liberal phase at Oxford. The same was true of Clem Attlee, though his family was anything but Socialist. Just like Clem Attlee, Harold Wilson *is part of* the Labour movement, indistinguishable from it in a way that is true of few Socialist intellectuals, however dedicated. Without conscious effort, Harold Wilson finds himself sharing the feelings of the 'typical' Party man. His natural place is somewhere in the middle of it, or slightly left of centre, which was Clem Attlee's natural position also.

It was pure accident that circumstances before and after 1951 cast him for the role of Bevanite number two. For years he was operating well to the left of his 'natural' situation. By any standards his action in standing against Hugh Gaitskell for the leadership in 1960 can be seen in retrospect to have been unwise. It created, or at least enhanced, unnecessary antagonisms, it gave a false impression of his personality. But he honestly believed that the Party was being unnecessarily divided and this, coupled with his dependence on the Left for his own support, led him into steps which were out of character.

When he became leader he recovered, with one or two masterly strokes, his true position in the middle. For someone supposed to be impersonal, his man-to-man achievements have been notable—Patrick Gordon Walker, Frank Cousins, Cecil King and Willy Brandt are but a few of those whose names come to mind here. On my own plane I have always found him, as Gladstone said of Chamberlain (before the fatal break), 'a good man to talk to'. He has a quick and shrewd and sympathetic idea of what one is after. More than most politicians and business men he puts his own cards on the table.

The triumph at Scarborough of his speech on 'Socialism and Science' was colossal. The faithful son of an industrial chemist in Huddersfield, he would feel that kind of future in his bones, while some of us Old Etonians and Old Wykehamists from the South of England could think it out at best with our minds. (I except from this comparison Dick Crossman, the Labour Party's Shadow Minister for Science.) He indeed can be lit up by a far-reaching intellectual idea, however fresh and external. But Dick is law to himself. Harold Wilson possesses, as Scarborough notably showed, the sharp, witty, deadly phraseology to make his convictions as formidable for his opponents as they are stirring to his own side. His humour, too, as distinct from his verbal wit, is ever more in evidence. Certainly his speech at Scarborough and his whole suggested revelation of what science could accomplish for the mass of the people has opened the door to a long new vista of Labour philosophy and action. I am happy to think that he will be leader of the Labour Party as long as I expect myself to be in active politics.

4

... To Each According to His Needs

By the time these words first appear, though I hope they will bear subsequent reading, we may well be standing on the brink of a general election, perhaps the most interesting and fiercely contested election since 1945. Education and housing could prove, and rightly prove, the decisive issues. But it would be inappropriate to end this book with election propaganda on behalf of individuals and policies. There is, however, one question to which I should attempt some kind of answer. Just over thirty years ago I began to question the assumptions of the Conservative Party in which I had expected to spend a political lifetime. Twenty-eight years ago (1936) I joined the Labour Party which five years earlier would have seemed as inconceivable as emigrating to China. Am I quite sure that I took the right step at that time? To that question I reply without a trace of difficulty, I have never for a moment doubted the wisdom of what I did. And I would add that the difference between the underlying outlooks of the two main parties seem to me as fundamental today as thirty years ago, though the practical programmes have drawn much closer.

Where is the difference to be discovered? It is sometimes said, and not by Marxists only, to derive from a contrast in class or group interests. And this aspect is far too important to be ignored. The higher-income men in the City are probably right to suppose that at least under a good Conservative Government they would be better off financially as individuals than under a good Labour one. It is the other way round with the miners. But it is of the essence of my political convictions that the poor or weak will always have a larger interest than the rich and powerful in policies of justice, communal provision, humanity, and mercy. The real purposes that spring from a poor man's Party are much more likely than those of a rich man's Party to be, for instance, international rather than national, to be ardently concerned for the poor, the maimed, the lame, and the blind, and on that account to be blessed.

Millions of poor men, or at least working men, vote Conservative, and a handful, relatively speaking, of the well-to-do vote Labour. But neither of these groups determines basically the philosophies of their parties. It is not unfair to say that the Conservative Party philosophies reflect what rich men consider, the Labour Party's reflect what poor men think is good for the nation. On neither side are the leaders thinking of their own pockets. I would like to say that once and say it again. But in each case they are reflecting attitudes which are typical of what Sir Winston Churchill once called, in a different connection, 'their slice of the nation'. (I am distinguishing the areas where the party philosophies differ. There is, of course, much common ground.) For myself I have never regretted my irrevocable commitment to the ideas of the 'Labour slice'.

In so doing, like many of my friends, some mentioned here, I was committing myself not only against my own economic interests but against the interests of the world in which I was brought up and educated. It is a world in which as a don, a business man, and a member of the House of Lords I have continued to spend much of my life. And what of my future now? I remember entering a provincial bookshop while a publisher's representative was displaying his latest list of titles and recommending a life of Nehru. 'Nehru,' said the book-seller doubtfully, 'he isn't much in the picture nowadays, is he?' To which the 'rep' replied, tapping him reassuringly on the shoulder, 'No, old boy, but you can take it from me he's

coming back any moment now.' Who knows if I shall be more
in the picture in the next few years, or indeed what picture
there will be to be in? But if I am granted more scope how do
I hope to render more service?

I am sometimes asked whether I am a Socialist for reasons of
justice or for those of efficiency. Once again my answer is
simple. Basically I am a Socialist for reasons of justice, but I
could never preach the supremacy of the Labour Party with
much conviction unless I were sure that they would be at least
as efficient as the Conservatives. Today I can go as far as that
in terms of efficiency and indeed much further. I am ready to
accept the challenge of a personal comparison between the
respective leaders, but find a much deeper superiority in the
whole Labour Party approach to the planned use of our
national resources. In terms of justice there seems to be no
comparison between a Conservative Party which roughly
defends the present distribution of wealth and a Labour Party
which will never accept it.

The dichotomy between justice and efficiency is not exhaustive. From the earliest days of the Labour Party there has
been a vision of a society inspired by higher, more unselfish
motives than those which drive round the wheels of capitalism.
Much of the best in recent Socialist writing by such men as
Raymond Williams and Richard Hoggart has tried to grope its
way beyond economics and politics and towards the production of a nobler *quality* of life.

Here at the end I would like to insert my own small ambition.
The representative image man of the Labour Party at the
moment is a white-collared young technologist, educated
anywhere but at Oxbridge, insistently keeping abreast of the
spirit of the space age. A retired bank chairman, educated at
Eton and Oxford, an hereditary earl—I may not at first sight
appear to be sufficiently 'with it'. Yet one cannot be other
than one is.

The two supreme decisions which have shaped my life
since I grew up were the decisions to become a Socialist
and a Catholic, described, as far as I was able, in an earlier book.
On a lower plane the acceptance of a peerage (1945) has meant

that when out of office I have had to earn my living in non-political work. And the National Bank gave me a rare and choice opportunity.

'What is Stalin like?' Ernest Bevin was asked on his first meeting with one whom Sir Winston Churchill had described as 'Ivan the Terrible'. 'Just a working chap,' he replied, 'like you and me, trying to make his way in the world.' Few of us are spared the necessity altogether of paying by our own exertions for ourselves and our families, not always in occupations in which we would have been expected to shine. I might have shirked that duty, if it had not in fact been inescapable. I am glad to have shared the lot of the vast majority, in some respects at least; to have learnt that those who work in the City are no less and no more human than the rest of us. I ought to have learnt, moreover, some lessons in commercial efficiency which have come the way of few Socialists.

If I am pressed again, and finally, as to where I suppose that I could render most service in the future, I would point to a different sphere and one where efficiency takes on a more subtle form. A year or two ago I might have singled out higher education. When I pleaded in the House of Lords in 1957 for a vast expansion I was treated as an amiable illusionist. But we are all expansionists now.

I turn instead to Luke v, 31, 'They that are whole need not the physician; but they that are sick.' This is not to say that domestic subjects are necessarily more urgent than international ones, that compassion is the only virtue or that the topics I have concentrated on are superior to others. Archbishop Heenan in his enthronement speech picked out the old and the widows as demanding our particular concern. I am aware, too, that all social advance depends on economic achievement, on which also depends our chance of performing our Christian duty to the undernourished millions abroad.

But the wind bloweth where it listeth. A flood of communal endeavour derives from many tiny streams of personal inspiration. For me, the call to serve has always been most insistent when unheeded by others. There has always been a special poignancy about the neglected cause. Hence my association with the New Bridge for ex-prisoners, with compensation for victims of violence, with penal reform generally, with the mentally handicapped, with the youth services, with Germany when she was starving.

To none of these have ordinary Labour men shown themselves indifferent, but the party, like other parties, has given them no high priority, inevitably preoccupied with issues which bear more obviously on the political struggle. Yet the moral quality that the Labour Party (or any party) can offer our country, or the world, is likely to be as great or as little as its own warmth of charity. That charity will not be measured by the testimony of large gatherings or electoral pronouncements but by the uncalculated tenderness, individual and corporate, which is shown in practice to all who strive against adversity and all who suffer.

EPILOGUE

The Author as a Father

BY JUDITH KAZANTZIS

My FATHER was the most mild, beneficent, and loving parent you could hope for. No one was less stern, more totally unable to mete out the discipline we constantly merited. I am sorry to say he was often a laughing-stock among us sophisticated hooligans in the middle section of the family. When 'X'—usually the same 'X'—ambled reluctantly into my father's study in order to receive a diatribe about his disgusting behaviour in thrashing a younger sister, that younger sister knew very well that in ten minutes the two of them would emerge cheerfully discussing some obscure point of cricket. Or if someone was unusually unbearable at lunchtime, with her waspish tongue and sarcastic retorts, only on a last desperate appeal from my mother—'Frank, would you really ask . . .!'—would my father say mildly, 'I do think, "Y", you must leave the table if you go on being such a nuisance!'—a remark that was usually received with giggles.

Sparing the rod was, to him, only one way of spoiling his children. I am sure that his failure to cope with our evil natures stemmed directly from the same humility about himself which has made him a most loved parent. I sometimes thought this humility overdone, possibly insincere, at any rate a character defect, probably from early childhood. But at the same time, and more and more, I saw that it was unique, and had been worked into the origin of so much good action that occasional idiosyncratic expressions of it could be tolerated. Perhaps it was the same characteristic of my father's that made him withdraw from his children; I don't mean that he did not love us dearly. He was never, never cold or putting off; he never forgot to ask what we were doing, or how we were getting on, could he help in any way, would we like a little present (if one were particularly depressed), and so on. Like the Holy Ghost, he used to kiss each one of us on the forehead right round the breakfast table when we came down in the morning, a ritual which I feel he still offers wherever he is, to whatever persons he happens to be with. But fatherhood did not come naturally to him. He was too shy, too intellectual, to find the crude, boisterous relationship with any one of his eight children an easy one. The nursery was very red in tooth and claw, and my father found it difficult to know how to deal with our scratches.

The gold dolphins upon the fish furniture in the Admiralty, where my father spent the last months of it, are my last and almost only memories of the great Attlee Government. Suddenly my father no longer had a Government chauffeur in a big black coat and a peaked cap to come and take him off to work at nine every morning from our Hampstead home. I, eleven at the time, and militantly on the defensive at a county boarding school of the most Tory sort, thought it all a great pity. It was not nearly such fun to be in the Opposition, now my father was a business man.

For the last twelve years my mother has valiantly kept running two homes: Bernhurst, idyllic within its great Sussex garden, and a tall gloomy house in Cheyne Gardens for weekdays and term-times. The four youngest children were scattered at Catholic day and boarding schools. The three oldest were, more or less, off and away, Antonia to marry a Conservative M.P., Thomas to spend a year in Ethiopia, write a book to show that Paradise was on top of a mountain in the middle of it, and become a professional journalist, Paddy to start as a barrister after gaieties at Oxford unsurpassed by any of us. I, veering towards Oxford also, was betwixt and between.

I was rebellious and critical in those years. My father in turn irritated me and inspired me. Perhaps the two went together. For example, why was he so slow, so over-patient, in argument, and yet always managing to deflate my splendidly positive and independent position at the end? And why should he use cheap verbal tricks in order to ridicule us? These tricks outflanked more splendid positions than mine, before loftier company. I thought it mean to use his debating technique on us. But how exhilarating as I got older and calmer about airing my views, and was able to discuss things with him in what seemed to me the most adult and Socratic way.

It was not only in direct conversation that my father made us aware of the value of speech, or indeed of the word, the thought, the idea. He loved to be articulate above all things. He adored, and adores, dinner conversation, and his and my mother's friends are all extremely vocal. The subject can be politics, gossip, why wars start, why peace starts, why anything starts, but it does always seem to come back to politics in the end. He taught us also the nature of a joke, the sly, throw-away humour that used to annoy me until I saw how grown-up visitors loved it. Jokes like wine, and particularly with wine, flowed freely amidst his conversation, never for a moment ribald or cozy, but discreetly balanced between the two.

One of my father's most endearing traits, the privilege, I suppose, of an occupied mind, was that he would always start talking about his immediate thoughts: the book he had been reading, the interview he had just had. And if it was important enough a theme that would be worked out for several days until it petered out of its own accord. For instance, being immersed in Wesley's *Journal*, he could quote nothing but Wesley for any circumstances that arose for two or three weeks. He found it most unfair that Mummy, writing a biography of Queen Victoria, could bring in her subject once or twice a day.

An inveterate reader, my father has passed this on to most of his children, including myself, though I wish he could have taught me how to skip through a 400-page volume in a weekend in order to get in a review by Monday. I like his habit of picking up and gutting, or appearing to gut, any book which may be under his hand as he wanders into a room, a genuine addict, ready to try any brand of the drug. Another ancient habit is rather more unfortunate: that of heavily underscoring any phrase or word in the book which strikes him. He then makes copious notes in the back page in a completely illegible handwriting, so that the next user is not even compensated with a few extra edifying thoughts for the vandalism. My father admires great prose above everything else, for I don't think he ever read any poetry in his life, nor drama for that matter, though he once wrote a play in a week. He is proud that it received every honour (including a play-reading by an Oxford drama group) except, he is forced to admit, that of production. He likes the rolling declamatory glories of the great essayists, and retires to a piece of fine prose as to a hot bath. Gladstone's rolling speeches on Irish Home Rule come top of all with him, and at the drop of a hat he will burst into the thunderous appeals: 'She is at the bar. She cannot be denied, etc., etc.' These speeches combine the thrill of the illustrious oratory which my father feels he can never quite bring off himself, and a passion for Ireland, which my father certainly shares. He had the special classicist's method of declaiming, which made even a newspaper report seem magnificent. As a constant speaker and writer, he is devoted to the art of composition and to techniques of delivery. He will explore endlessly the reasons for the success of some public man's speaking style, with what might be called Christian envy.

He faces with absolute horror the prospect of any lengthy composition himself, but he has at times wanted to write a great biography on, say, Newman, or to travel the length and the breadth of his total reading of Christian philosophy and ethics in an exhaustive history of morals. But, apart from time, he has always disliked the mechanical process of writing, the fiddling with unsharpened pencils, the inability to understand his own handwriting; and the almost physical task of wrestling with a great mental project stretching ahead for unforeseeable months is not softened by a natural delight for the handling of words and language which he so much admires in others. He loves literature so much, I think, because he has little to do with other art forms. He is quite unmusical, having no ear. Once only, he has tried out his gifts as a performer and that ended ignominiously. Someone had told him that only training stood between him and a fine baritone voice. Elated, he insisted on lessons. A singing teacher was eventually brought to the house. They shut themselves in the dining-room, and the first lesson began. But as the scales started, so did giggles on the other side of the door, where many sons and daughters had gathered. Dada's crescendos mounted, but so did the chuckles, the cackles, and finally the convulsed peals of laughter until the lesson had to be abandoned in despair. The teacher rushed from the house and was never brought back. My father still feels that only the wintry winds of our unkind laughter blew away a voice which could well have been that of another Gobbi.

Though manifestly bored by any lengthy discourses on them, my father has a humble simplicity of heart before the great gods of opera, ballet, or painting. He has always wished he knew more about them. One day he brought home a Penguin on opera which he had picked up on impulse, as he might a book on fly-fishing, and which was at last to reveal to him the mysteries which others, in close touch with him on all other subjects, enjoyed. I remember he gave it to me the next day.

On the other hand he has always liked going to great plays, though I suppose it is natural that he should fall for, above all, dramatizations of novels, such as C. P. Snow's *The Affair*.

Oxford, home of the written word, has always stood for the good life in my father's vocabulary. When I was at Oxford he seemed to come up at least once a term, either to address some undergraduate society about world government, where he seemed to get no more barracking than a bishop might, or to go off to some cozy dinner with some dons he had known since Christ Church days. From the second I generally reaped a quick drink at the Randolph; from the first I got maybe a full meal at the Capri, which was very nice indeed. Partly his love for Oxford and partly love of learning made my father intensely ambitious for any child who showed the slightest intelligence to go there—or at any rate to Cambridge—and to come away with a First. The situation has become more desperate through the years, since Antonia, Thomas, Paddy, myself, and Rachel all crawled away with nothing better than a Second. The list of possibles becomes despondently shorter. He once turned to an old friend of his at Oxford when he noticed Paddy and Thomas playing in a Dragon School match at the ages of seven and nine, and said, 'I wish my children weren't so competitive.' And the friend told me years later she thought maybe he made them so. Maybe he and my mother were too interested in exam results.

It was easier for him to be fatherly towards small boys than towards small girls, for he could talk to them for hours on

cricket, or football, or swimming, or tennis. And the letters
of my younger brothers home from school, full of detail about
this failure or that success at some sport, have always been
eagerly received by my father. He always seemed to be going
to Cup Finals, though apparently they happen only once a
year. My younger brothers, Michael and Kevin, greatly excited,
would be with him. When it was England *v.* Ireland they would
return bursting with tales in wild brogue, having temporarily
deserted the English side for what was felt to be their more
native country. At Christ Church he ran in a race of which a
photograph is still extant, showing him, a mighty man,
pushing himself forward beyond the puny undergraduates—
obviously before the starter had said 'Go'. This has always
been hotly denied, though he won.

At the root of the passion for sport, I think, lay a passion for
bodily as much as for mental excellence. The other half of
the classicist's ideal, I suppose. Thus my father has always
had almost an obsession for keeping fit, keeping in trim, seeing
gay business friends go literally to pot, and their chins multiply with their years. He has, for as long as I can remember,
kept himself under extraordinarily strict control as far as diet
is concerned. The Pakenhams have always been rather large,
well proportioned, and ample; overweight is a sort of family
curse which, taken with the love of second helpings, has
descended to this generation, and at certain moments the
house has been filled with nothing but excited talk about
seaweed pills, sawdust in the tummy, steaks, and the slimming
farm that James Bond went to. During my adolescence my
father's introductory cries, 'How's the work going?' 'How's
the weight going?' were almost interchangeable, oblivious of
my fury when the room was full of attractive visiting men.

He was fascinated by the whole slimming business. Once
when I was particularly fat he kindly sent me to a wise old
physiotherapist friend of his. This man had taught him excer-
cises when he was in his twenties, which he had practised for
thirty odd years regularly in the morning. No one was dis-
mayed if, coming into my parents' bedroom before breakfast,
they found my father writhing around in a Fijian belly-dance,
back to the floor, while above him my mother composedly

did her hair. He was very proud of this feat, as of several others. I remember as a child being invited quite often to punch the rock-hard tummy, and the biceps, which were supposed to be the result. It has given him real satisfaction that the artificial life of the twentieth-century man has not got him down. One up to Socialism maybe, in a world of flabby Tory commuters. At any rate, it has always pleased me that my mother, about whose figure older women have constantly exclaimed to me, 'Goodness, and after eight of you too!' should have as elegant an escort as well.

Excluding sport, my father is an absent-minded professor in many ways. He never did a bit of science at school, and he no more knows how to mend a plug than to wash up without breaking everthing or adjusting a television set. There have been suspicions from time to time that he deliberately kept himself ignorant. My mother has, from early marriage, reluctantly been forced to become the fuse-mender. When the moment comes that good faith is strained to the uttermost my father shows such naïve goodwill, ready to learn to do absolutely everything, that accusations are put away as unworthy. It becomes clear to you only later that the detailed lecture you gave him has fallen on stony ground, and that you will have to do it yourself in the end.

My own incredulity reached high-water mark one moment at Cheyne Gardens after breakfast. From the top of the stairs my mother shouted down could I please turn off the heaters in the dining-room before I finished, as she had forgotten? Already a quarter-way up the stairs, I tried to pass the buck to my father by shouting could he do it. The buck bounced back with lightning speed. He said he would have loved to, but he had no idea how. How did they work? In twelve years the heaters had been in constant use, but probably my father had not even noticed the source of warmth. He is so unmechanical that he often practically executes himself shaving, and has to disappear to the House of Lords with pieces of white cotton wool sticking up all over his chin. They were always removed by the time he spoke, which was just as well, for they would not have suited his speaking style. This was, as I have heard it, lofty and full of noble compassion. It always had the effect of raising the moral tone by half, even on rougher public platforms than the Lords.

His background and education have made him eminently clubable. He loves Eton and Oxford and he loves the House of Lords. Sadly he knows he is committed to abolish, or, at any rate, reform them, for political, backed by Christian, convictions come first. But in their ritual and their rather jolly traditions they remain seductive, warring just a little with my father's temperamental devotion to justice. But not irreconcilable. Almost in a way they are complementary. My father's Socialism is first and foremost a passion to help the needy, to oppose the mighty, and this would lack something positive, something vital, if he did not also appreciate some of our older social benefits, whether or not the mighty ones had sole enjoyment of them. He made his political decision a long time ago, and I am sure that he is intellectually at peace with himself. Nevertheless, to live in two nations mutually hostile is not easy, even when attempted out of sincere conviction.

The particular rub for my father lies in his deep-seated fascination with men of power. What makes a man great, in whatever field, is a subject which is sure to draw him and he will endlessly discuss the success and failures of public men and the reasons and circumstances for them, comparing one against the other. He has always liked drawing up a list of the ten best of everything. A public man can always count on my father's fascinated scrutiny, be he pop-singer, great athlete, statesman, or worse. But his appreciation of worldly excitements makes his devotion to an egalitarian philosophy seem more admirable.

If England has two ways of life I think of my father as having three. For the first, he has forayed into the Tory drawing-room of an old friend and political enemy in search of the latest tasty political morsel; for the second, two battered old ex-prisoners made good, waiting patiently at Cheyne Gardens for him to come back from work so that they can present him with an enormous and magnificent brief-case in return for past help; or, again, he is travelling to perhaps a remote northern constituency to speak to four farm labourers in a deserted school-room on a wet Tuesday by-election evening; for the third he is on his knees beside the drawing-room sofa saying his goodnight prayers before he goes up to bed. A little comic, so large on the floor, not sitting up like any civilized man on the sofa, it has always seemed character-istic of my father's gentle persistent effort to do as he thought right, however uncomfortable it might look to others.

Index

ACTON, Antony, 26, 35, 44, 59
Addison, Lord, 67, 69, 79, 80–1, 83
Adenauer, Dr., 11, 111
Aiken, Frank, 95
Albermarle, 11
Aldenham, Lord, 53, 54
Alexander of Hillsborough, Lord, 69–70, 74, 79, 81–2, 83, 202, 203, 208–9, 210
Alexander, Lady, 70
Alington, C. A., 113, 165
Alton, Cardinal d', 100, 102
Amory, Heathcote, 56, 59
Andrew, Father Agnellus, 200
Andrews, Eamonn, 197
Arran, Lord, 92, 161, 207
Ashbrook, Harry, 142
Astor, David, 122, 128, 241
Astor, Lady (Bronwen), 160
Astor, Lord, 160
Attlee, Lord, 12, 29, 69, 74, 78, 79–80, 85, 99, 169, 187, 188–9, 190, 195, 219, 220, 222, 232, 245–6, 254, 264
Avon, Lord, 22, 46, 187
Ayer, Freddy, 172

BACON, Alice, 241

Baird, José, 128
Baker, Peter, 132
Balfour of Burleigh, Lord, 22, 41
Balfour of Inchrye, Harold, Lord, 159
Balfour, Prime Minister, 136–7
Beauvoir, Simone de, 248
Beavan, John, 238–9
Beaverbrook, Lord, 67, 86, 169
Beck, Bishop, 202
Beckley, John, 124, 141
Beeching, Dr., 63
Behan, Brendan, 105
Bell, Mr., 197
Bellenger, Fred, 211
Bentley, Derek, 135
Berlin, Aline, 225
Berlin, Sir Isaiah, 14, 167–8, 225
Bernstein, Sidney, 22
Berry, Michael, 251
Berry, Pam, 251
Betjeman, John, 105, 167, 225
Bevan, Aneurin, 48, 187
Beveridge, Lord, 72, 121–2, 189, 209–10, 253
Bevin, Ernest, 118, 189, 209, 228, 259
Biggs, Norman, 45, 46

Birk, Ellis, 237
Birkenhead, Lady, 251
Birkenhead, Lord, 27, 169, 251
Blake, George, 140
Blake, Robert, 168, 171
Blyton, Bill, 253
Bodkin, Professor, 11, 97, 98, 101, 102
Boland, Fred, 95
Bonham-Carter, Lady Violet, 71, 247
Boothby, Lord, 69
Bourne, Joan, 121
Bowlby, John, 72, 122–3
Bowra, Sir Maurice, 14, 167, 225
Boyle, Sir Edward, 197
Brabazon, Lord, 195
Brandt, Willy, 255
Brierley, Barbara, 68
Broad, Professor, 123
Brown, Curtis, 171
Brown, George, 253
Burns, 197
Burrows, Henry, 82, 92
Burton, Lady, 71
Butler, R. A., 56, 148, 149–50, 185
Buxton, Jane, 128

Callaghan, James, 48–9
Canterbury, Archbishop of, 70, 195
Carrington, Lord, 79
Carrington, Sir William, 198, 240
Catlin, George, 211
Cecil, Lord David, 14, 167–8
Chadwick, Father, 197
Chamberlain, Joseph, 170–1, 218, 248, 255
Chamberlain, Neville, 72, 166, 170
Champion, Joe, 76
Chandos, Lord, 22, 78, 101
Chardin, Teilhard de, 172
Cherwell, Lord, 34
Chetwode, Roger, 169

Chichester, Bishop of, 184
Childers, Erskine, 106
Churchill, Randolph, 16, 37, 166–7, 232, 239
Churchill, Sir Winston, 14, 34, 37, 57, 88, 96, 131, 137, 150, 166, 187, 257, 259
Clark, Dr. Stafford, 156
Clark, William, 122
Clarke, Thom, 141
Clery, Gabriel, 33
Cobbold, Kim, 55
Cohen, Lewis, 22, 201
Cole, G., 167
Coleman, Ronald, 144
Collins, John, 247
Collins, Norman, 246
Conesford, Lord, 76
Connolly, Cyril, 16
Cooke, Michael, 25–6, 27, 28–9, 30, 31, 32, 33, 35, 44, 54, 215
Cooke, Michael, junior, 34, 215
Cooper, Duff, 187
Corbishley, Rev. T., s.j., 209
Costello, J. A., 98, 101
Cousins, Frank, 48, 222, 229, 255
Cousins, Nance, 229
Craig, Christopher, 135–6, 137–9
Craig, Mr., 136
Craig, Niven, 136, 137, 138, 139
Crawford, Virginia, 171
Crawley, Aidan, 225
Crawley, Virginia, 225
Cremin, Con, 101
Cripps, Sir Stafford, 183, 218
Croft, Michael, 130
Cromer, Lord, 55
Crosland, Tony, 230–1
Crossman, Anne, 249
Crossman, Richard, 16, 169, 185, 238, 248–50, 255
Crossman, Zita, 249
Crowther, 11

Cudlipp, Hugh, 237
Curzon, Lord, 97

DAMIEN, Father, 162
D'Arcy, Father Eric, 204
D'Arcy, Father Martin, s.j., 113, 116, 172, 196
Davies, Joyce, 143
Davies, Michael, 124, 141-4
Davies, Pat, 153
Davies, Richard Llewellyn, 153
Davis, Thomas, 103
Davitt, Michael, 141
Davy, James, 33
Dawtry, Frank, 125
Day, Robin, 172
De Gaulle, President, 232
De Valera, Eamon, 98, 101, 102, 103, 104-5, 106
De Valera, Mrs., 104
Denning, Lord, 70, 158
Devlin, Lord, 11
Devonshire, Duke of, 99
Dilke, Sir Charles Wentworth, 171
Disraeli, Benjamin, 166
Donaldson, Jack, 111-12, 123
Douglas, Sholto, 118
Doyle, John, 140-1
Driberg, Tom, 167
Drogheda, Lord, 41
Duggan, Paddy, 33
Dulanty, John, 27-8
Dundas, Robin, 87
Dundee, Lord, 69
Dunsany, Eddy, 106, 165
Durbin, Evan, 218
Durbin, Marjorie, 236

EDINBURGH, Duke of, 11
Eichmann, Adolf, 154, 246-7
Eliot, Lady, 71
Elizabeth, Queen Mother, 211
Empson, William, 200

Escriva, Joseph, 191
Exeter, Bishop of, 70

FARRER-BROWN, Leslie, 27, 122
Fawcett, Bice, 197
Field, Xenia, 125
Filmer, Jack, 125, 128, 129
Fisher, H. A. L., 115, 246, 248
Fisher, Lord, 207-8, 209
Fitzgerald, Peggy, 58, 68
Fleming, Anne, 127
Fleming, Ian, 16
Fleming, Peter, 114
Foot, Michael, 16, 229
Foyle, Christina, 168
Fox, Sir Lionel, 131
Franco, General, 96
Franks, Lord, 21, 31, 40, 51, 53
Fraser, Antonia, 12, 127, 168, 185, 188, 189, 198, 264, 267
Fraser, Hugh, 12, 105, 198, 264
Fraser, Lionel, 41, 42, 46, 47, 62-3
Freeman, John, 187
Fuller, Thomas, 192
Furneaux, Rupert, 142

GAGE, Lord, 92
Gaitskell, Cressida, 244
Gaitskell, Dora, 217, 224, 229, 232, 239, 240, 244
Gaitskell, Hugh, 29, 38, 48, 167, 183, 187, 191, 217-27, 228-44, 249, 250, 251, 253, 254
Gaitskell, Julia, 244
Gallagher, Frank, 107
Gardiner, Gerald, 247
Gibbens, Dr., 156
Gilleman, Father, s.j., 206
Gladstone, W. E., 87, 230, 255, 266
Gladwyn, Lord, 69, 78
Gollancz, Victor, 128, 154, 169, 184, 189, 246-8
Goodhart, Arthur, 125, 168

Gordon Walker, Audrey, 252
Gordon Walker, Patrick, 231, 237, 249, 250–2, 253, 255
Gore, Bishop, 124
Gormley, Jack, 46
Goulding, Basil, 33
Goulding, Valerie, 33
Greene, Graham, 200
Green, Maurice, 237
Greenwood, Anthony, 222
Gregory, Lady, 97
Grey, of Falloden, Lord, 83, 250
Griffin, Cardinal, 143, 197–8
Grimond, Jo, 185
Grisewood, 197
Grunhut, Dr., 125, 133, 156
Guiness, Alec, 197

HAILSHAM, Lord, 69, 73, 79, 82, 83, 84, 87–90, 99, 159, 166, 187, 207, 208, 209, 210, 205, 216, 250, 251
Hair, Gilbert, 126, 133–4, 138
Haley, Sir William, 237
Halifax, Lord, 79–80, 86, 183
Hall, George, 245
Hall, Robert, 242–3
Harding, Gilbert, 14, 88, 172, 197
Harlech, Lord, 22
Harman, John, 166
Harman, Kitty, 166
Harman, Michael, 166
Harris, John, 235–6
Harrod, Billa, 168
Harrod, Roy, 168
Hart, Herbert, 124
Hart-Davis, Rupert, 246
Hawkins, Father, 124
Headlam-Morley, Agnes, 14, 168, 197
Healey, Denis, 221, 231
Heath, Edward, 231
Heenan, Archbishop, 200, 259
Hemingford, Dennis, 247

Henderson, Lord, 67
Henderson, Mary, 107
Henderson, Nicko, 107
Henriques, Basil, 199
Hern, Tony, 168
Hewitt, Bill, 125, 128
Higgins, Phyllis, 128
Hignett, Norman, 134–5, 136
Hinden, Rita, 222, 233
Hirshfield, Desmond, 240, 242
Hoare, Christopher, 28, 46
Hobson, Valerie, 212
Hodson, Harold, 170
Hoggart, Richard, 258
Hollis, Chris, 198
Home, Lord, 69, 79, 82–3, 84, 85, 90, 215, 216
Home, Sir Nutcombe, 45
Hope, Christine, 167
Hope, Michael, 167
Horsbrugh, Lady, 71
Howard, Tony, 236
Hughes, Hector, 98
Huxley, Sir Julian, 171, 184

IDDESLEIGH, Lord, 195, 196, 208
Ingleby, Lord, 75
Ivanov, 160–1

JACOB, Sir Ian, 200
James, Lord, 78
James, Walter, 181, 183, 186
Jay, Douglas, 218, 230–1
Jay, Peggy, 226, 231
Jeger, Lena, 237
Jellicoe, Lord, 78
Jenkins, Arthur, 245
Jenkins, Sir Evan, 38–9, 44, 45
Jenkins, Mr., 34
Jenkins, Roy, 230, 234, 241
Jessel, Lord, 92
John, Augustus, 14

John XXIII, Pope, 178–80, 195, 206, 207, 208
Johnson, Paul, 237
Jowitt, Lord, 67, 79, 81, 83

KAZANTZIS, Alec, 12
Kazantzis, Judith, 12, 88, 168, 262–71
Kedlestone, Marquis Curzon of, 51
Kelly, Marie-Noël, 197
Kennedy, Ludovic, 128
Kennedy, President, 185–6, 228
Keynes, Lord, 86
Khama, Seretse, 252
Khrushchev, N., 161
Killearn, Lord, 78
Kilmuir, Lord, 89–90, 142
King, Cecil, 237, 242, 255
King, Ruth, 237, 242
Kirkpatrick, Sir Ivone, 32, 45, 217
Klare, Hugh, 125
Knight, Margaret, 200, 201
Kung, Dr., 205–6

LAMB, Henry, 12
Lamb, Pansy, 12
Lambert, Angela, 68, 69, 111
Lancaster, Osbert, 167
Lane, Sir Hugh, 97, 100, 101
Lansbury, George, 183
Latham, Lord, 76
Law, Bonar, 169
Lawrence, D. H., 177
Lawrence, T. E., 205–6
Lawson, Jack, 203, 245
Lee, Sir Frank, 252
Lee, George, 210
Leen, Father, 16
Leicester, Bishop of, 210
Lemass, Prime Minister, 33, 101–2
Lenin, V. I., 137
Levin, Bernard, 168
Lewis, C. S., 177

Leydon, John, 33, 96
Lindgren, George, 76
Lindsay, Sandy, 99
Lippmann, Walter, 185
Listowel, Lord, 67, 75
Littlewood, Joan, 105
Lloyd, Selwyn, 56
Lloyd George, David, 150, 169, 218, 248
Longford, Edward, sixth Earl, 12, 104–5, 106, 111, 215–16, 223
Longford, Elizabeth Countess of, 12, 13, 14, 88, 96, 113, 116, 142, 165–73, 188, 196, 200, 216, 219, 224, 225, 233, 240, 241, 242, 248, 249, 250, 252–3, 264, 265, 268–9
Lothian, Peter, 208
Lucan, Lord, 75

McCANN, Hugh, 101
McCarthy, Desmond, 177–8
McCarthy, Mary, 128
McCorquodale, Lord, 77
MacDonald, Lord, 202
MacDonald, Ramsay, 97
McElligott, Mr., 33
McGroaty, Congressman, 185
McGuire, Ned, 33
McKeown, General, 95
McLachlan, Donald, 59
Macleod, Iain, 89, 90
Macmillan, Harold, 56, 98–101, 102, 184–5, 187, 232, 239, 242
McNair, Lord, 86
Makarios, Archbishop, 85
Mancroft, Stormont, 148
Mander, Rosalie, 167
Mankowitz, Wolf, 169
Mansergh, Professor Nicolas, 103
Marston, Mr., 34
Martelli, Anne, 197
Martelli, George, 197
Martin, Sir Alec, 97

Martin, Sir Hugh, 97
Martin, Kingsley, 154
Martindale, Father, 17
Masefield, John, 166
Mathew, Father Gervase, 196–7
Mathieson, Dr., 143
Matthew, Archbishop, 196–7
Maudling, Reginald, 56, 238, 250
Mauriac, François, 195
Mayhew, Christopher, 234–5, 236
Meade, Professor James, 242
Mellish, Bob, 198
Mill, John Stuart, 180
Mills, Lord, 69
Milton, Frank, 156
Moberley, Sir Walter, 124
Monckton, Lord, 11, 22, 31, 33, 51,
    53–4, 55, 142
Montagu, David, 45, 46, 47, 199
Montagu, Samuel, 46
Montgomery, Lord, 69, 131–2
Moore, George, 14
More, St. Thomas, 186–7
Morley, John, 218, 230
Morrison, Lord, 69, 74, 76, 78, 99,
    203
Mortimer, Raymond, 194
Mosley, Sir Oswald, 114, 246
Moyle, Arthur, 245
Moyne, Lord, 11, 97–8, 102
Muggeridge, Malcolm, 16, 237
Murphy, Donal, 140–1

NASSER, President, 86
Nathan, Harry, 199
Nehru, Pandit, 257
Neill, A. S., 200
Nelson, Lord, 88
Newman, Cardinal, 136, 266
Nickalls, Roger, 167
Nicolson, Sir Harold, 51
Norfolk, Duke of, 195, 197–8
Norman-Butler, Belinda, 130

Nuffield, Lord, 27, 112, 116, 121, 122,
    123, 124, 126, 133, 143, 147, 156

O'BRIEN, Conor Cruise, 95
O'Connell, Daniel, 23, 26
O'Donovan, Patrick, 68, 69, 71, 77,
    90
O'Hara, Archbishop, 221
O'Higgins, Kevin, 107
O'Kelly, Miss, 104
Ogmore, David, 70
Oliver, Matt, 142
Oliver, Mr., 197
Opie, Roger, 122
Owen, Frank, 250

PAGE, Leo, 116
Pakenham, Catherine, 12
Pakenham, Kevin, 12, 168, 268
Pakenham, Michael, 12, 268
Pakenham, Paddy, 12, 264, 267
Pakenham, Paul Mary, 27, 104, 105,
    106
Pakenham, Rachel, 12, 168, 267
Pakenham, Thomas, 12, 107, 206,
    224, 264, 267
Pannell, Charles, 221
Peel, Sir Robert, 26–7, 114
Perth, Lord, 195
Pethick-Lawrence, Lady, 140
Pethick-Lawrence, Lord, 67, 77
Phipps, Frances, 197
Piercy, Lord, 21
Piggott, Julian, 211
Plato, 127, 154, 248
Plowden, Edwin, 201, 242
Pollen, Arthur, 197
Pollen, Daphne, 197
Pollen, Francis, 197
Poole, Oliver, 247
Powell, Anthony, 12, 16
Prendergast, Mr., 34
Profumo, John, 192

QUIRKE, Anthony, 33

RADCLIFFE, Lord, 11, 36
Rait, Cecil, 45-6
Ravensdale, Lady, 71
Rea, Philip, 70
Reading, Lady, 71, 72
Reed, Joan, 130
Reith, Lord, 200
Rendel, George, 195
Renoir, Pierre Auguste, 97
Richardson, Maurice, 172
Rickaby, Father, 124
Riddell, Lord, 150
Robarts, David, 49, 53, 54
Robbins, Lionel, 78, 101
Roberts, Dorothy, 128
Robertson, Brian, 118
Robertson, Lord, 78
Rodgers, Bill, 231
Roper, Hugh Trevor, 14
Rose, Kenneth, 237
Rosebery, Lord (5th Earl), 75, 136
Rosebery, Lord (6th Earl), 76
Rothschild, Lord, 46, 48
Rowse, A. L., 200-1
Russell, Lord, 124, 184, 189

SAINSBURY, Alan, 22
Sales, St. Francis de, 190-1, 192
Salisbury, third Marquess, 75-6, 84, 87
Salisbury, Lord, fifth Marquess, 22, 67, 68, 69, 75, 79, 82, 83-4, 85, 86-7, 89-90, 187
Salvesen, Harold, 113, 233
Sampson, Anthony, 68, 69, 76, 90
Samuel, Lord, 67, 77, 79
Samuel, M., 46
Sartre, Jean-Paul, 124
Scott, Michael, 247
Shackleton, Lord, 74
Shakespeare, William, 177

Shaw, G. B., 37, 106
Shawcross, Sir Hartley W., 225
Shepherd, Malcolm, 76
Silkin, Lord, 69, 76, 91, 202
Simon, Lord, 85
Sitwell, Sir Osbert, 120
Snow, C. P., 267
Sorel, Georges, 172
Soskice, Frank, 220
Sparrow, John, 167, 225
Speaight, 197
Spearman, Alec, 61
Spender, Stephen, 128, 167
Stalin, Joseph, 259
Stansgate, Lord, 67, 77, 89
Stevenson, Robert Louis, 196
Stewart, Michael, 76, 235
Stokes, Dick, 184, 189
Stonham, Lord, 74, 121, 131, 210
Strang, Lord, 78
Summerskill, Lady, 71, 72-3
Swinton, Lord, 67, 75

TAYLOR, A. J. P., 14, 168
Taylor, Charity, 147
Taylor, Lord, 74, 131
Temple, Dr. William, 157
Temple, Mrs., 157
Thomas, George, 235
Thompson, John, 128
Thompson, Peter, 123-4, 131
Thomson, Roy, 170
Thorneycroft, Peter, 56
Toynbee, Philip, 114
Trefethin and Oaksey, Lord, 215
Tuke, Tony, 30, 31, 51, 53
Tullett, Tom, 142
Tyerman, Donald, 38

VICTORIA, Queen, 76, 170, 171, 265
Vidler, John, 150
Villiers, Arthur, 43, 44

WALSTON, Lord, 74, 236
Ward, Dr. Stephen, 153, 159-60, 161-2, 199, 200
Warnock, Mary, 124
Warrell, Mr., 34
Watson, Graham, 171
Watson, Sam, 238
Waugh, Evelyn, 14-15, 16, 17, 105, 166, 196, 200
Webb, Beatrice, 171
Wedgwood-Benn, Anthony, 215
Wellington, Duke of, 98, 100
Wellington, first Duke of, 26, 27, 114
Wells, C. M., 113
Wesley, John, 157, 265
West, Rebecca, 16
Whitaker, Mr., 33, 95
Williams, Raymond, 258
Williams, Shirley, 221
Wilson, Harold, 38, 48, 49, 57, 59, 187, 202, 203, 250, 251, 252-5
Wilson, Mary, 253
Windlesham, Lord, 102

Windsor, Duke of, 54, 216
Winn, Godfrey, 237
Winterton, Eddie, 124
Witt, John, 101
Wolfe, Mr., 34
Wolfenden, John, 11, 83, 91, 125, 159, 205
Wood, 'Splinter', 144
Woodcock, George, 198
Woodham-Smith, Cecil, 170
Woodman, Dorothy, 154
Woodruff, Douglas, 195, 198
Woodruff, Mia, 198
Woods, Oliver, 237
Woollard, Mr., 34
Woolton, Lord, 22, 67
Wootton, Lady, 69, 71-2, 74-5, 121, 122-3, 125, 155, 156-7, 172-3

YEATS, W. B., 14, 97, 106, 195
Younghusband, 11

ZULUETA, Father de, 197